Irish
Women
Writers

Irish Women Writers

An Uncharted Tradition

ANN OWENS WEEKES

THE UNIVERSITY PRESS OF KENTUCKY

Scholary publisher for the Commonwealth,
serving Bellarmine College, Berea College, Centre
College of Kentucky, Eastern Kentucky University,
The Filson Club, Georgetown College, Kentucky
Historical Society, Kentucky State University,
Morehead State University, Murray State University,
Northern Kentucky University, Transylvania University,
University of Kentucky, University of Louisville,
and Western Kentucky University.

Editorial and Sales Offices: Lexington, Kentucky 40506-0336

Library of Congress Cataloging-in-Publication Data

Weekes, Ann Owens, 1941-
    Irish women writers : an uncharted tradition / Ann Owens Weekes.
      p. cm.

    Includes bibliographical references.
    ISBN 0-8131-1714-3
    1. English fiction—Irish authors—History and criticism.
2. English fiction—Women authors—History and criticism. 3. Women
and literature—Ireland—History. 4. Ireland—Intellectual life.
5. Ireland in literature. I. Title.
PR8733.W44 1990
823.009'9287—dc20   90-12122

For Trevor,
and for our mothers, sisters, and daughters

Contents

Acknowledgments

FAMILY, friends, and colleagues have helped me to think and write this book. I thank them all and list but a few: the writers themselves, Jennifer Johnston, Molly Keane, Mary Lavin, and Julia O'Faolain, who have been generous and gracious with their time and thoughts; Susan Hardy Aiken, whose help and expertise were invaluable; Sid Smith, who first suggested my working on writers whose work I love; Rachel Burrowes of the *Irish Times* and Joseph Keller of Harvard College Library, who assisted in the search for photographs; the staff of the National Museum in Dublin, who provided access to the Edgeworth papers; my husband, Trevor Weekes, who read, reread, and helped with the word-processing; my daughters, Karina, Fiona, and Lara, who read and commented on most of the texts; and my family in Ireland who provided early copies of new work. Thank you all.

1. Seeking a Tradition
Irish Women's Fiction

I came to explore the wreck.
The words are purposes.
The words are maps.
　　—Adrienne Rich, "Diving into the Wreck"

AN IRISH literary tradition is, of course, a given, is perhaps the one unchallenged cliché about Ireland and its people. "I must be talking to my friends," Yeats has the country "herself" cry, and through long centuries the Irish people have talked and sung their tears and joys.[1] The recitation began with Oisin, poet of the mythical Fianna, was taken up by the bards who entertained and abused the ancient high kings, and then concealed itself in Gaelic from the colonizer. We can hear the recitation today in the music of the *seanachie*, the storytellers who linger in isolated parts of the country. Indeed, library shelves stocked with Yeats, Joyce, Beckett—to name but the most illustrious—bear witness to this tradition; many more shelves groan beneath volumes of exegesis, classification, and definition. From the mundane to the esoteric, Irish literature would seem to have been separated, classified, and analyzed in every meaningful division. And yet the student who searches the shelves for works on Irish women's fiction—surely, one thinks, an obvious subdivision—feels very much as Virginia Woolf did when she searched the British Museum for work on women by women. The most determined researcher detects only a few slim volumes. Thus one is forced to ask whether Irish women have written fiction; and if so whether this fiction has any artistic or even historic value; and finally whether this fiction differs sufficiently from that of Irish men to merit the recognition of yet another category.

A recent critic confronted with this problem suggested that "modern Irish literature is dominated by men so brilliant in their misanthropy . . . [that] the self-respect of Irish women is radically and paradoxically checkmated by respect for an Irish national achievement."[2] The brilliance and misanthropy of Irish men's writing is not in question; the latter half of the hypothesis is. But critics, I suggest, not Irish women, are, or have allowed themselves to be, checkmated. Despite centuries of oppressive conditions, Irish women have written, initially in Gaelic and English and latterly chiefly in English, and judging by what survives of their writing, they have written well.[3] The problem lies not in their work but in the single lens with which critics have traditionally viewed most fiction, Irish included.

Analyzing the neglect of women's writing in 1928, Virginia Woolf wrote: "This is an important book, the critic assumes, because it deals with war. This is an insignificant book because it deals with the feelings of women in a drawing-room. A scene in a battlefield is more important than a scene in a shop—everywhere and much more subtly the difference of value persists."[4] Approaching texts with expectations about the appropriateness of ideas and treatments, critics validate and perpetuate traditional subjects and techniques. Unable or unwilling to recognize the value in difference, they perhaps thus ignore women's work. Indeed, Frank O'Connor's 1963 criticism of Irish fiction validates Woolf's insight. Men have written the literature of the Irish renaissance, O'Connor argues, because politics (which usually in Ireland entails war) is the stuff of literature. In such a climate, a woman must act like the Girl at the Gaol Gate; that is, she must bring food to, or serve, the men actively engaged in the fight. In support of his own argument on the subject of literature, O'Connor notes that the Irish man reading Mary Lavin's work is lost when the revolution "practically disappears" to be replaced by a "sensual richness" quite foreign to him.[5]

The cavalier dismissal of Irish women's writing is not surprising given the similar treatment until recent times of women's literature in general. Consider, for example, the long absence of Mary Shelley from the section on romanticism in that bible of orthodoxy, *The Norton Anthology of English Literature*, or the inclusion, with little attempt to distinguish gender differences, of George Eliot with the male Victorians. Even in the United States, where scholars have long fought to integrate women's work into rigid curricula, acceptance is grudging and minimal. Susan Hardy Aiken remarks on the progress after two decades of feminist criticism: "Many professors will add a woman here and there to their syllabi, but all too few move on to question how and why the system into which she is introduced has by its very presuppositions about such categories as 'literature,' 'greatness,' and 'significance' inevitably excluded her and her sisters."[6]

Similarly, critics of Irish literature fail to distinguish difference, or the marks of gender, in women's writing, but rather they view the whole spectrum through a single lens fashioned by male dictums of "literature," "greatness," and "significance." Even contemporary critics who note the importance of the woman's perspective in certain female-authored texts fail to consider the deeper implications of this perspective. The failure to recognize the possibility of real difference between women's and men's depictions of women may have reached its zenith in a recent study of the Irish short story; a critic unattracted by the work of recent women writers nevertheless welcomes it as providing much-needed sisters for Molly Bloom. In the case of American and English women's literature, however, Ellen Moers, Elaine Showalter, Nina Baym, and Sandra Gilbert and Susan Gubar have begun optimistic and often beautiful excavations and interpretations. Irish writers have been included in some of these studies, notably Gilbert and Gubar's *Madwoman in the Attic*.[7] My study differs from earlier ones, however, in its quest for a specifically *Irish* women's tradition.

In attempting to sketch uncharted territory, one is naturally guided by reflection on the known territory, on the texts that, for whatever reason, show themselves and whose features we can identify. Of the women's texts in print today, a few have retained a long popularity, being steadily reprinted over the centuries. Others have been retrieved and reprinted by Virago (the British publisher that specializes in women's work), and still other, more recent works have captured an immediate, if limited, audience. The earliest texts considered in this study are those that stand out distinctly on the literary horizon and thus demand to be included in any map of the territory. The limited number of early works makes those choices simple, but recent texts are more numerous; here we must select, rather than include all the distinctive, rich work. A comprehensive approach, while eventually desirable, would make this exploratory work unwieldy and properly awaits critical recognition of the women's tradition in Irish literature.

More important, perhaps, are the forgotten writers of the nineteenth century, the women whose valuable work may remain hidden beneath the surface of acknowledged literature. An intrepid diver must rescue them. This diver's work will be easier, however, if a blueprint, however hazy, exists, enabling her to recognize some of the salient features.

That differences in male and female perspectives exist is a commonplace; what are important here are the implications of these differences in positing a tradition of Irish women's literature. Psychologists and psychoanalysts trace gender difference to the earliest years, suggesting that men and women reared to expect and seek different sources of fulfillment routinely develop different perspectives. But if a woman, as the father of psychoanalysis suggests, is no more than a blighted man—one who must adopt uncomfortably to her castrated second-class status, one who must accept her inferior and secondary sexual organs and role, one whose natural sphere is the devalued one of childbearing and care, one who is, in fact, no more than an adjunct to man—critics might be justified in applying the only logical criteria of value, that of the male perspective, or in charitably ignoring her work. The work of the brilliant and influential anthropologist Claude Levi-Strauss also seems to support the Freudian thesis. Based on examinations of tribal societies, Levi-Strauss's work suggests that the system of exchange of words, gifts, and women is the beginning of the social state as distinguished from the natural one. The rules of exogamy in earliest societies attest, he claims, not to concern for biological dangers inherent in consanguineous marriage but to the social value of the exchange itself. This social value, attained by the giving of the most precious gifts, one's daughters, is, he argues, the essential basis of human culture.[8]

The problem of exclusion, then, extends beyond male dominance of the academies to dominance of the disciplines that define human conditions, the disciplines upon which the academies draw. But feminist critics have been quick to note that what

Freud and Levi-Strauss present are descriptions of the ways in which culture has repressed women rather than valid empirical evidence of women's inferiority or of the exchange of women as a necessary basis of culture. Indeed, a recent critic notes that the whole system of nature versus culture is itself a product of culture and, as such, is suspect.[9] We could say that Freud and his followers, Levi-Strauss included, made intellectually respectable the neglect, ascribed by Woolf to myopia if not chauvinism, of women and their works.

Their own experience, however, and education that allows them to articulate this experience cause twentieth-century women to reject the Freudian cripple. Margaret Mead was one of the first anthropologists to suggest that the differences in women's and men's temperaments were not the results of biology but of culture. Like Levi-Strauss, Mead based her assertion on observation and analysis of several tribal societies. She noted that when the allocation of activities that in the Western world are viewed as male or female is reversed in certain societies, reversals in temperaments also take place, and men adopt attitudes traditionally associated in Western culture with women.[10] Mead's work thus implied that not biology but culture is responsible for observed and alleged attitudinal differences in men and women. This being the case, a complete picture of human culture is more likely to emerge from an empirical consideration of all human experience, from, to paraphrase Simone de Beauvoir, an analysis of the becoming of a woman as well as the becoming of a man, than from acceptance of male-generated biological theories that, whatever their inspiration, attempt to explain and justify inequalities. Such a picture, of course, can most readily be drawn by women.

Psychologists and anthropologists have responded to Mead's challenge of the biology/destiny theory, and theoretical models based on women's experiences have been constructed over the past twenty years. Building on her predecessors' work, Nancy Chodorow presents a clear, well-documented picture of the development of female personality defining "itself in relation and connection to other people more than masculine personality does." In the first place, Chodorow notes, this development is not the result of "parental intention," but of the human child's

habit of internalizing perceived patterns and relationships. This
of course makes identification and analysis more difficult: because
the patterns are intuited, we have no overt evidence of the cul-
turing, and the fact that small children conform to "untaught"
patterns seems to suggest that the patterns are those of nature.
But Chodorow examines the usual process of early parent-child
interaction. The separation and individuation from the mother
that takes place during a child's first years is experienced differently by male and female children, she notes. Some socio-
logical evidence suggests that mothers identify more with their
daughters than with their sons, and hence they tend to perpetuate the primary identification with the one and hasten the separation from the other, thus establishing "gender personality
differentiation" even before gender identity.[11]

Because in Western society women tend to be almost exclusively responsible for the care of young children, the young boy
becoming conscious of gender must learn to identify with the
role, not the person, of the absent father, identifying "masculine"
in the negative sense of what is not his mother's, what is not
feminine. This identification entails the rejection of what he perceives to be feminine, then, in himself and in outside society and
is the basis, Chodorow argues, of the universal devaluation of
the female sphere. The female child, however, need not totally
reject the primary identification: often restricted to the kitchen,
or at least to the house, she is exposed to adult women and consequently identifies with the person as well as the role of the
mother. Neither do all psychoanalysts accept Freud's model of
female penis envy; the daughter's transference of sexual preference from the mother to the father is seen as gradual rather
than sudden. "It is erroneous to say that the little girl gives up
her first mother relation in favor of the father," Chodorow quotes
Helene Deutsch. "She only gradually draws him into the alliance,
develops from the mother-child exclusiveness toward the tri-
angular parent-child relationship and continues the latter, just
as she does the former, although in a weaker and less elemental
form, all her life."[12] Ultimately, as a result of this relational
model, women form closer emotional and relational ties with
other women than men form with members of their sex.

Purposeful training and socialization are imposed at a later age on the largely unconscious, internalized organization. Boys are encouraged to form their own separate groups; girls are encouraged to become members of the often intergenerational female group and to partake of its activities. Self-reliance and achievement is stressed in boys' training, nurturance and responsibility in girls'. This results in men's perceiving and describing their experiences in "agentic" terms and women's perceiving and describing theirs in "communal" terms. Chodorow uses David Bakan's definitions here; the terms agency and communion define the essential duality he remarks in human personality. Agency is used, he explains, "for the existence of an organism as an individual, and communion for the participation of the individual in some larger organism of which the individual is a part. Agency manifests itself in self-protection, self-assertion, and self-expansion: communion manifests itself in the sense of being at one with other organisms. Agency manifests itself in the formation of separations: communion in the lack of separations."[13]

Indeed, Chodorow notes, society itself adopts these terms, describing women relationally and men by the jobs they perform. Although her study has been questioned, Carol Gilligan's results seem to confirm many women's experiences. Separate training, Gilligan asserts, affects men's and women's moral perspectives. Men tend to base their judgments on objective factors, as they have learned to do in the games they play as equals, while women tend to base their judgments on the expected results of an action, the effect on the community, and the context. The real danger for women in overidentification, Chodorow and others note, is the loss of self that results from the mother's allowing no room for difference between herself and her child and in the child's attempt to escape by projecting whatever she perceives to be "bad" in herself onto her mother. The loss of ego boundaries that results from this overidentification infuses mothers and daughters with guilt, shame, and embarrassment for the other's actions.[14]

In essence, then, women's experiences—the results of their early training and the perspectives this training engendered—will be different from men's and as such would seem to demand recording. But in fact, as anthropologists note, women's experiences are in every instance denigrated in comparison to men's. Referring to Mead, Michelle Zimbalist Rosaldo notes that however different were the descent, property arrangements, or labor divisions in the tribes she studied, the "prestige values always attach to the activities of men." Rosaldo concludes that even when traditional roles are reversed, value is assigned to those activities performed by males.[15] The value, we must presume, lies in the actor, not in the deed.

Given this almost universal cyclopsic perspective, it is hardly surprising to find sensitive and astute literary critics studying literature through a single, limited lens. Indeed Gilbert and Gubar suggest that male authors and critics alike, equating the penis with the pen and imagining the author as pregnant with his text, have reserved both the origin and the nurturance of texts for themselves, have, we may say, devised an unnatural dynasty of texts sired, conceived, and borne by fathers. Harold Bloom, for instance, traces both poetic achievement and "anxiety" to a bitter struggle "between strong equals, father and son as mighty opposites" in a history that is one of "sonship." But anxiety about one's inheritance, Gilbert and Gubar counter, is preferable to the madness that confronted the female who, given the metaphor, foolishly and grotesquely attempted to employ the male tool. The very theorists to whom we turn for help in articulating the "monocentrism" and "ethnocentrism" that have dominated Western literature fail to recognize their own androcentric exclusion of women. Edward Said, for example, insists on the ever-present "central patriarchal text" and asserts the author's legal and material assumption of the role of father. Roland Barthes suggests that every narrative "is a staging of the (absent, hidden, or hypostatized) father," and M.M. Bakhtin fails to distinguish women's in the cacophony of voices he hears rise from the novel.[16]

In light (or dark) of the centuries-long and pervasive myopia of Western culture that imagines the impetus to literature as primed by the "search for the father," women's exclusion from the *Norton Anthology* and from the canon of Irish literature is hardly surprising. Back in 1929, when women were locked out of both anthologies and the very buildings that housed them, Virginia Woolf understood that inclusion was a kind of incarceration. Observing the fellows as they approached the chapel, she was reminded of "giant crabs and crayfish who heave with difficulty across the sand of an aquarium." The university, she concluded, "seemed a sanctuary in which are preserved rare types which would soon be obsolete if left to fight for existence on the pavement of the Strand." Inevitably this rarefied atmosphere bred an idiosyncratic creature. And when women students were finally admitted to the university sanctuary, they were, Elaine Showalter reports, expected to revere—since by definition they could not participate in—this version of propagation, to venerate the same values, and to think like men.[17]

But the infusion of new, strong blood was irresistible, and the value and energy of the present contribution was undeniable, implying also the value of earlier, ignored strains. In response, critics finally reassessed pedigrees and examined their canons anew. That task is now recognized as essential, though dispute on methods of genealogical reorganization is loud, as evidenced in a special issue of *Critical Inquiry* devoted to the subject. The challenge of the marginal voices will, of course, be resisted; as Christine Froula argues, the opening up of the canon entails not only the inclusion of women's texts but the revision of the venerated male texts themselves and, more important, of the cultural and institutional authority they enact.[18]

Considering the recent voices raised both in opposition to and in praise of new inclusions and revisions, Aiken warns those who would form a separate canon of the danger of reifying the very power they oppose and thus of further "ghettoizing" women's texts. Further, she rejects the distortion implicit in any theory of exclusive maternity as similar in kind to that perpetuated by the male canon. I agree with Aiken. This study is not an attempt to set up an alternate or competing canon, nor to ask that these women's work be privileged over any others. Rather, remembering Rich, this exploration seeks the purposes the women share, the map of Irish female experience their words may reveal. As Elaine Showalter notes, "When women are studied as a group, their history and experience reveal patterns which are almost impossible to perceive if they are studied only in their relation to male writers." Reading women's texts not for the war or the search for the father, not, that is, for what has been considered important, I may perhaps, to use Nancy Miller's terms, "overread" the "underread." This is no sin, but a necessary corrective, as Siobhan Kilfeather suggests in her reading of the work of the seventeenth- and eighteenth-century Irish woman, Mary Davys.[19]

These directed readings are essential in helping us to identify what is female and unique in the writing of Irish women. Having identified these female elements in the visible structure, in the work of women who are accepted if not highly honored, we can with a great deal more confidence plunge into Rich's depths to identify and salvage the buried planks, the forgotten texts of other women.

At first glance a tradition of Irish women's writing seems more problematic than that of British or American women. In the first place relatively little writing in English by nineteenth-century Irish women has surfaced, and in the second place two separate cultural traditions divided, and to a lesser degree continue to divide, the people of Ireland. A brief sketch of the history and development of these traditions as they pertain to this argument is perhaps necessary for the non-Irish reader. Such a sketch generalizes rather than details the variety and difference that always persisted over space and time.

Having settled Irish land with a small number of English and Scottish landlords in the seventeenth century, the government of England and Ireland through the provisions of the Settlement of Ireland Acts aimed to assimilate the Gaelic people. This goal might have been accomplished, as some argue it was in Scotland and Wales, had Ireland like England been affected by the Reformation. However, the acts had to instill not only a new language and a new political allegiance but also a new religion. With assimilation in mind, the government imposed severe penalties for the practice of the Roman Catholic religion, the speaking of the Gaelic language, and the serving of Gaelic chieftains.

Ironically the acts, by impoverishing, disenfranchising, and reducing the Gaelic-Irish to ignorance, succeeded only in making visible the previously invisible religious difference, and thus the acts ultimately buttressed differences rather than promoted assimilation. By 1800 Ireland was a country with an English-speaking, Protestant government and was served by a minority of English-speaking professional, religious, and landed gentry. The majority of Irish citizens, however, spoke Gaelic, attended furtive Roman Catholic services, and were prohibited from voting, being educated, practicing professions, and owning sizable estates. The descendants of the British who settled in the seventeenth and eighteenth centuries (the Anglo-Irish) traced their linguistic and cultural heritage back to *Beowulf*, while the descendants of the Celts and of the ancient Tuatha de Danann and Firbolg (the Gaelic-Irish) traced their linguistic and cultural patterns back to the Cuchulain sagas. The terms *Anglo-Irish* and *Gaelic-Irish* are used in this text to distinguish the two traditions. *Irish* was the common name both groups applied to themselves until the late nineteenth and early twentieth centuries. Then those attempting to free Ireland from political subordination to England—predominantly the descendants of the Celts—coined the *Anglo* prefix in an effort to valorize their own Irishness.

Although the eighteenth century saw a lessening of the suffering of the minority, if not of the privilege of the majority, the nineteenth century, in which this study begins, still saw two clearly distinct groups.[20] The privileged Ireland of Charles Maturin, Oscar Wilde, George Bernard Shaw, and William Butler Yeats differed greatly from the dispossessed Ireland of the Banim brothers, William Carleton, James Joyce, and Sean O'Casey. Although English was the language of these writers and increasingly of Ireland itself after 1800 (the year of the union of the English and Irish parliaments and hence the end of any pretense of independence), the English spoken by descendants of Gaelic speakers followed and still follows different idiomatic, structural, and even grammatical forms than that spoken by descendants of English speakers. For example, Denis Donoghue suggests that the Irish refusal to employ the neutral pronoun *one* comes from both historical and Gaelic grammatical roots. "One," he conjectures, denotes in the work of English writers a shared "superior experience," one that springs from intuitive understanding that Oxbridge is the "centre of the universe, the place where all experiences worth having are fully understood if not fully enjoyed." The Irish experience, in contrast, is "fractured."[21] The Anglo-Irish, generally speaking only English and sending their sons to English public schools and universities, would have shared the British linguistic/cultural experience.

Secondly, Donoghue notes, the Gaelic language has no equivalent for either the neutral pronoun or the passive voice; the neglect of *one* thus betrays the direct translation of Gaelic idiom into English. Such translation always carries within it the dual inheritance, the language itself incorporating the history—the resistance, conquest, uncomfortable but enriching compromise. Stephen Dedalus's shock—his discovery of his history in the language he spoke—was and is still a Gaelic-Irish experience.[22] Thus even when speaking the same language, Anglo- and Gaelic-Irish writers spoke, and to a lesser degree continue to speak, from different cultural, linguistic, and political roots, united only by a common absorption of English literary traditions.

Despite the vast economic, political, religious, cultural, and linguistic divide that separated the Irish peoples, women's experience in both cultures differed, in important ways, more in degree than in kind. Although prior to the conquest and plantations Irish women had enjoyed considerably more economic independence and security than had English women, they lost these rights during the seventeenth and eighteenth centuries. Before the conquest, for example, the property Irish women brought into marriage remained their own; a husband could not dispose of this property, as an English husband could, nor could he make unfavorable contracts with others that would affect its use without his wife's permission. If the marriage dissolved, the property reverted to the original owners. Again, unlike English husbands, Irish husbands were not granted sole responsibility for their wives; the women's families retained partial responsibility, and husbands had to answer to these families in cases of mistreatment. Indeed, the wife of an Irish chieftain had some small political independence, being "entitled to certain rents and taxes from her husband's subjects, sometimes called 'lady's rent,' or 'little rent.' "[23]

Of course these rights pertained only to a small privileged group, but their existence may imply a fairer attitude toward women in general. One could argue that from the plantations until the famine Gaelic-Irish women of the poorest classes retained more economic independence than their Anglo-Irish sisters who were generally upper-class. The poor were engaged in the textile industries, and "as late as 1841 women accounted for more than half the total non-agricultural labour force" in a country that was admittedly largely agricultural. Summing up the situation, however, Gearoid O'Tuathaigh notes that "The conquest and plantations of the sixteenth and seventeenth centuries transformed the political, social and economic structure of Irish society. From then until the great famine of the mid-nineteenth century there are only three general statements which can with any confidence be made concerning the roles of women in that society. Firstly, they were totally without formal political rights; secondly, their property and inheritance rights both within and outside marriage were now governed by English common law, and thirdly, theirs was a subject and subsidiary role to the male, and it was performed, for the most part within a domestic context."[24]

Gaelic-Irish women had some economic independence before the famine, but they had little independence of any kind after this event. Now although the circumstances varied cruelly, women's lives in both cultures centered chiefly on their families and their homes. Indeed, the family no longer consisted of a woman's husband and children but often also included her husband's parents, brothers, and sisters. Ironically, as J.J. Lee notes, a country that professed to value the domestic virtues excluded, after the famine, a large percent of its women from marriage. Early marriage had been the previous pattern in Gaelic Ireland; tiny plots of land were indefinitely subdivided to provide subsistence for new families. Consolidation became the goal after the famine, a consolidation that, in an agricultural society, depended on fewer divisions and hence fewer marriages.[25]

A similar situation developed in the predominantly Anglo-Irish world of the landlords: impoverished by the famine, many estate owners and their sons sought employment in England. The situation was exacerbated in 1869 when the Church of Ireland, the traditional sinecure of younger sons, lost its right to levy a tithe on the large population of Irish Catholics. The results of the consolidation and emigration were devastating for Irish women of both cultures: before the famine, the historian Lee notes, 10 percent of women remained unmarried at age forty-five; by 1926 this number had risen to 25 percent.[26] Excluded from participation in political and economic life and increasingly from the primary domestic role, Irish women might have competed for the limited prizes within their own Anglo or Gaelic culture but would not have competed with the women of the other culture. Irish men, however, were in active opposition: while Anglo-Irish men controlled the church (until 1869), government, professions, and land of Ireland, Gaelic-Irish men alternately served and opposed these masters.

This universality in women's lot is implicitly recognized by writers who link colonization to feminization. Yeats's Kathleen Ni Houlihan—the Ireland who must be talking to her friends—and the silent Ireland—the auditor in Seamus Heaney's poem: "I caress / The heaving province where our past has grown. / I am the tall kingdom over your shoulder / That you would neither cajole nor ignore"—are but the latest in a long series of such visions. The "stretchmarked" female body in Heaney's poem is Ireland, and the "imperially male" I is the England whose 1800 "act of union" Ireland sees as rape. The possible responses, too, are revealing: as a woman, Ireland's choices are to "cajole," to humor or tease, or to "ignore" the intruder.[27]

Centuries before Heaney, poets writing in both Gaelic and English could only picture their enslaved country as female, "the old hag of Beare," "the *Sean Bhean Bhoct*" (poor old woman), "Dark Rosaleen"; later disillusioned writers would depict the country as "harridan" and "crone" or, in James Joyce's characteristic terminology, "the old sow who eats her farrow." The convention of seeing Ireland as a wronged woman was by the eighteenth century so popular that whole schools of poets wrote *Aislingi*, or dream-visions, poems that foretold the Stuart protector's freeing of the beautiful woman. The sad, passive figure of Ireland awaiting deliverance by a male poet represents to some degree the eighteenth-century feminine ideal. Patrick Pearse, the leader of the 1916 rising, might be said to continue or perhaps to bring to fruition this tradition. Decrying the loss of the "ancient glory," he laments, "My mother bore me in bondage, in bondage my mother was born."[28]

Ringing with Pearse's cadences, the 1916 proclamation of the new Irish Republic reveals a curious gender transformation. Speaking for the enslaved Ireland, the terms of the proclamation are feminine: "In the name of God and of the dead generations from which she receives her old tradition of nationhood, Ireland, through us, summons her children to her flag and strikes for her freedom." Briefly the proclamation notes the period of enslavement just prior to the rebellion, when "her" sons trained and "her" allies aided Ireland. But the newly created, independent country which Pearse and the provisional government proclaim is no longer feminine: "We pledge our lives . . . to . . . its freedom . . . its welfare . . . and its exaltation." The Republic, in turn, "guarantees its citizens, "declares its resolve."[29] Colonization, then, makes female both country and people, ironically bonding both the women "of" the colonizers and the peoples colonized.

Less purely poetic and more analytical minds have also seen similarities between the situation of women and of colonized people. Taking on the school of male educators who prescribed female obedience and submissiveness and denied women the exercise of reason or taste, Mary Wollstonecraft in 1792 saw those conditions, for even the most fortunate of beauties, as those of slavery. Studying the subjection of women in the second half of the nineteenth century, Harriet and John Stuart Mill reasoned that marriage and mothering could hardly be as natural as Englishmen proclaimed, for if they were, then laws denying women other opportunities and enforcing their economic, legal, and social dependence in marriage would not be necessary. Indeed, the Mills continued, the only rational defense for these laws was the belief that "the alleged natural vocation of women was of all things the most repugnant to their nature." Hence men denied women opportunity, they suggested, fearing that if allowed alternatives, women would demand marriages of equality rather than of dependence. The laws of England, in order to support women's "natural vocation," had rendered them less free economically and legally than the slaves of ancient Rome. Both Wollstonecraft and the Mills found women's adoption of degrading, dishonest attitudes, the flirting and effort to gain male attention, for example, or the refusal to tell the truth to those who held all power over them, to be self-preserving acts of the disempowered, not examples of the essentially inferior character which chauvinists had cited as reason for women's subordination.[30]

Contemporary writers continue to study women's strategies. In an analysis of "the weak," disempowered groups worldwide, Elizabeth Janeway concentrates on women's conditions, because "it is paradigmatic of the existence of all the governed, of those whom their betters see and define as 'other'; paradigmatic because women are present in all groups of the weak." As identified by Janeway, the weak do not constitute democratic groups that elect one of their own number to government but are like slaves or colonized people. Yet Janeway also suggests that the weak have some power: like the husbands the Mills caricature, the powerful need the consent of the weak. This power of consent is similar in some ways to the influence that Louise Lamphere finds women wielding in many traditional societies in which men make the decisions and women must achieve their goals through fathers, brothers, or husbands. Over the centuries, Janeway observes, women have survived by shrinking their expectations, by clinging to the median in tests, and by refusing to seek success, thus rendering themselves as immune as possible to shock, "for shock precipitates panic," by becoming, to use Showalter's word, "muted." In their citadel of internal dissent from which they reject the values of the dominant, women have resorted to strategies of survival, strategies which men, forgetting that women had no part in the establishment of accepted codes, condemn as women's lack of morality. To survive, Janeway notes, the weak distrust and reject the definitions of the powerful, believe in their own value, and, refusing the isolation which benefits the powerful, embrace their own community and their mutual goals, making points "by endurance and repetition" rather than by force.[31]

Cut off from authority, wealth, and overt decision-making, Janeway's women resemble the Gaelic-Irish of the eighteenth century. "Excluded from landed wealth, from political life, from the 'official' church," the historian Karl Bottigheimer notes, "the Irish erected a counter-culture, not so much rebellious as evasive," a strategy, like women's, decreed by their similar repression, and one whose end was also survival.[32] By 1800, then,

despite the number of Gaelic-Irish women engaged in manufac-
turing textiles, Irish women's lot on the whole—their economic,
social, and legal statuses, those important determinants of personality and perspective—was, unlike men's, different in degree
rather than in kind. This similarity makes possible the consideration of a shared perspective, the similar objects of which
would emerge in both Anglo- and Gaelic-Irish women's literature.

Awareness of their "foreign" audience also links women writers in general to the colonized and weak. Explaining why women
have slumbered, or appeared to, for centuries, Adrienne Rich
notes, "Every woman writer has written for men even when,
like Virginia Woolf, she was supposed to be addressing women."
Irish writers (male and female) from Maria Edgeworth in 1780
to Molly Keane in 1980 have also been forced, initially by culture,
language, and economics and latterly by economics alone, to address their work to a foreign, imperially male, English audience.
Obviously this relationship bred resentment: Maria Edgeworth's
glossary and her comments in *Castle Rackrent* on the English
reader's "ignorance" of the sister country and Somerville and
Ross's and Elizabeth Bowen's caricaturing of English characters
in their fiction are obvious examples.[33] Happily, perhaps not totally unrelated to the independence of the country and the recent
beginnings of women's liberation, this defensive criticism has
virtually disappeared from contemporary Irish women's writing.

This analysis spans the period in which the novel developed in
Ireland, opening with Maria Edgeworth's *Castle Rackrent* (1800)
and concluding with Jennifer Johnston's *The Railway Station
Man* (1984). Given the goal of seeking a cross-cultural tradition,
an equal number of Anglo- and Gaelic-Irish novelists is desirable,
but nineteenth-century Gaelic-Irish women, uneducated and impoverished, have left few written records. When they did write,
poetry was the preferred genre, and Eilean Ni Chuilleanain suggests the likelihood of a female tradition, much of the love poetry
of the Old- and Middle-Irish periods being attributed to women.
Indeed, the most distinguished Gaelic lament of the eighteenth
century is that of Eibhlin Dubh Ni Chonaill, whose mother was
also a poet. Gaelic poetry deteriorated in the nineteenth century,

Ni Chuilleanain suggests, both in quality and as feminine expression. The twentieth century, however, has seen a dramatic increase in Irish poets writing both in English and Gaelic; many deserve praise—too many to name, but Ni Chuilleanain herself should be cited, as well as Eavan Boland and Medbh McGuckian.[34] As noted earlier, poetry and fiction may yet remain submerged, but the identification of the feminine must begin with what is available.

The dearth of writing by Irish women in the nineteenth century measures to some extent the lack of devotion of the Anglo-Irish to a literary culture. Unlike their counterparts in England, the inhabitants of the Big Houses in Ireland were not given to intellectual or cultural pursuit and did not see themselves as guardians or promoters of the culture that privileged them. Although exaggerated, the picture Maria Edgeworth presented in her novel *Castle Rackrent* (1800) and that E.OE. Somerville and Violet Martin presented in *Some Experiences of an Irish R.M.* (1889) of the jovial, drinking, Anglo-Irish sportsman may be closer to the actual than is the received picture of the Anglo-Irish man.[35]

Briefly let us consider the source of the received impression. Terence de Vere White, scion of Gaelic- and Anglo-Irish parents, suggests that Yeats, out of his own need to claim membership in an aristocracy, conceived the notion of the Anglo-Irish as the guardians of an ancient civilization. Conceived without material agency (another cerebral, male phenomenon), this illusion was born in Yeats's famous 1925 Irish senate speech that, coming from the best-known poet of the century, received global attention. Upbraiding the new state for denying divorce to its Protestant citizens, Yeats soared into eloquent, if imaginary, genealogies: "I am proud to consider myself a typical man of that minority [Anglo-Irish Protestants]. We against whom you have done this thing are no petty people. We are the people of Burke; we are the people of Grattan; we are the people of Swift, the people of Emmet, the people of Parnell. We have created the most of the modern literature of this country. We have created the best of its political intelligence." The Anglo-Irish were not a race, however, White asserts, but a class. Yeats, though he professed to speak for them, would not have been chosen as their representative. For despite his friendship with that unusual, scholarly aristocrat, Lady Gregory, Yeats was not of the company of the landed Irish gentry, as his trouble in gaining admission to their Kildare Street Club reveals. "Coming forward in the Senate as the spokesman for the Protestant Ascendancy . . . [Yeats] flattered the people he spoke for by admitting them *en bloc* to the company of his fellows; what he had in common with Swift and Burke was genius. This was by no means widely distributed among the Protestant Ascendancy," White concludes. The members of the latter group were not in general lovers of literature or of the Gaelic revival, nor were they interested in Irish Catholics or in Yeat's Abbey theater.[36]

Maria Edgeworth's development as reader, scholar, and writer in this inimical background was largely the result of her formidable father's efforts. Although he initially banned novels as potentially dangerous influences on young women (Richard Lovell Edgeworth adhered to many of Rousseau's doctrines), Edgeworth did encourage his daughter to read widely. His own head was filled with schemes to improve many aspects of life, and Edgeworth turned his eldest daughter into an apprentice/secretary. Written largely under his guidance and at his direction, Maria Edgeworth's early educational tracts and later novels reflect his beliefs. As Edgeworth's biographer, Marilyn Butler, notes, *Practical Education*, for example, articulates what Richard Lovell Edgeworth and his second wife, Honoria, had hoped to compile, and the idealized landlords of the later novels reflect both the father's high morality and the model he would have his countrymen embrace.[37] But Maria Edgeworth was not solely her father's creation. *Castle Rackrent*, for instance, suggests doubts about the extent—and even the existence—of the landlord ideal she so frequently painted. Not only does this subversive novel question the status of the Anglo-Irish landlord but it also looks askance at, indeed even ridicules, those who unquestioningly accept the absurd position of Irish and/or English women. Indeed Edgeworth implies that this condition is in part the logical result of its inscription and preservation in the great works of English literature. It is no accident that Edgeworth's masterpiece, this inquisitive, challenging novel, was written without any direction or assistance from Richard Lovell Edgeworth, a fact which also makes it an appropriate place to begin the study of modern fiction by Irish women.

Sydney Owenson (Lady Morgan) shared the early nineteenth-century spotlight with Edgeworth. Excluded from this study on the basis of its excessive romanticism and sentimentalism, Owenson's work still deserves mention. Her celebration of Gaelic civilization, history, and aspirations was the first sympathetic presentation of Gaelic Ireland to reach a wide audience. But the land problems that swept Ireland in the 1830s changed the literary as well as political focus from the relatively secure societies presented by Edgeworth and Owenson. Saddened by the increasing alienation of tenants and landlords, Edgeworth wrote: "It is impossible to draw Ireland as she now is in a book of fiction—realities are too strong, party passions too violent to bear to see, or care to look at their faces in the looking-glass." The famine followed in the 1840s, enfolding the country in a pall that silenced all but the voices of mourning. Indeed a generation had to pass before writers could once again see beyond the grief. The land wars that the famine hastened exacerbated the insecurity and comparative impoverishment of the once-powerful ascendancy. Emily Lawless's *Hurrish* attempted to explore the land problem from the peasants' perspective, and though her work is also excluded because of its sentimentality and sensationalism, her sympathetic inquiry deserves mention, as do her lovely descriptions—in *Hurrish* and in other novels—of the Irish countryside.[38]

The land question—the threat to Anglo-Ireland—prompted Edith Somerville and Violet Martin to raise their voices in defense of their class. Publishing their work under the names E.OE. Somerville and Martin Ross, the cousins produced many comic sketches and several fine novels, including the excellent *The Real Charlotte* (1894). Received well initially, the novel was neglected in an Ireland preoccupied with wars in the early twentieth century. Later, in a country that saw the members of the Anglo-Irish ascendancy as tools of the former oppressors, the lament of Somerville and Ross seemed anachronistic and irrelevant. *The Real Charlotte* went out of print and was virtually forgotten until it was reprinted in the 1970s, when the richness and diversity of the work attracted attention. No other nine-

teenth-century Irish novel spans such a wide section of, nor
delves so deeply into, Irish society; George Moore's *Drama in
Muslin*, for example, seems limited and conventional beside *The
Real Charlotte*.[39] Apart from the thematic richness, this product
of two voices is also a fascinating literary anomaly, mothered by
two women rather than a single father. Also narrated by a double
voice, the work constantly forces the reader to consider the narrators' biases and prejudices toward their characters, to consider
indeed the narrational "contamination" and what such a stance
might suggest about the approach to literature itself.

The latter part of the nineteenth century produced several
excellent Irish women writers. But as evidenced in a recent volume of short stories, these writers are almost without exception
Anglo-Irish.[40] Hence it seemed reasonable to limit the nineteenth-century writers to those who reach beyond the concerns
of their contemporaries both thematically and structurally—
Edgeworth, and Somerville and Ross.

Selecting writers from the plenty of the twentieth century
was more difficult. Because I seek a tradition that spans time
and class, I chose an equal number of Anglo- and Gaelic-Irish
writers from different periods of the century. Inevitably personal taste was also a factor. Future studies will include the
valuable writers simply celebrated here by name: Dorothy Ma-
cardle, Mary Manning, Maura Laverty, Janet MacNeill, Edna
O'Brien, Caroline Blackwood, Maeve Kelly, Mary Beckett, Clare
Boylan, Polly Devlin—a full listing would exhaust both chapter
and reader. Elizabeth Bowen is the first twentieth-century
writer studied; although her work has received a great deal of
attention, it has not yet been treated within the context of Irish
women's fiction. *The Last September*, the story of the demise in
the 1920 Irish Troubles of a Big House and the parallel release
from Eden of a young girl, seems an appropriate Bowen text
since the relationship between the two events is more than co-
incidental. Begun by Edgeworth, the Big House theme is now
seen as a subgenre in Irish literature. The condition of the house
itself often acts as an extended metaphor for the condition of the
ascendancy. Writing at approximately the same time as Bowen,
Kate O'Brien, the first Gaelic-Irish novelist examined, attempts
to articulate a woman's position in the new Ireland.[41] Despite

the Catholic, Gaelic, and middle-class qualities of this Ireland, O'Brien suggests that the structures the newly powerful embrace are those of the old ascendancy, derived, then, from the patterns of kinship Levi-Strauss uncovered in early societies. Thus women are no more free in the Ireland of the rebel Eamon De Valera than they were in that of Queen Victoria.

The sheer beauty and poetic allusiveness of her prose wins a place for Mary Lavin, the "disturbingly different" writer. Despite Frank O'Connor's comments, the difference and richness in Lavin's first collection of short stories were welcomed in 1942 by the established writer Lord Dunsany. Lavin's subjects range from the highly sensitive to the almost insensate; she is the first writer under consideration to examine the mundane areas of women's existence, bringing to this perusal a poet's eye for the unusual, beautiful, and universal in the ordinary. Leaving the realistic novels of Kate O'Brien behind, Lavin reveals and places in cosmic patterns the most delicate nuances of human emotions.[42] Her work, like her vision, is organic, developing in the natural sequence of her life, moving from the early interest in young love to a consideration of the role of widows in society and more recently to detailed examination of the ties that bind mother and daughter. To demonstrate Lavin's organic vision, I consider stories that span her career.

Roughly contemporaneous with Lavin, Molly Keane began her first writing career in the 1930s. Although her early work was both daring and colorful, *Good Behaviour*, the masterpiece (to date) of her second writing career, is the focus of this study. Finally published by Alfred A. Knopf in 1981—after several rejections—this black comedy testifies to the variety as well as the continuity within Irish women's fiction.[43] This satirical glance down fifty years to the last September of Anglo-Ireland, like Bowen's the September of a young girl's awakening, presents another Ireland, caricatured but perhaps also a needed corrective, or widening, of Bowen's picture.

Daughters of mothers and fathers who epitomize the two Irish traditions, Julia O'Faolain and Jennifer Johnston represent the most current writers of fiction. O'Faolain's parents are both writers. In early enthusiasm for the new Irish state, her father changed his name from the English Whelan, spoke the Gaelic language in his home, joined the Irish Republican Army, and addressed traditional Irish subjects. He was, however, to become as disillusioned with the republicans as he had been with the British empire. On the other side, Johnston's mother, Shelah Richards, was an Abbey actress; her father, Denis Johnston, was a playwright, whose most famous play received its title from Lady Gregory's refusal to accept it—*The Old Lady Says No.* Johnston's parents, then, come directly from the Anglo-Irish tradition.[44]

In the works of O'Faolain and Johnston, the contemporary representatives of the two traditions, we find initially a returning to the roots of the past, to the roots of their traditions. But this returning is not what it was for their ancestors; rather, O'Faolain and Johnston seem to feel a need to reassess history for themselves, to dive into the wreck, not passively accepting but examining in person the map they have inherited. Only when this reassessment, which becomes a re-vision in Rich's sense of the term, is complete are the writers free to concentrate on women's contemporary situations. Because O'Faolain evokes Irish myths and history which may be unfamiliar to readers and thus may need explication, I discuss only one of her novels in detail— *No Country for Young Men.* On the other hand, the brevity of Johnston's first seven novels allows examination of each, an examination that is important because these works enact both Johnston's own personal journey to selfhood and that of many contemporary women.[45]

The work of the feminist anthropologists and psychologists already introduced is used to elucidate the themes and to analyze the underlying relationships in the fictions, and this work is referred to throughout. Awareness, for example, of both the value and the cost of human relationships forms a constant undercurrent in Irish women's writings, the emphasis shifting from cost to value. While Irish women writers seem to espouse community more than do their male counterparts, important differences exist between traditions. These may indeed be the fruit of the two cultures. The emphasis, for instance, on the individual in Anglo-Irish writing may reflect the agency David Bakan associates with the Protestant ethic as conceived by Max Weber. The Protestant relationship with God, Bakan notes, is private, salvation being "essentially an individual matter." Concluding from the responses of Protestantism to economic and scientific advances that the Protestant ethic is allied with capitalism, Bakan argues that the exaggeration of the agentic (or the individual), essential to this alliance, entails the "repression of the communion component."[46] The emphases and shadings, then, the often difficult balancing of relationships and individual responsibility, which may seem but the loose strands or abstruse corners of women's texts, are the evidences both of gender and culture that I seek in the work of early writers.

Elaine Showalter's analysis of feminist criticism suggests the importance of these marginal areas. Using the Ardener model of human communication, Showalter explains that male and female experience may be represented by two circles. These circles overlap but are not concentric, since a crescent of each remains free of the other. Each of these crescents represents an area of exclusively male or female experience. Women are cognizant of the male crescent, Showalter asserts, because male culture has been seen and represented in art and indeed in political, economic, and social life as human culture. The female crescent, on the other hand, the exclusive area of women's experience, is to men an unknown, wild territory because this experience has been either ignored (consider women's exclusion from the *Norton Anthology*, for example), devalued as the product of nature rather than culture (see Sherry Ortner's work), or regarded as an inferior adjunct, not worth analysis for its own sake (as the work of Freud and Levi-Strauss attests). Consequently women partake of a dual culture, participating at once in the large circle of "human" and in the small crescent of women's experience. Paraphrasing the Ardeners, Showalter notes the problem of rendering women's own experience, for "all language is the language of the dominant order, and women, if they speak at all, must speak through it."[47] Not only has women's experience been largely ignored, then, but women must attempt to speak that experience through the very language that denies it or must, to put it another way, speak doubly.

Doubleness itself is not, of course, unique to women. Speaking of the dispossessed in general, Tony Tanner argues that discourse from Roman times on has been the property of the powerful: "Not only do the propertied classes own land, capital, and machinery, but they also own the discourses that serve to define and regulate the various strata and groups within society."[48]

But in another context, M.M. Bakhtin suggests that the lower classes, or the "weak" to use Janeway's term, are not completely silenced. Relevant here and worth summarizing briefly is Bakhtin's argument for the conflicting novelistic voices. Parody and ultimately the novel, Bakhtin suggests, are the rich fruits of "the common people's creative culture of laughter." Supplying the needed corrective of laughter to the monoglossia of the epic, which valorized both the discourse and the values of a closed era, parody ridicules not the heroes but the language of epic. Whether in Greece, ancient Rome, or medieval Europe, two styles cross in parody, he argues. Even when only the language of the genre being parodied is present, we can recognize the implicit presence and perspective of the other point of view, the "dialogizing backdrop." The questioning and parodying have developed into such heteroglossia in the modern novel, Bakhtin concludes, that "one often does not know where the direct authorial word ends and where a parodic or stylized playing with the characters' language begins."[49]

The Ardeners, on whose work Showalter builds, suggest that women, like the lower orders Bakhtin posits, would also find expression through established ritual and art; this expression, they suggest, would take the form of a muted voice or text not obvious to the dominant culture. While some critics espouse the idea of an entirely female text outside the bounds of the "dominant structure," Showalter argues that "women's writing is a 'double-voiced discourse' that always embodies the social, literary and cultural heritages of both the muted and the dominant." Tanner also suggests a secondary or subversive text, but an unspoken one. The knowledge of the world forbidden or ignored by the powerful, he asserts, speaks its presence in the "gap, or silence, in the bourgeois novel," while Bakhtin identifies the weak in the heteroglossia, the multiple voices of the repressed that threaten to break the fictional surface.[50]

Nancy Miller's work on the "emphasis added" in female-authored texts also helps us to read the muted texts of Irish women. Considering *La Princesse de Clèves*, Miller notes Bussy-

Rabutin's objection that Mme de Clèves's confession to her husband is the material of life, not fiction. This means, Miller notes,
that "art should not imitate life but *re*inscribe received ideas
about the representation of life in art." Rejecting the confession's
implausibility in the first place on the basis of textual patterns—
the "maternal discourse," the advice of Mme de Chartres to avoid
the "misery of a love affair," and the precedent of confession set
by the prince—Miller finds a more basic fault with Bussy-Rabutin's criterion. The problem is that "the fictions of desire behind the desiderata of fiction are masculine and not universal
constructs." As articulated by Freud, two "impelling wishes"
dominate men and women respectively; these are either ambitious, "serving to exalt the person creating them, or they are
erotic." But the male text, while valorizing the egoistic wish,
still, Freud suggests, preserves an erotic subtext: "We can discover a woman in some corner, for whom the dreamer performs
all his heroic deeds and at whose feet all his triumphs are to be
laid." Miller asks the obvious question: "Is there a *place* in which
the ambitious wish of a young woman asserts itself? Has she an
egoistic desire to be discovered 'in some corner'?"[51]

This is the subtext Miller finds operative in *La Princesse de
Clèves*, one at work also in George Eliot's novels of heroines who
demand something vague, they know not what but something
other than that offered: the fulfillment of erotic desires. The princess, Miller quotes Claudine Hermann, "knows that *love as she
imagines it* is not realizable. What is realizable is a counterfeit
she does not want. Her education permits her to glimpse this
fact: men and women exchange feelings that are not equivalent."
Hence, Miller notes, in retreating the princess preserves her
desires "in and as fantasy, she both performs maternal discourse
and italicizes it as repossession." Maggie Tulliver in Eliot's *The
Mill on the Floss*, on the other hand, refuses her lover because
"she will not build her happiness on the unhappiness of others."
The women's rejection of the Freudian paradigm, the implausibility of their seeking egoistic desires, is subtle, unemphasized,
or "demaximized." This is an instance, Miller believes, of the
italicizing we can expect in women's fiction, hence it is a likely
characteristic of the muted plot.[52] Similarly we might also see
the lacunae created by disconnections in dialogue as important

instances of italicizing by demaximization, by women's traditional retreat from the center of the stage.

Miller's analysis suggests another important consideration: remarking on women writers' rejection of the male "desiderata of fiction," she notes that "the plots of women's literature are not about 'life' and solutions in any therapeutic sense, nor should they be. They are about the plots of literature itself, about the constraints the maxim places on rendering a female life in fiction." Similarly many Irish women's plots also criticize these constraints and often successfully evade them. Female bildungsromane or novels of awakening are especially at odds with the demands of genre, with the constraints of the male desire inscribed therein. These texts begin the work of inscribing their own different paradigms. Drawing on the theories of Chodorow and others, the editors of a recent volume on fictions of female development, *The Voyage In*, remark the essential difference in the male and female experience but note that critics of bildungsroman have classified experience only as it relates to the male paradigm. Excluded from generic fulfillment, women's fictions have often concluded with death for the awakened woman who will not "accept an adulthood that denies profound convictions and desires." The editors also note the frequent late awakening of women, whose development often takes place only after traditional expectations of marriage and children have been tried and found wanting, a pattern that also emerges in Irish writing.[53] The pattern of early awakening occurs occasionally in Irish work, sometimes triggered by sheer accident, more frequently by education and maternal direction. We are always aware, however, that these are isolated, fortunate exceptions.

The development of the bildungsromane as described by the editors of *The Voyage In* accords with the muted and de-emphasized plots described earlier: "The tensions that shape female development may lead to a disjunction between a surface plot, which affirms social conventions, and a submerged plot, which encodes rebellion; between a plot governed by age-old female story patterns, such as myths and fairy tales, and a plot that reconceives these limiting possibilities; between a plot that charts development and a plot that unravels it. The development tale may itself be concealed in coded memories, as in *Mrs. Dal-*

loway, or deflected through recurrent dreams, as in *Wide Sargasso Sea*."[54] Whether muted or not, the female bildungsromane by its very nature, its assertion of an alternate paradigm, contests the patterns inscribed in male fictions.

Revision of myth and history, as well as fairy tale, is a recurrent element in the muted "undercurrent" of women's texts. Adrienne Rich explains that re-vision, "the act of looking back— of seeing, with fresh eyes, of entering an old text from a new critical direction—is for us more than a chapter in cultural history: it is an act of survival." In "Diving into the Wreck" Rich describes such a quest: "the thing I came for / the wreck and not the story of the wreck / the thing itself and not the myth." In a way we can see "the story of the wreck" as the canon of Irish literature in English; the "thing," the work of Irish women. Although women must delve beneath the huge mythic surface to re-touch themselves and not what others say they are, the myth has so deeply encrusted our forms that we cannot without risking destruction break these cleanly away. Rich's diver, too, having found the place, claims a necessary doubleness: "And I am here, the mermaid whose dark hair / streams black, the merman in his armored body." "I am she: I am he." The myth is as inescapable as is our human form, for the myth, like the early relational structures Chodorow considered, has been internalized and is now part of human culture.[55]

Speaking specifically of the Demeter/Persephone story but generally of myths which perpetuate "destructive stereotypes of female passivity and masochism," Susan Gubar argues that "gender definitions reflect and enforce the terrible recurrence of the myth." Consequently "the myth must be rewritten to be evaded." The triumph of the artist over the earth mother has, Gubar notes, been celebrated by women poets, by Mary Shelley's *Proserpine* and by Elizabeth Barrett Browning's *Aurora Leigh*, for example, and more subtly by Virginia Woolf in *To the Lighthouse*. This re-(en)visioning of Demeter/Persephone allows women to redefine and reinscribe female consciousness. But reflecting Rich's insight, Gubar also remarks Woolf's need to celebrate the earth mother, Mrs. Ramsey (a creation of the myth), in the first part of *To the Lighthouse* before being liberated to celebrate the artist Lily in the third section.[56]

Perhaps the most repressive myth from women's viewpoint is that of Milton's Eve. Characteristically, Charlotte Brontë had her Shirley rage impotently against the restrictive boundaries of Eve interpretation, while Virginia Woolf humorously advised her readers to "look past Milton's bogey." In delving beneath the surface of Milton's text to a deeper deposit, that of the repressed mother goddess, Christine Froula answers Woolf's call. The goddess, we recall, was almost silenced in Genesis and was silenced totally in Milton's creation, but she remains implicit in Eve's memory of a sort of golden-age origin, Froula argues, one governed not by the "patriarchal indoctrination" Adam supplies but by feminine metaphor.[57] Although Milton's Eve still hides the sun from many women, Elizabeth Bowen overtly inverts the Miltonic sequence and allows her Eve to turn from the ignorance paternal discourse decrees to the light of the wider world. Other Irish writers, Kate O'Brien and Molly Keane, for example, align their Eves less directly with the Miltonic or biblical versions, but they release them just as surely from centuries of Edenic bonds.

It may indeed be difficult to find a woman writer who does not invoke myth in order to revise it. Advising readers to expect such revision, Alicia Ostriker includes historical or quasi-historical figures such as Helen, Sappho, and Napoleon in her definition of myth. An important element in the revision may be the reversing of traditional values: Ostriker notes, for example, that Denise Levertov in identifying "an active, aggressive woman with Truth" in "The Goddess" is defying "a very long tradition that identifies strong females with deception." Passivity, on the other hand, will be suspect in women's work, and woman's traditional power for evil, so long associated with destructive sexuality, is seen as "a direct function of her powerlessness to do anything else."[58]

Ostriker sees four common elements in the revisions of women poets, elements worth noting here because they occur also in the revisionist work of the Irish writers examined in this study. In the first place women poets treat "existing texts as fence posts surrounding the terrain of mythic truth but by no means identical to it." Second, the poems "involve reevaluations of social, political, and philosophical values," particularly those that enshrine the separation of earth and body from mind and spirit.

Third, unlike male poets, women revisionists do not hearken back to a golden age. And finally, "revisionism correlates with formal experiment." The Irish writers apply these strategies to literature as well as to myth and history. Ostriker has warned us to be awake to the potential for revision in recalling myth; John Hollander also elaborates on the reshaping he sees implicit in the use of literary allusion, direct or implied. The echoing or alluding to previous texts, he notes, always takes on shades and associations different from, if not in direct opposition to, those of the original.[59] Just as they re-envision myths, Irish writers also re-envision—by their echoing—their history and literature.

The living writers in this study all agreed to interviews.[60] Mary Lavin, Julia O'Faolain, and Jennifer Johnston do not see themselves as feminists. They object to being considered members of a particular group with whose politics and actions they frequently disagree. Jennifer Johnston, for example, suggests that while Irish feminists have a real injustice to combat, their actions, like those of the Provisional Irish Republican Army who seek to overthrow an unjust system in the north of Ireland, alienate rather than gain them support. All labeling is divisive and limiting, these writers argue, and though their characters are women, their characters' situations are simply human.

Johnston sees all separation as destructive, and class as the most damaging separation of all. Not that these women are content with the status quo: Johnston notes that traditional marriage was diminishing but that what must change is attitude, a change that can most readily be effected by education. Courageously straightforward in her own life, Johnston rejects the pessimism that breeds political inaction. She insists on an end to hypocrisy north and south of the Irish border but relies herself on honest individual human relations.

Lavin does not have much confidence in politics either, though she does admire individual politicians. Like Johnston, she believes in "family politics" that can be extended to the community and perhaps one day to the nation. "Women are out of their boxes, everywhere," she notes gladly, and they will remain so. Her admiration extends from the traditional work of nuns, like those who taught her, to the efforts of the young women who, like her own daughter, visit Nicaragua in search of truth and peace. "Individual conscience," she insists, must always have priority over any group belief, religious or political. She sees the contemporary movement in fiction away from father-son to mother-daughter and to grandmother-mother-daughter in her own latest work—the fruit of women's own focus on themselves—as enriching.

Having edited the feminist study *Not in God's Image*, a consideration of the legal status of Western women from Greek to Victorian times, Julia O'Faolain notes that she has moved on. She absorbed those influences and can now concentrate on women without being bound by their political concerns. Of Carla's return to her chauvinistic husband in *The Obedient Wife* (1982), a return that disappointed both her own father and feminist reviewers, O'Faolain notes that Marco, the husband, was not really important. What Carla was returning to was a way of life, an environment, a life in skeptical, sophisticated Italy rather than in naive, romantic Los Angeles. The idea that a particular man (Carla's lover Leo in this case) is essential to a woman's happiness is, O'Faolain notes, a Hollywood illusion. But having said that, O'Faolain sees no reason to throw out the traditional job of mother/hostess/lover that Carla and many women like her perform so well.[61]

Molly Keane, on the other hand, while not claiming to be a feminist herself, is full of admiration for those she calls the "tearaways," the young women writers who are outspoken about their goals. Delighted with women's increasing involvement in extradomestic activities, Keane does not, however, devalue the domestic scene. Indeed she recently published a lovely cookbook, prompted by the desire to pass to the busy working mothers she admires her recipes for good, tasty, quick meals.[62]

Given the writers' emphasis on the total community, the reader may question an analysis that extracts their work from the body of Irish fiction or indeed from the larger body of fiction in general. In the first place, I do not distort their writing. I interpret it based on the paradigms of women's experiences as described by psychologists and anthropologists and of women's fiction as described by feminist critics. An understanding of these paradigms is as essential to our understanding of all literature as is knowledge of Freud's insights. Secondly, I extract the strand of women's writing not to keep it separate, isolated from that of their brothers, but only to examine it for what may be unseen in the larger kaleidoscope of Irish literature. In that larger context, so many elements compete for attention that critics may, indeed must, ignore some in order to develop a manageable analysis. In this selection process, since women's work has been in the minority and critics have until recently been largely unaware of women's experience and hence of the strategies for encoding that experience, women's texts have been ignored or—as we saw in Bussy-Rabutin's analysis of *La Princesse de Clèves*—misinterpreted. Finally, as I said initially, I wish to consider women's writings in relation to each other to determine if women may have inherited some forms, techniques, or themes from their mothers. I do not suggest a conscious borrowing or, to paraphrase Woolf, a deliberate thinking back through their mothers, but an intuitive response acquired, like so much else in human personality, unconsciously.

2. Maria Edgeworth
Domestic Saga

> We are surely justified in this eager desire to collect the most
> minute facts relative to the domestic lives, not only of the
> great and good, but even of the worthless and insignificant,
> since it is only by a comparison of their actual happiness or
> misery in the privacy of domestic life, that we can form a
> just estimate of the real reward of virtue, or the real punish-
> ment of vice.
> —Maria Edgeworth, Preface to *Castle Rackrent*

"AN INORDINATE desire to be beloved," was, according to Richard Lovell Edgeworth, the greatest defect in the character of
his daughter Maria Edgeworth. A glance at any selection of the
novelist's voluminous correspondence confirms his estimate. The
contemporary reader moves from sympathy to impatience at the
writer's constant professions of love for her readers, delight in
her readers' love, and coy denials of her own merits and worth.[1]
The insecurity that inspired such professions can be traced, I
suggest, to the neglect Maria Edgeworth endured as a small
child, a neglect that fostered the "inordinate desire" that dominated not only her personal relationships but also her literary
endeavors.

Born to Anna Maria Elers Edgeworth and Richard Lovell
Edgeworth on 1 January 1768, Maria spent her first five years
at Black Bourton, her mother's family home in England. Little
information about her early childhood is recorded; we may indeed
infer the relative unimportance and neglect of the child from the
father's lack of comment. Having married Anna Maria in haste,
if not under duress, the young, ambitious, and inquisitive Richard Lovell Edgeworth soon found her company tedious. Home,
he would report in his memoirs, was not rendered "delightful"
by his wife's constant lamenting of "trifles." Consequently Richard Lovell Edgeworth, spent most of his time away from home;

his own education or that of his eldest son, Richard, who accompanied him, was his ostensible object. Maria was thus deprived of the company of her father and, perhaps more important, of her brother, her favorite companion, and left to the sad woman she remembers as "always crying." Edgeworth senior reports that he was "obliged" to return to England when Anna Maria died bearing her fifth child, but within four months he had married Honora Sneyd, the woman with whom he had been infatuated during his first wife's lifetime and who would become his intellectual and emotional companion. Noting that his "virtue" (presumably sexual fidelity to the wife he ignored) had been rewarded in his finding Honora well, Edgeworth reports their immediate removal to the estate he had inherited from his father in Ireland.[2]

Absorbed with wife and estate, Edgeworth records neither Maria's reactions to her mother's death—to the ending of the only security, sad though it had been, she had ever known—nor her early response to Honora and Ireland. Marilyn Butler, Maria Edgeworth's biographer, has recovered some details that testify to the child's terrible loneliness. Arriving in the strange city of Dublin accompanied by adults who must have seemed equally strange, the child was scolded by a maid for climbing through a high garret window. You could have broken your neck, the maid reprimanded. "I wish I had—I'm very unhappy," replied the five year old.[3] During two years at Edgeworthstown, Maria expressed her unrecognized loss in willful and destructive behavior, which finally resulted in the senior Edgeworths' enrolling the child in boarding school in England. Cut off from her own mother and the early Black Bourton relatives, Maria may not have tried (she was only five) to establish a relationship with Honora. And Honora, principled, theoretical, and honorable, seems not to have exhibited much warmth or understanding to the difficult child.

Once at school, however, Maria appeared anxious to maintain what must have seemed a fragile link with home. Eagerly she wrote, "Dear Mamma, It is with the greatest pleasure I write to you, as I flatter myself it will make you happy to hear from me." But the letters from Edgeworthstown were chilly. Honora expressed pleasure at Maria's being taught to dance: it "may enable you to alter your common method of holding yourself if you pay attention to it, & I must say you wanted improvement in this respect very much when you were here." In another letter she chided the child for writing first: "I shall not be displeased with you for omitting anything which I had before told you, I did not expect." The father's advice was hardly more soothing: "With a benevolent heart, complying Temper, & obliging manners, I should make no doubt, that by your mother's assistance you might become a very excellent, & an highly improved woman—Your person, my dear Maria, will be exactly in the middle point, between beauty and plainness—handsome enough to be upon a level with the generality of your Sex, if accompanied with gentleness, Reserve, & real good sense—Plain enough to become contemptible, if unattended with good qualities of the head & heart."[4]

If we look at the situation in light of the psychological theories discussed in chapter 1, we may understand the child's responses. The female child reared in the extended female family sees herself as an essential part of that group, committed to their interests as they are to hers, whereas the male child is encouraged to engage with his own age group and sees himself as an autonomous individual, governed by objective rules. Suddenly removed from the female community and the ensuing relatedness of Black Bourton, Maria Edgeworth was plunged into a strange world, a world where directives and the consequences of disobeying these directives were clearly stated, a fair world in the objective sense but an alien and male one to the female child. Lonely, unmoored, unable to cope or understand, the child sought attention by misbehaving, by violating the rules. Rewarded with expulsion, she at some level reassessed the situation and endeavored to win affection by a constant assertion of both her love for and gratitude to her parents, by an overeager desire to become the daughter they desired. Thus she strove to be accepted into a communion like that she once knew.

With Honora's death in 1782, the Edgeworth family life changed; Maria was brought by her father and his new wife, Honora's sister Elizabeth, to live at Edgeworthstown. Unlike Honora, Elizabeth saw her role as that of guide and guardian of her husband's children, and Richard Lovell Edgeworth also turned to his daughter—for assistance. Possibly for the first time since her mother's death, Maria Edgeworth felt loved and needed. Unsure, perhaps of her ability to retain this love, Maria Edgeworth, I suggest, now consciously sought to be in her person and in her work everything the father desired, sought intuitively to replace the estimable Honora. Acting as her father's estate-assistant, bookkeeper, and secretary and as a teacher to several of his many children, the daughter was exposed to the practical, energetic, and industrious side of Richard Lovell Edgeworth. The memoirs she completed after his death attest to her admiration for his moral and principled behavior with his tenants and to his practical, mechanical abilities.[5]

The first writing assignments he gave Maria underline his concern with the useful: the fourteen-year-old girl was advised to read about the Irish economy and constitution and to write "an enquiry into the causes of poverty in Ireland." When this was complete, she was set to translate *Adèle et Théodore; ou, Lettres sur l'éducation*. Edgeworth and Honora had devoted much of their time together to studying education, and Maria now worked on *The Parent's Assistant* (1796), stories for children, and was also included in the study begun with Honora, *Practical Education* (1798). Although Richard Lovell Edgeworth encouraged his daughter to write novels, she always professed to value the practical more than the imaginative work, valuing it thus, I believe, because again at some indeterminate level she thought her father so valued it. Possibly she misinterpreted his interest in the practical as a desire for the didactic. Of this interest there is much evidence: In *Memoirs*, for example, she noted that her father, who read, advised her on, and corrected her material, always asked for the plan of any new story. But if Maria presented the details, he waved them away as "drapery," asking only to see the "bare skeleton." An 1805 letter from Maria to her cousin Sophy Ruxton suggests the father's low opinion of novelettes, if Maria read him correctly, an opinion that Maria may have sought to change by writing novels that taught a lesson. "He has pointed out to me," she wrote, "that to be a mere writer of pretty stories and novelettes would be unworthy of his partner, pupil and daughter."[6]

Citing the merits of *Castle Rackrent*, the one novel written without the father's advice and assistance, critics blame Richard Lovell Edgeworth for the didacticism that mars much of his daughter's work. The source of this flaw, I suggest, lies not in the father's advice but in the daughter's internalized perception of his values. To justify the writing of "pretty stories and nov- elettes," the daughter of a father who values utility must teach a lesson. Thus, for example, *Ennui* (1809) contrasts negative and positive land agents and stresses the need for peasant education (something the Edgeworths strongly believed in and worked to- ward in founding a small school) and some measure of financial security. *The Absentee* (1812) blames much of the evils of poverty and mismanagement on absentee landlords who must learn, as Richard Lovell Edgeworth did, to oversee their own estates. Maria's own letters suggest that Richard Lovell Edgeworth may not have valued didacticism as much as his critics assert. An 1804 letter to Mrs. Ruxton notes: "My father continues to think Olivia and Lenora flat and spiritless and stuffed with morality." The evidence Marilyn Butler presents in her detailed chapter on authorship also strongly suggests that Edgeworth senior did not contribute overtly to the didacticism of his daughter's work.[7] Rather, I suggest, the didacticism is the ultimate if indirect re- sult of the neglect and loneliness of Maria's childhood and of the consequent desire never to risk exile again.

In this atmosphere of willing, perhaps mistaken, conformity, the origin of the subversive, original *Castle Rackrent* demands explanation. Maria Edgeworth's letters and the biographies all suggest the writer's reliance on an audience during the com- posing process for both assistance and assurance. Richard Lovell Edgeworth, father, teacher, and companion, most often played this role, but *Castle Rackrent* was the one work he neither com- missioned nor saw until its completion. Certainly, however, the writer who always sought assurance must have sought it in writ- ing her most experimental and original work. The many Edge- worth siblings, audience to countless schoolroom tales, were unlikely candidates for this particular text for, as Butler notes, Maria's superior role with her father was resented, and she lacked confidantes in her immediate family circle.[8] But there was one audience to whom she could always pour out her heart—the Ruxton family, in particular her Aunt Ruxton and Cousin Sophy.

Pages of letters flowed back and forth between Edgeworthstown and the Ruxton home, Black Castle, a home close enough
for frequent visits, though never as frequent as Maria desired.
Confidences, plans, jokes, observations were exchanged, but
however much she wrote Maria noted that it was not "half I
intended." "How I did laugh," she wrote her aunt of evenings
spent by the fire in Black Castle, "and how impossible it is not
to laugh in some company, or to laugh in others." Even when
her father's advice was readily available, Maria consulted the
Ruxtons, requesting both content and advice. She noted that she
had rewritten some forty pages of *Leonora* as a result of Ruxton
suggestions. Frequently she noted, coyly and childishly, that she
wrote in secret lest her father be annoyed by her constant need
to commune with her aunt and cousin. "I have been very prudent
in not bringing forward in conversation the joys of Black Castle—I was very near it once or twice but checked myself in
time!" Or she wrote, "My father seems to think that I have been
fed up into a little glutton at Black Castle—All things considered
I do not believe I have lost any considerable portion of my father's affection by my six weeks absence—and I hope dearest
aunt it has increased your love for me a tiny bit."[9]

All Maria's letters suggest a confidence and ease, a certainty
of acceptance that the Ruxton letters in their turn confirm. It is
not surprising then to find Maria mimicking in some letters the
dialect of John Langan, her father's steward and the model for
Thady Quirk, the purported narrator and retainer of *Rackrent*.
The brevity of the notations suggests a long-standing joke, one
so familiar to both writer and reader that a word serves to evoke
it. As early as 1792, for example, in a letter to Sophy "larning"
is used for "learning" in imitation of the Gaelic accent. In teasing
her aunt about who had written the most letters, Maria wrote,
"We'll leave it all to your honor's honor," a direct "Thadyism."
Butler reports that the "dramatic monologue" was first performed to entertain the sick Mrs. Ruxton, and Edgeworth herself suggested that the Ruxtons were both the initiators and the
frequent auditors of *Rackrent*. Writing her aunt in 1822 she
noted, "How many things we have talked over together! 'Rackrent' especially, which you first suggested to me and encouraged
me to go on with."[10]

Most revealing perhaps of the closeness of the Edgeworth/ Ruxton relationship are the letters concerning Maria's proposal. Traveling with her parents, Maria wrote frequently to her aunt. She broke off one letter because M. Edelcrantz, a Swedish diplomat, had called to see her. Returning in Pamela fashion to her letter, Maria confided to the "dearest Aunt" the news of Edelcrantz's proposal. Addressing Sophy five days later, however, she revealed her concerns: "I persist in refusing to leave my country and my friends to live at the Court of Stockholm, and he tells me (of course) that there is nothing he would not sacrifice for me except his duty; . . . He says he should not fear the ridicule or blame that would be thrown upon him by his countrymen for quitting his country at his age, but that he should despise himself if he abandoned his duty for any passion. This is all very reasonable, but reasonable for him only, not for me—I have not ever felt anything for him but esteem & gratitude." This frankness, not to say cynicism, emerges only in Maria's letters to her dear friends. After Maria's death, Edgeworth's fourth wife, Frances, who with her daughters published a memoir of the author, suggested that Maria was "mistaken as to her feelings," and evidence suggests that Richard Lovell Edgeworth favored the match.[11] But Maria's concerns about Edelcrantz's feelings for her (rather than hers for him) were apparently voiced only to the Ruxton family, the intimate circle in which she felt free to explore the ambiguities of her personal and political situation.

This lengthy introduction is necessary to correct some of the explanations of the Edgeworth partnership and to suggest the likely source of *Castle Rackrent*. The genesis of this text is important not simply as an historical note but because it accounts to a large extent for *Castle Rackrent*'s excellencies. Writing "for amusement only" and thus freed from the restraints she felt when publishing or going public, Edgeworth explored with her intimate confidantes the contradictions in the landlord-tenant relationships and the uncertainties and potential dangers in the marriage contract.[12] A questioning of either situation could only be undertaken in the company of those whom she knew and trusted thoroughly, who would not consequently misinterpret or suggest a betrayal of class or gender. It could only be undertaken, in short, in the security of the Ruxton home.

Persuaded by her Aunt Ruxton to publish the novel, Maria Edgeworth penned a preface intended to distance the manners and habits of the Rackrent landlords from her time and hence from any allegorical relationship or reflection on her father or on his family and friends. The prefatory passage I quote as epigraph to this chapter serves this deflective purpose but also points to the important patterns Edgeworth has inscribed in the text, patterns that identify the domestic life as a more reliable criterion of virtue than the public life and that further imply that performance in one sphere is an indication of performance in the other. In spite of text and preface, however, for nearly two hundred years critics have read only the public plot. As one of *Rackrent*'s most ardent admirers, George Watson is worth quoting at some length: "This vast literary revolution, which inspired Scott and perhaps Turgenev, and which informed the historical sensibility of a whole century and more, was set on foot (in the novel at least) by a diminutive thirty-year-old Anglo-Irish spinster in a remote house in the middle of Ireland in the last years of the eighteenth century, and it is a triumph that is still largely unknown. The best studies of the historical novel do not mention it. It is difficult to believe, even now, but Scott himself, who called her 'the great Maria,' seems to have been in no doubt where the credit lay." But even Watson ignores the domestic life. The critical tendency Virginia Woolf identified to validate one subject over another is at work here (see chapter 1). Another factor partially excuses these critics: Richard Lovell Edgeworth's belief in contract as the basis of social justice in Ireland is itself common knowledge and is the subject of his daughter's high praise in *Memoirs*. But *Rackrent* reveals what historians have long known, that contract was less than useless in eighteenth-century Ireland given the tenants' dependency and the landlords' greed.[13] This implied contradiction in the usual critical area of interest, the public life, attracts and distracts critics from other concerns.

Recent criticism, for example, reveals this public focus. Thomas Flanagan, the first of the contemporary critics, concludes his perceptive study by attributing the Rackrent downfall to betrayal and greed: "The family owes its origin to a triple denial, Patrick's rejection of his name, his blood, and his creed.

The denial has been made for the sake of land and the money which land brings, but these, despite every frantic measure, run through their fingers." Turning to Thady, Bruce Teets sees the retainer as "at once servant of lovable wastrels and father of a son who unlovably profits at their expense." James Newcomer continues to analyze the enigmatic narrator: Thady, he says, "reflects intellect and power in the afflicted Irish peasant. . . . He is artful rather than artless, unsentimental rather than sentimental, shrewd rather than obtuse, clear-headed rather than confused, calculating rather than trusting." Looking again to the Rackrent men, W.B. Coley notes that "extinction of the direct Rackrent line is an early hint of the frailty of the aristocratic ideal, particularly as the basis for organizing a modern society, and it becomes the implicit aim of the novel to demonstrate this frailty in all its forms." O. Elizabeth M. Harden sees the Rackrent vices, the causes of their fall, shine clearly through the transparencies of Thady's deliberately opaque paean, and Gerry H. Brookes finds the work a didactic "apologue."[14]

Following Flanagan's lead, John Cronin sees Thady as "a magnificently realized slave, a terrifying vision of the results of colonial misrule," whereas W.J. McCormack notes that *Rackrent* reveals the division in the Anglo-Irish class and the changing modes of inheritance. Remarking on the importance of the woman's perspective, McCormack seems to limit that perspective to architectural details. The most recent criticism to date continues the public focus: *Castle Rackrent*, says Robert Tracy, is "an object lesson in how *not* to be an Irish landlord."[15] Perceptive and probing as these criticisms are, they remain incomplete because they disregard the complicating, ironic foil of the domestic plot.

While *Castle Rackrent* is most certainly the story of four Irish landlords, it is also the story of the Rackrents as husbands, seen through the eyes of a Gaelic-Irish retainer, a servant, and, perhaps more important in the domestic context, a man. The first Rackrent, Sir Patrick, assumes the estate and name on the death of a distant cousin. Hard-drinking and jovial, Sir Patrick ignores the estate, feasts the countryside, and dies as he has lived, drinking and entertaining. Sir Murtagh succeeds—a lawyer and miser who brings the full force of the penal laws to bear upon his tenants, denies them customary rights, and sues rather than entertains his neighbors. Marrying Skinflint, a woman who shares his acquisitive ardor, Murtagh acquires not the rich estate he had hoped for but a competitor. With Murtagh's blessing Skinflint exploits the tenants, but she also extracts monies unapproved by and infuriating to Murtagh. In a final debate over these monies, Murtagh bursts a blood vessel and dies.

The childless squire is succeeded by his younger brother, Sir Kit, a gambler whose only interest is in extracting every penny he can from his estate to wager in England. The charming Kit commissions an agent to do his gouging, and the tenants are driven ever closer to economic ruin and starvation. Seeking financial salvation, Kit marries Jessica, a rich English Jewess. Despite Kit's limiting the household meat to pork and locking Jessica away for seven years, Jessica refuses to part with her money. She is finally freed when Kit dies in a duel with the brother of one of the women he courted during his wife's seclusion. Childless like Murtagh, Kit is followed by his cousin Condy. Lazy, slovenly, and weak, Condy flatters the gentry, incurs enormous debts (in part because he runs for parliament to please this gentry), and allows his "castle" to fall into ruins and his estate and tenants to be bought out by Thady's son Jason. Despite his friendship with Thady's niece Judy, Condy runs off with the rich Isabella whose father refused Condy's overtures to his daughter. Her own money spent and with Jason closing in for the kill, Isabella leaves Condy, who sells Jason the jointure he had generously bestowed on Isabella. Condy dies childless; he is friendless too because he is penniless, as the poor spectacle of his funeral shows.

Within the text itself Edgeworth draws clear parallels between the behavior of the Rackrents as landlords and of the Rackrents as husbands, the comparison she points to in the preface. Another element that should draw attention to the domestic plot, an element noted by Sandra Gilbert and Susan Gubar but unobserved in analyses of the novel, is the reversal of the traditional romance ending. In *Rackrent* each wife escapes upon her husband's death, her fortune intact and indeed in two cases increased. In Edgeworth's own life such escapes would have been anomalies—pregnancy and childbirth took a heavy toll on married women. Edgeworth's father, for example, had four wives, who between them bore him twenty-two children. Although Edgeworth portrays strong women and virtuous women elsewhere—Lady Geraldine in *Ennui*, for example, and Grace in *The Absentee*—their roles are traditional, circumscribed by their relationships to males. The parallels and reversal of plot, then, in *Castle Rackrent* are overt and unusual both in Edgeworth's and in traditional fiction. There seems little excuse to ignore them. Related elements, however, which support this unconventional perspective constitute the muted or secondary plot of women's fiction and are by definition recessive; hence, neglect is understandable.[16]

Important in this latter context are Edgeworth's allusions to and revisions of earlier texts, allusions that implicitly condemn traditional narrative paradigms. Yet another important element in this muted plot is the narrator's disinterest in the fate of the Rackrent wives. If Thady Quirk, the purported narrator, is, to borrow from Watson again, "an observer fully within a society he exemplifies as well as describes," then his attitude, which the reader must condemn, is also to some degree that of his society, which, by extension, we must also condemn. Subversively recounting the troubles of his people, the tenants, while apparently praising their tormentors, the Rackrents, Thady dismisses the Rackrent women's problems. Ironically, as a colonized Gaelic-Irish servant, one of Elizabeth Janeway's weak, Thady can be seen as a surrogate woman, one prevented from supporting her natural allies by the need to remain in the good grace of the powerful. But the extent of Thady's neglect demands explication. Joanne Altieri suggests that "a description of Thady's speech is a picture of the novel's world, its refusal to see causality, to make choices, to think." Altieri terms the disruptions in Thady's speech, the incomplete sentences, and the apparently illogical syntax "parataxis." I suggest that the persistent jettisoning of the women's, or domestic, plot into the lacunae created by Thady's parataxis calls attention to the discarded plot, an instance of the italicizing by underemphasizing that Nancy Miller discusses.[17] Another irony is present in *Rackrent*: Edgeworth pictures this jettisoning, this dismissal of women's concerns, as the immediate, unquestioned, instinctive mode of the male narrator. Thady's behavior thus, in this and in other respects, calls into

question the implied contract between writer and reader, just
as the Rackrents' behavior as landlords and husbands questions,
I argue, the contracts advocated by eminent eighteenth-century
figures as the bases of social justice.

In his study of contracts in the nineteenth-century novel, Tony
Tanner examines the historical relationship of property and marriage laws. Marriage contracts, he notes, were intended to constitute an essential "harmonious interrelationship of patterns of
property and patterns of passion and feeling." A wife's fidelity
insured that a man's son would inherit his land; in return a
woman received her husband's attention and protection. The
other side of the marriage contract—the side that ties this contract securely to the public landlord contract, the side understandably taken for granted in the England Tanner studies—was
the husband's duty to procreate with his wife, to beget an heir
to the property. This contract-making power of the propertied
classes is, Tanner believes, derived from the power to define
terms and to control discourse. Like Tanner, Edgeworth aligns
the property and marriage contracts, but *Castle Rackrent*, as
we shall see, also implies knowledge of other property laws—
the property laws of Gaelic Ireland, for example, that allowed
the wives of chiefs to extract rent from the subjects or tenants—
and the equity laws. A comparatively new field in the eighteenth
century, equity laws were designed to redress some of the injustices of common law and were the first English laws to attempt protection of women's property rights in marriage.
Further, also like Tanner, Edgeworth realizes the power that
control of discourse confers, a control she ties in *Castle Rackrent*
to the Rackrents' economic power. Their power enables them, as
Tanner notes of Clarissa Harlowe's father, to "distort terminolo-
gies and vocabularies."[18] Finally, in alluding to Shakespeare,
Edgeworth implicitly extends this control to another group—to
the writers and interpreters of canonical works whose views
often become gospel for following generations.

This thematic triad—landlord and marital contracts and control of discourse—runs through all three marriages in *Castle
Rackrent*, revealing ironic distances between principle and practice. The first conflict Thady is made to detail, that of Sir Murtagh
and his tenants and Sir Murtagh and his wife, Lady Skinflint, is

explicitly presented as a struggle between conflicting interpretations based on the bodies of law concerned in each case. Murtagh, we are told, is a "legal expert" who keeps the tenants in shape through "driving for rent" and fear of lawsuits. The epitome of the corrupt eighteenth-century Irish landlord, Murtagh, Thady tells us, is "always driving and driving, and pounding and pounding, and canting and canting, and replevying and replevying, and he made a good living of trespassing cattle—there was always some tenant's pig, or horse, or cow, or calf, or goose, trespassing, which was so great a gain to Sir Murtagh, that he did not like to hear me talk of repairing fences. Then his herriots and duty work brought him in something—his turf was cut—his potatoes set and dug—his hay brought home, and in short all the work about his house was done for nothing; for in all our leases there were strict clauses with heavy penalties, which Sir Murtagh knew well how to enforce."[19]

Refusing the tenants their customary rights, those rights of security extended under old Gaelic law and under English law, rights which Thady synecdochically represents as "their whiskey," Murtagh enforces the onerous repressions of the penal laws, repressions that Edgeworth's grandfather imposed but that the ideal landlord, Richard Lovell Edgeworth, "never claimed or would he accept of them." Yet, Thady muses, Murtagh, the great lawyer, loses money and is forced to sell Rackrent land.[20] Although Murtagh can drive his unprotected tenants to poverty and force them to work his land at the expense of their own miserable harvest, his compulsive suits against his neighbors cost him heavily. Despite his legal training, Murtagh, blinded by excessive greed, misreads the legal code, whereas Lady Skinflint, as we shall see, reads closely and correctly.

The litigious, avaricious landlord whose activities lead to decrease is also presented through the gaps in Thady's narrative as an equally litigious, avaricious husband. Murtagh has sinned against the harmonious alignment of the marriage and property contracts in marrying only for "the great Skinflint estate." But there, Thady admits dolefully, "he overshot himself," for though Lady Skinflint is "one of the co-heiresses, he was never the better for her." Never the better for her, Murtagh must have had no access to the income from the Skinflint estate. The estate must, therefore, have been protected from him in equity. Under common law the income from the estate as well as all other income Lady Skinflint accumulated would have been legally Murtagh's to use as he pleased. Murtagh's legal losses to his neighbors may also stem from his ignorance of equity law: the proceedings that he undertook and lost so often are referred to as "suits," the term used for proceedings in equity, whereas "actions" referred to proceedings in common law. Not only does Lady Skinflint outwit Sir Murtagh in her lifetime, but Thady begrudgingly admits that "she had a fine jointure settled upon her," that is, a financial interest in some Rackrent land for her lifetime.[21] Although Murtagh's greed as a landlord allows him to ignore the old Gaelic rights and to exploit the newer penal law against his tenants, his greed as a husband blinds him to the fact that another new system of law might protect his wife's fortune from him.

Control of discourse alone allows Murtagh to bully and cheat; loss of this control means death for Murtagh, freedom for his wife, and a new form of bondage for the tenants. When the body of his predecessor, Sir Patrick, is seized for debt, Murtagh refuses to "pay a shilling of the debts," asserting that he had meant to honor all of them, "but the moment the law was taken of him, there was an end of honor to be sure." This comes from Murtagh, the man who taught his tenants "to know the law of landlord and tenant." Dismissing the alternative perspective of Murtagh's behavior as the derogatory story of enemies, Thady, in an overt example of double-voiced discourse, reports the enemies' belief that "this was all a sham seizure to get quit of the debts, which he had bound himself to pay in honor." The "derogatory story," of course, illustrates Murtagh's ability to twist concepts. The last debate, however, takes place not in a courtroom but in Lady Skinflint's chamber. The subject is one that has long incensed Murtagh—Lady Skinflint's interpretation of landlord-tenant contracts. For the Lady, a quick learner, appropriates, besides her dues, many extras from the tenants. Most infuriating to her husband is the money she receives to "speak" for the tenants "about abatements and renewals," monies not unlike the lady's rent or little rent received by wives of Gaelic-Irish chieftains as their dues. Usually alert to his own interests, Murtagh has, to his terrible anger, overlooked these customs. In "his last speech," Thady reports, Murtagh becomes so "mad" at his wife's insistence on the "last word" and shouts "so loud" that he bursts a blood vessel.[22] The outraged figure of the rapacious landlord and husband is finally silenced by the volcanic eruption of his own distorted discourse.

Another parallel runs through the three marriages: the Rackrents are all childless. Exceptional in itself, this condition also rebounds to the Rackrents' discredit as husbands and landlords. Thady glides quickly over this area, the source of the Rackrent condition becoming lost in the gaps of his language, gaps which act as a scaffolding in both hiding and drawing attention to the muted plot. Even the fact of Sir Murtagh's childlessness is reported in an offhand manner, a mere aside as Thady introduces the next Rackrent, the brother, not the son, of Murtagh. We must return to the introduction of Murtagh for explanation. The local people, Thady told us, were surprised at Murtagh's marriage, thinking "he demeaned himself greatly." No explanation of the demeaning is offered, and the reader must explore the space of Thady's silence. Marriage, we recall from Tony Tanner, was a method of effecting property security through physical alliances. The bride's financial status, the property half of the equation, is not the cause of Murtagh's demeaning himself, for Thady knows Murtagh "looked to the great Skinflint estate."[23] Thady, the Rackrent interpreter, however, says nothing to the locals, thus controlling their image of Murtagh. This leaves the physical alliance and Murtagh's childless condition. Is this, then, the reason Murtagh's marriage was demeaning? Lady Skinflint was a widow, but since no children are mentioned, we may presume she has none. The widow could be barren, a condition the locals would sense, and hence they would find Murtagh's marriage demeaning. Perhaps the widow is too old to bear children (hence Murtagh, as Thady notes, would not have foreseen her survival). Or, again, she may be physically repulsive. If any of these conditions exists, Murtagh's demeaning marriage is directly related to his childlessness. If this is the case, then Murtagh, who has already perverted the harmonious alignment by marrying only for money, is doubly a contract-breaker. By ne-

glecting his duty as husband he has also neglected the duty of
a landlord to provide for his estate, the one act (or absence
thereof) rendering void the hearths of both contracts.

In the more detailed presentation of the next Rackrent, Sir
Kit, Edgeworth parodies a popular type. Unlike the dour Murtagh, Kit is "so fine a gentleman" that Thady can easily understand Jessica's acceptance of the charming gambler. From Bath
Kit calls for monies and more monies to finance his gambling,
forcing the agent to "rackrent," to ignore tenants' improvements
at renewal time and to lease the land to the highest bidder. The
leaseholder must in turn take what he can and then abscond,
since the lease is too high to allow him a living.[24] Popular fiction,
and tradition as espoused by Thady, fostered the idea of the noble
and innocent landlord behind whose back the agents, characterized as avaricious "middle men," cheated and gouged the tenants.

In *Memoirs*, Maria Edgeworth also blames the problems
Richard Lovell Edgeworth encountered upon his return to Ireland on the agent; the rackrenting, "driving," and "fining down
the year's rent" that "came into fashion" with Kit are all abuses
Edgeworth senior discovered in Edgeworthstown. Time and
again throughout her career in novels such as *The Absentee*,
Maria Edgeworth rails against these abuses of the agents or middle men, but in *Castle Rackrent* the hypocrisy of the landlord's
delegation of responsibility is exposed. "Money" to Kit is no
"more than dirt," and so he writes his agent in Ireland for sum
after exorbitant sum. Tenants are driven to destitution (those
forced to give up land were deprived of their only livelihood),
but Thady passes over this as quickly in *Rackrent* as Edgeworth
does in *Memoirs*. Rents are called in early to finance Kit's gambling, and finally the agent resigns, not having, Thady reports,
"any more to lend himself."[25]

Kit's greed and subsequent need for funds distinguishes him,
of course, from Richard Lovell Edgeworth, who "not being in
want of ready money . . . was not obliged to let his land to the
highest bidder." But as historians note and as Edgeworth implies
in the irony of Thady's conclusion, the absentees were themselves responsible for all the abuses inflicted in their names on
the tenants. Thady summarizes the awful conditions: "I walked
about, thinking if his honour Sir Kit, (long may he live to reign

over us!) knew all this, it would go hard with him, but he'd see us righted."[26] The paralleling of prayer and opinion emphasizes the duplicity: Kit's return, as Thady knows, brought as little amelioration to the tenants as his own prayer for long life is likely to bring increase of years to the dead man.

The same patterns of hypocrisy prevail in Kit's marriage. As he courts Jessica, Kit writes to Thady that "he was going to be married . . . to the grandest heiress in England, and had only immediate occasion at present for £200, as he would not choose to touch his lady's fortune for travelling expences home to Castle Rackrent." Kit, we must assume, is putting on a show of his own financial stability for Jessica. This Thady denies later, noting that "it was a shame for her, being his wife, not to show more duty, and to have given it [money] up when he condescended to ask so often for such a bit of a trifle in his distresses, especially when he all along made it no secret he married for money." The person Kit made it no secret from was Thady, however, not Jessica. Otherwise why would he pretend financial stability? And in marrying thus, Kit, of course, also abuses the harmonious alignment clause of the marital contract. In attempting to compel Jessica's financial surrender, he again resorts to hypocrisy. Initially isolating Jessica in a foreign country away from society, then having his cook serve only "pig-meat" to his Jewess wife, and finally locking her in her room for seven years, the charming host, Kit, toasts his "ladyship's health" and—ultimate hypocrisy—sends servants "to know if there was any thing [always sausages or bacon, or pig meat] at table he might send her." All the while Kit pays court to other women. But try as he may, he cannot touch Jessica's money, which Thady represents as her "diamond cross."[27]

Again only the laws of equity can protect both Jessica's income and her personal property from the unprincipled gambler's greed. Inadvertently Thady points us to these laws again: referring to the women who pursued Kit during Jessica's enforced isolation, the canny retainer notes wryly that they did not know "how my lady's fortune was settled in her will." Under common law Kit would have had a lifetime interest in Jessica's estate after her death, even though the estate itself were not willed to him. Under equity, however, Jessica devises the property as she desires, and Kit can benefit only if she wishes. "Never cured of his gaming tricks," as Thady reports indulgently, Kit has ruined his tenants and his agent and most certainly would have wasted Jessica's fortune also had he had access to it.[28]

Once again it is control of discourse that allows Kit to prevail. A "sad crisis" arises when two of the three ladies Kit has promised himself to while his wife, Jessica, still lives show his letters of promise to their brothers. Sir Kit responds to the brothers' anger by challenging them to duel. And local society—defined by Thady as the "gentlemen"—not knowing of Jessica's will nor of the mortgages and debts against Rackrent, bends easily to what it perceives to be the source of economic, and hence narrative, control: "Upon this, as upon all former occasions, Sir Kit had the voice of the country with him because of the great spirit and propriety he acted with." It is only, Thady continues, when Kit is carried home "speechless" that the gentlemen understand that Jessica was "shut up" "against her own consent." Then they come to protest her confinement and release her. Kit must lose control of discourse before the fawning neighbors pretend to notice Jessica's predicament. Indeed, since Jessica is wealthy, their motives are again as suspect as Thady's; he reports that he would have been quite a favorite had she stayed: "But when I saw she had made up her mind to spend the rest of her days upon her own income and jewels in England, I considered her quite as a foreigner."[29] Hence the praise that Thady might have bestowed is lost, and Jessica is abused as a "foreigner" instead.

The pattern of childlessness is repeated in Kit Rackrent's life, and we must again repair Thady's parataxis for explanation. On the morning after the honeymoon night in the stateroom of Rackrent, Thady notes sagely that he saw "how things were" and remarks, apparently irrelevantly, that Kit inquired if the barrack room were dry. Edgeworth's glossary note on the fitting of barrack rooms with beds for extra guests hints at the importance of Kit's question. We next hear of this room when Thady extracts a key from the pocket of the dead Kit and releases Jessica from the barrack room. Jessica, then, has been banished from the nuptial chamber, the stateroom, since her second day in Rackrent. Kit's condition, then, is of his own making. The absentee landlord is also an absentee husband. Thady confirms this reconstruction at a later point in the narrative: "Latterly," he says of Condy, "seeing how Sir Kit and the *Jewish* lived together, and that there was no one between him and the Castle Rackrent estate, he neglected to apply to the law as much as was expected of him." Not only does Kit violate the land customs with his tenants and the harmonious alignment tenets of the marriage contract, but his sexual abstinence with Jessica also undermines both contracts. Adultery, as Tony Tanner notes, seeps through the silences of the nineteenth-century novel, undermining the very basis of the writer-reader contract.[30] Ironically it is sexual abstinence that seeps through the cracks in Thady's narrative, also undermining the narrator-auditor contract and suggesting the appropriateness of a more pervasive skepticism than that already applied to Thady's unvarnished tale.

The patterns of the third Rackrent are by this time obvious and would be ignored except that critics, following Thady's bias to his white-headed boy, have found Condy likable and the "only honest member of the clan." One need only glance at Condy's parliamentary record to appreciate his "honesty": Condy, Thady reports, was astonished by the lawyers asking his friends "had they ever been upon the ground where their freeholds lay?" as the law demanded of voters. "Being tender of the consciences of them that had not been on the ground," Condy sent a servant for sods from the lands and had his friends stand on these. "We gained the day by this piece of honesty," Thady reports. As for Condy the parliamentarian, Thady tells us that he looked daily to no avail for word of his master in the paper, for "he never spoke good or bad." But word does come that Condy "was very ill used by the government about a place that was promised him and never given, after his supporting them against his conscience very honorably, and being greatly abused for it, which hurt him greatly, he having the name of a great patriot in the country before." The daughter who admired Richard Lovell Edgeworth's parliamentary stands against what he saw as the powerful, monied interests in government must have seen Condy's actions as far from honest or likable. Condy's final dealings with Jason also bespeak deception.[31]

Accurately Thady defines Condy as "not willing to take his affairs into his own hands." Refusing to cope with the debts he keeps incurring, Condy allows Jason to buy him out bit by bit. Drinking constantly, he ignores the decline of Rackrent, tenants, and marriage. This refusal of responsibility is part of a servile mentality; Condy often acts not from any conviction but to ingratiate himself with either his acquaintances or with the local squires. Although in dire need of money, Condy, fearful of displeasing his gentry debtors, never requests payment and cheerfully does their bidding, even to his ruin. Again fawning on the Rackrent tenants, he borrows their money with promises of bargain leases, even before Sir Kit's death.[32]

This pattern is similar to Thady's own patterns of speaking and acting: I have already noted the narrator's assuring the editor of his unbelievable trust in Sir Kit's willingness to save the Rackrent tenants. Throughout, the story is the same. Thady frequently notes his premonitions of disaster but adds, "I said nothing for fear of gaining myself ill will." Thady, of course, unlike Condy, is a member of the weak, colonized class, and his tactics—those, Cronin notes, of a "magnificently realized slave"—are thus a matter of survival. Condy, however, is gentry, the head of Castle Rackrent; his tactics are not necessary but are the result of, presumably, his early training by Thady himself, cowardice, and inertia. Again, Condy's activities as landlord are in sharp contrast with those of Richard Lovell Edgeworth, whose daughter notes that despite the difficulties presented by his own generous nature, her father persisted in a just course in dealings with his tenants. "If the people had found or suspected him to be weak, or, as they call it, *easy*, there would have been an end of all hope of really doing them good. They would have cheated, loved, and despised a mere *easy* landlord; and his property would have gone to ruin, without either permanently bettering their interest or their morals." Although he does not harass the tenants personally as Sir Murtagh did or through an agent as Sir Kit did, Condy's neglect of his affairs proves disastrous, as Edgeworth predicts of "easy" landlords, throwing the tenants under the terror of Jason's landlordship.[33]

Condy's marriage duplicates the landlord patterns. Afraid of displeasing either Judy, the woman to whom he is promised and whom Thady thinks he loves, or Isabella, the woman who seems to love him and whose father rejects him, Condy tosses a coin, allowing chance to select his bride. Refusing to take responsibility, Condy acts as we see Thady talk; that is, he refuses to connect events in his life with his actions, just as Thady refuses to connect elements in his speech. While Isabella's own money lasts, the "easy" Condy is happy to spend it with her. When there are no prospects of any further monies, Condy is equally easy to stay at home in discomfort, poverty, and squalor. As the broken windows in Rackrent are patched with slates and as the furniture is "canted," Condy, ever agreeable, consents to Isabella's request that he shave, though he notes, "I shaved the day before yesterday." (Ironically, the Big House—whose decay parallels the decline of the Anglo-Irish in later work—makes its natal appearance in *Castle Rackrent* as a fully-fledged wreck!) And as Isabella deplores her lot in having opposed her father and insisted on marrying a man who was—unbeknownst to her—already ruined, Condy comforts her: "Don't cry and make yourself *uneasy* about it now, when it's all over, and you have the man of your own choice in spite of 'em all" (my italics).[34]

In settling the jointure on Isabella prior to settling his debts with Jason, Condy, the unpracticed lawyer, reveals his knowledge of equity. Although under common law jointures could be arranged before marriage, as in Lady Skinflint's case, they could not be so arranged after the marriage. Husband and wife being one, there was no "other" for whom a spouse could plan. In his initial willingness to do the generous thing by Isabella, Condy is true to his "easy" character; in his equal willingness to renege on this act when tempted by Jason's gold, the pliable Condy remains constantly inconstant.[35] Excessive drinking is, of course, both the source of Condy's troubles and his refuge from them, but again Thady and Condy are presented as being unable to recognize the consequences of this habit, both for the Rackrent tenants and for Isabella.

The third marriage is also childless. In the early days of the marriage Thady reports that Isabella sobbed and begged Condy to give up his drinking, for the smell made her sick. Reporting "faithfully," Thady notes that Condy could not understand this, for the smell had never made Isabella sick before her marriage. "I never smelt it, or I assure you I should never have prevailed upon myself to marry you," Isabella asserts. Condy answers, confirming Isabella's worse fear, that he neither loves nor desires her: "I am sorry you did not smell it, but we can't help that now." Despite Condy's "reasonableness," Thady notes that Isabella continued to provoke him, asking if he was "fit company for her, and he drinking all night." The "fit company" Isabella desires is of course a lover—this is the reason the romantic woman ran away with Condy. The effects of a night's drinking on the lover's performance are commonplace, but, unwilling as always to "look" his affairs "in the face," Condy misreads Isabella's plea and, Thady reports, picks up the candle and retires to "his" room. Drinking all night and every night, the flexible, "easy" Condy is, even before he sinks totally into squalor, impotent, physically incapable of sexual intercourse. Isabella, though not subjected to the conscious harassment her predecessors endured, is bereft indeed of the "father, brother, husband, and friend" she expected to find in Condy.[36]

Attempts to control discourse and to manipulate peers' and subordinates' perceptions of reality characterize each Rackrent's attempt to control his land and his wife. Murtagh tries to enforce his will through legal declarations; Kit, through agents; and Condy, through a refusal to understand the implications of words, similar to the Rackrent refusal to recognize the implications of contracts. Ignoring the transformation between what he seemed to be and to promise and what he has become, Condy cannot understand Isabella's complaints. In response to her plea that he not drink so he can be a husband, Condy answers, "Am not I your husband, and of your own chusing." Forgetting that words, like contracts, must have a basis in the actual as well as in the legal and linguistic worlds, Condy implies that the legalization and formalization of the title constitutes the physical relationship itself. When Isabella reproaches him for failing to inform her before marriage of his financial position, Condy says: "Tell you, my dear, . . . did you ever ask me one word about it? and had not you friends enough of your own, that were telling you nothing else from morning to night, if you'd have listened to them slanders."[37] Condy distorts discourse as does Thady, and the effects on his tenants and on his wife are similar to the effects of the deliberate perversion of discourse by his ancestors. While

equity attempts to repair the gap left by the decay of the natural
basis of the common law tenets on property in marriage, other
breaches, which the Rackrents exploit, remain. Ignoring the mutuality of commitments implied by the words *husband* and *landlord*, the Rackrents, while insisting on their legal positions,
reduce and destroy the "natural" basis of semantic and legal definitions. Their own barren natural conditions symbolize their true
standing as both husbands and landlords.

Other elements in the muted plot support this interpretation.
As noted already, this plot resides in the literary allusions and
revisions, the gaps and patterns (or patterns of gaps) in Thady's
speech, in, to use Nancy Miller's terminology again, the italicizing of demaximization. The pattern of childlessness in the
Rackrent family is an instance of such italicizing; the pattern
becomes visible through an analysis of Thady's oblique remarks
and silences. Another instance of de-emphasis is Thady's ignoring of the plight of the Rackrent wives, his grotesquely casual
dismissal of Jessica's seven-year entombment and of the squalor
in which Isabella must live. The cavalier attitude of the Rackrents toward their religion also highlights Jessica's steadfastness. Thady reports that Patrick O'Shaughlin had to change his
name to Rackrent to inherit the estate, but Thomas Flanagan
points out that he also had to change his religion, a precondition
that Thady would certainly have known but that, like so much
else, gets lost in the parataxis of his language. In contrast with
Patrick's perversion, Jessica's steadfastness is admirable and
ironically suggests, as Elizabeth Harden notes, not the "financial
salvation" Kit had expected from his marriage but damnation.
Edgeworth links the last Rackrent, Condy, to the first, not only
through his alcoholism and his death by drinking but also through
the presentation of his marriage decision. Thady tells us that the
coin Condy tosses to decide his bride is marked with Judy's sign,
the sign of a cross, and the editor repeats (for emphasis?) this
information in a footnote.[38] Combined with the other religious
references in this passage—Condy's swearing his oath on a bal-
lad book he took to be a Bible, Thady's blessing himself and
praying for Condy—the cross highlights Condy's attitude to religion. In abrogating his duty to rationally enter the marriage

contract that should, according to St. Paul, mirror for the Christian the contract of Christ and his church, Condy, by implication, like Sir Patrick, also abrogates his religious duty.

In alluding to Shakespeare, the muted plot suggests a more subtle and enduring power over discourse than that of Thady, a mere narrator (though a manipulative one), or of the Rackrents. At the most obvious level the Rackrents exercise control because the weak, tenants and wives, must agree with their definitions. Thady, as narrator of the Rackrents' story to both the townspeople and the editor, controls the locals' opinion of Rackrent wives and husbands and, as we have seen, has controlled readers' opinions to an excessive, embarrassing extent. But ultimate control of the word rests with the author, who, Gilbert and Gubar note, as "owner of his [sic] text . . . is also, of course, owner/possessor of the subjects of his text." As such, Edgeworth is in control, and it is ultimately she who manipulates Thady, not he who controls the editor. This "owner/possessor" has Thady tell us that Kit formerly wooed the Jewess as "my pretty Jessica," and thus she calls our attention to the parallels between the marriage of Kit and Jessica Rackrent and that of Lorenzo and Jessica in Shakespeare's *The Merchant of Venice*.[39]

Shakespeare's control of his discourse allowed him to depict approvingly a young woman's robbing of her revengeful but protective father and abandonment of family, race, and creed for romantic love. Traditional interpretation has followed Shakespeare's lead, implying by its silence the wisdom of Jessica's choice and commenting only on the rough fate of Shylock. Edgeworth's reversal, her female text, in which Jessica is incarcerated for her refusal to surrender her ducats, suggests the hideous alternative to the fantasized happiness. Jessica Rackrent's escape, her ability to leave Rackrent on Kit's death, is the direct result of the preservation of her economic independence through the equity law and of Jessica's acting contrary to Shakespeare's character. Invoking Shakespeare in the first place, Edgeworth recalls for us the romantic myth; revising him in a shocking manner, she implies the dangerous consequences of a woman's accepting the myth. Further, the fact that Jessica has to her regret initially conformed suggests the enduring and pernicious power of unreasonable patterns when such patterns are encoded and therefore apparently legitimized in powerful artistic discourses. Jessica, in effect, has attempted to act out a Shakespearean role.[40]

The suggestion is even stronger that the self-destructive foolishness of Isabella's marrying Condy may be the logical result of centuries of male control of discourse. Unlike the suave Kit, Condy is a "laughing stock and a butt for the whole company" in Isabella's house. And Isabella, we understand—despite Thady's partiality to his niece Judy—is fashionable, lovely, and wealthy. So why would she marry Condy? Again we must look beyond the narrational summation for Isabella's motives: Isabella lives in Mount Juliet, where, according to her brother, she "plays" Juliet "better than any woman on or *off* the stage" (my italics). She sends messages through her servants to the oath-loving Condy and, when her father locks her in her room, runs away to a furtive marriage. Belatedly Isabella recognizes the source of her actions: "My father was wrong to lock me up, I own; . . . for if he had not locked me up, I should never have had a serious thought of running away as I did."[41] Although the limited narrator is unaware of the echoes, the implication is clear that, like Jessica before her, Isabella acted out the Shakespearean drama in real life. Such replays, Edgeworth's repetitive plot suggests, are inevitable as long as texts conclude "optimistically" with women's surrendering of all ties for romantic love. Denied any respectable livelihood outside marriage and nurtured on the ideal of romantic love, eighteenth- and nineteenth-century women "naturally" modeled their expectations and their acquaintances on the life they knew only through literature, often with disastrous results.

If, as Isabella discovers, romantic marriages are optimistic deceptions, then the structure of traditional narrative is also at fault. In terminating women's stories with their marriages, the structure as well as the content signals that marriage is the end of women's lives and of their interest as narrative subjects. Edgeworth reverses the schema, opening her sequences with the women's marriages and closing with their escapes. In the interval her heroines encounter vicissitudes comparable to those of male adventurers, from which they emerge not unscathed but wiser. Such a revolutionary reversal is not a matter of chance and, coupled with Edgeworth's critical revisions, suggests a critique of the reproduction of male as human desire in traditional narrative. These paradigms, Edgeworth implies, are adopted by young women who lack alternative patterns or the means to create them. Indeed, in alluding to Shakespearean dramas of female incarceration, Edgeworth by association suggests that for women marriage implies imprisonment and perhaps even death: Jessica's physical and Isabella's emotional constriction corresponds in some measure to Juliet's entombment.

In this context, I must mention Judy—Thady's niece—who is overthrown by Condy for the fashionable lady, Isabella. Hearing that Isabella has had an accident, Judy, now widowed, visits the destitute, ill Condy. Seeing the welcome she receives, Thady thinks Judy is likely to become "my lady Rackrent after all, if a vacancy should have happened." But Judy plans otherwise: "What signifies it to be my lady Rackrent and no Castle?" she asks, and she suggests that it is to Jason she will now look. And while Thady, but not his sister, is shocked at what he calls ingratitude, Edgeworth's structure suggests irony rather than disapproval. For Judy's intention duplicates the marital intentions of the Rackrent squires, repeats the egoistic pattern Freud identified as male rather than the erotic one he characterized as female, and appropriates in fact the male desiderata. Edgeworth's subversive revisions thus imply the revolutionary perspective that the writer-reader contract, like the landlord-tenant and husband-wife contracts, assumes when viewed from the wild zone of the weak: the "impartiality" of the contract is replaced by the partiality of a system designed and interpreted by and for only one of the contracting parties. Asserting the instability of all such contracts, the plot of *Castle Rackrent*, like the plots of women's works Nancy Miller analyzes, is not only about life, or the Rackrent lives, but "about the plots of literature itself, about the constraints the maxim places on rendering a female life in fiction."[42]

As I suggested earlier, the excellencies, the contradictions and novelties, in *Castle Rackrent* are due in large measure to its genesis. By "novelties" I mean the subversive domestic plot. By "contradictions" I mean that *Castle Rackrent* reveals that the contracts Richard Lovell Edgeworth favored, and which his daughter lauds him for so favoring, are less than useless in eighteenth-century Ireland, given the tenants' condition and the landlords' power. This dichotomy continues to tilt the critical focus toward the public story only and to cause Edgeworth supporters concern. Marilyn Butler, for example, suggests that Watson should not use the word *skill* in describing Maria Edgeworth's use of Thady as narrator. While agreeing that Thady's "dominance" gives the work unity, Butler asserts: "It certainly does not allow the story to speak for her. She found it unpalatable that she had made the quaint, archaic narrator more interesting than the Rackrents, who as landlords had in reality a more significant part to play in Irish life. Her motives in taking to fiction were not to act as an amanuensis to John Langan; on the contrary, the viewpoint she wanted to adopt was English and forward-looking."[43]

Of course it was. And the viewpoint Edgeworth did adopt in all the later, carefully constructed novels and in the *Memoirs* was that of the forward-looking landlord. This is the point: Edgeworth did not write *Castle Rackrent* to exemplify any principle, either her own or her father's. To repeat, she wrote it, as she tells us herself, "for mere amusement, without any ideas of publishing."[44] Consequently she was in this single instance not intent on polemic, either in favor of her father's practices or in behalf of a repressed Ireland. Freed thus from public view, Edgeworth drops her role of exemplum and adventures instead into ambiguous territories, registering there (whether fully conscious of the message or not) contradictory, conflicting voices, registering indeed the cacophony of conflicting voices that M.M. Bakhtin identifies with the uninhibited novel. Sadly, however, in Edgeworth's case, all future writing was undertaken to enlighten and reform and did present the ultimately less interesting forward-looking view that also isolated Edgeworth from the dangerously infectious, vitally compelling voices.

3. Somerville and Ross
Ignoble Tragedy

> It is hard to ask pity for Charlotte, whose many evil qualities
> have without pity been set down, but the seal of ignoble trage-
> dy had been set on her life; she had not asked for love, but it
> had come to her, twisted by the malign hand of fate. There is
> pathos as well as humiliation in the thought that such a thing
> as a soul can be stunted by the trivialities of personal appear-
> ance, and it is a fact not beyond the reach of sympathy that
> each time Charlotte stood before her glass her ugliness spoke
> to her of failure, and goaded her to revenge.
> —E.OE. Somerville and Martin Ross, *The Real Charlotte*

The Real Charlotte, published in 1894, nearly one hundred years
after *Castle Rackrent*, often evokes Maria Edgeworth, that
"brilliant pioneer of Irish novelists," by its energy and astringent
humor. In its narrational biases and calm acceptance of the unusual, *The Real Charlotte* recalls Edgeworth's narrator, Thady
Quirk. The novel was greeted initially with aversion; Edith Somerville noted that a "distinguished London literary paper" pronounced it "one of the most disagreeable novels we have ever
read." Soon, however, *The Real Charlotte* was recognized as a
very rich and funny work, and even the "loathing" of Edith's
mother's gave way in face of favorable reviews. After 1922, however, in an Ireland that saw the former ascendancy as a barrier
to its full political independence, the work of Somerville and Ross
was devalued and ignored. But time passes and attitudes change;
the novel has been reprinted in recent decades to applause in
both Ireland and England. Terence de Vere White, for example,
finds *The Real Charlotte* second only to "the great whale"
(Joyce's *Ulysses*), and V.S. Pritchett calls it the best Irish novel
of any period. Yet despite its success, the novel has not received
detailed analyses: only the themes of the Big House and the declining race have been examined in detail, and the perceptive

analysis of society therein has been applauded. Despite its emphasis on land and on the qualities of several houses, however, *The Real Charlotte* does not focus so much on the Big House as does a later novel by Somerville and Ross, *The Big House of Inver* (1925), which expands Edgeworth's theme by reaching into history to explain contemporary events.[1] Given American interest in exhuming valuable but forgotten work, it is surprising that *The Real Charlotte* remains virtually unknown in the United States.

One reason for the neglect may be the presence of certain resistant, almost inassimilable passages, which sprinkle the work with weedlike regularity and persistence. Another reason may be the narrational stance, often biased and sometimes heedless to or apparently unaware of human suffering. Not that one expects a naive identification with narrational values, but in a world increasingly aware of ethnic sensitivities the patronizing colonist's voice grates, especially in relation to the still unsolved problem of Irish/English relations. I suggest, however, that the difficult passages and the narrational stance are integral elements in *The Real Charlotte*, essential to any thorough analysis of the novel. These are indeed literary manifestations of the authors' personal and political situations and may finally be examples of the "formal experiment" Alicia Ostriker expects in women's texts.[2] In depicting the crumbling of the Anglo-Irish ascendancy, Somerville and Ross reveal the connections between the society and the patriarchal family on which it is modeled; the source of disintegration in their beloved society mirrors and can be seen as a logical extension of the source of injustice in the equally beloved family. The arbitrariness of the access to power—political, economic, and social—which membership in the ascendancy ordained, reflects the arbitrariness of gender-specific roles ordained by membership in the patriarchal family. The injustice and destructiveness—the ignoble tragedy—of the class and gender system is revealed almost against the will of the narrators, who never fully condemn it and who frequently stand in the same difficult, ambivalent relationship to the text as do the authors to their society.

The cousins Edith Somerville and Violet Martin, the E.OE. Somerville and Martin Ross of the title page, are, like Maria

Edgeworth, daughters of the ascendancy, but they were born at a time when the stable world of their literary ancestor was falling apart. Perhaps it was their keen awareness of the end of this era that caused them to look back nostalgically, maybe too brightly, on the past and to condemn the future system so harshly. Violet marked the passing with her father's death in 1872: "The curtain fell for ever on the old life of Ross," she noted, "and the keening of the tenants as they followed his coffin, a tremendous and sustained wail, like the voice of the grave itself, was the last music of the piece."[3]

Whatever the national outlook may have been, the personal future of Anglo-Irish women (and, of course, of Gaelic-Irish women) looked bleak. Famine, the disestablishment of the Church of Ireland, the land acts of 1870 and 1881 and the later act of 1903, which encouraged the ascendancy, by offering generous terms, to sell land to their tenants, all contributed to the impoverishment and decline of Anglo-Ireland. As employment and economic security slipped away, great numbers of men of the ascendancy were forced to seek service in England. The foreign wars, as wars will, engaged the excess. Turning away from Ireland for careers as well as education, the survivors frequently married British brides, contributing to increasing numbers of unmarried women at home. As a result, spinsterhood, as census figures show, increased dramatically between 1871 and 1911. *The Real Charlotte* reveals how this epidemic exacerbated the emotional, psychological, social, and economic deprivations of the status-less women in the man's world of Anglo-Ireland, where, Hilary Robinson observes, "hunting, shooting and fishing took precedence over other activities." In this Ireland, Robinson continues, a spinster's only uses were to act as unpaid nurse or to keep house "until the sons returned from England or outposts of the Empire with English or Anglo-Irish wives—to whom the daughter would give her keys."[4]

Coupled with the declining economic conditions, the absence of fathers and brothers forced many Anglo-Irish women not only to keep house but also to shoulder the burdens of running the estates. Violet Martin and Edith Somerville both undertook the management of their family homes, at the same time supporting them with their literary earnings. Ross House, the Martin family home in Galway, was closed in 1872 since the son and heir, Robert Martin, both resided and worked in England. Consequently Mrs. Martin and her five daughters led the life of genteel itinerants for sixteen years, paying extended visits to relative after relative. On one such visit in 1886, the cousins Violet and Edith met for the first time. When the Martin women returned in 1888 to a Ross House that was in need of a great deal of physical labor outside and inside, the "fragile, indomitable" Violet cleaned, painted, and even scythed the weeds. Edith wrote, "From her mother had come the initiative, but it was Martin who saved Ross." "Often she could not write at night," Hilary Robinson notes, "because her hands were trembling too much from a day with the scythe or the shears." But physical effort was not her only contribution: "Almost all of Violet's literary earnings were spent on the upkeep of the house."[5]

Although there was comparatively more money in the Somerville home, Drishane (in county Cork), in the late 1880s, Edith, the eldest of eight children, was tied by a demanding mother to an interminable round of hostessing duties. Seeing herself as "Head Dog," Edith from the start claimed a position between her father and her grandfather, superior to that of her mother, siblings, and servants. When her mother died in 1895, the Head Dog took over the care of her father as well as the running of both house and estate. Energetic and innovative, Edith not only used her literary earnings to support the estate, but she also became a successful horse dealer, started a dairy farm, and imported the first Friesian cattle into Ireland. (Had a majority or perhaps even a sizable minority of Anglo-Irish landlords been so diligent, the history of Ireland might have been different.) It is fair to say that both Violet and Edith expended enormous physical efforts in preserving the estates reserved not for them but for their brothers and the brothers' male children. This injustice did not end with the transfer of political power in 1922: having run and supported Drishane for decades, Edith, at age eighty-eight, had to move along with her sister into Tally-Ho Lodge when the son and heir of Alymer Somerville took possession.[6]

At the cousins' first meeting in 1886, a deep friendship and an extraordinary literary collaboration was born. Publishing Vio-

let's memoirs in 1918, Edith described their bond: "The out-
standing fact, as it seems to me, among women who live by their
brains, is friendship. A profound friendship that extends through
every phase and aspect of life, intellectual, social, pecuniary.
Anyone who has experience of the life of independent and artistic
women knows this; and it is noteworthy that these friendships
of women will stand even the strain of matrimony for one or both
friends." The friendship was emotional as well as intellectual,
although nothing suggests a physical relationship between these
Victorian women. Indeed years later Edith was to shrink from
such a relationship with the well-known lesbian Dame Ethel
Smith. Yet the sexual ambiguity of Edith and Violet's relationship is suggested by the fact that, in references to her friend,
Edith always used the masculine name that Violet herself selected, one which echoes and demonstrates her pride in the old
Irish family title, Martin of Ross. The depth of the bond is also
suggested by Edith's continued use of both their names on work
written after Violet's death. No one could replace Violet, and
Edith's simple expression best spoke the loss: "My share of the
world," she wrote her brother, "has gone with Martin and nothing can ever make that better."[7]

Although the literary collaboration was to be the high point
of Somerville and Ross's lives and although it contributed sub-
stantially to preserving the Big House life of Ross and Drishane,
the Somerville and Martin families constantly hindered the effort. The distance between Ross House in Galway and Drishane
in Cork, more than one hundred miles, was also a considerable
obstacle at the end of the nineteenth century. When the cousins
did meet, their collaboration was frequently cut short by affec-
tionate but peremptory calls to return home. Even their time
together was constantly interrupted by demands to give up the
"nonsense" and to attend to women's "real" duties of entertaining: the thirty-three-year-old Edith recorded hiding from her
mother in a clothes closet so that she might write rather than
visit. Seeking refuge from their families, Somerville and Ross
worked in a cold loft over the stables at Castle Townshend. Sir
Patrick Coghill, Edith's nephew, recalls this situation and their
"multifarious activities" fondly, noting that the women could be
uninterrupted in the loft from which they could spot intruders.

Hilary Mitchell reports, however, that Edith strained at the constant interruptions and "want of mental tranquillity" her duties imposed on her, finding "intellectual development is well nigh incompatible with domesticity."[8]

Violet also chafed at the distractions. Evening was the only time she could write, apparently, and the drawing room, the only place. But the sociable Mrs. Martin insisted on conversation. Humorously Violet reported how her attempts to shut out the parental distraction were stymied by her sister-in-law, who, with proper regard for the appropriate, would pick up and tidy both conversation and Violet's papers. Yet despite the demands and the constant frustration and exasperation, Violet and Edith enjoyed open, friendly relations with their mothers and left moving accounts of their great admiration and affection for these original, idiosyncratic women.[9] Under trying conditions, however, the cousins frequently turned not to novels but to short articles, which could be produced in the interrupted periods allowed them and which brought speedy financial returns.

Ironically *The Real Charlotte* benefited from the familial interruptions. Conceived in 1889, the novel was not completed until 1893, but Edith notes that, once imagined, the characters of *The Real Charlotte* were constantly in the collaborators' heads, *their* views affecting their creators' other work. Many years after Violet's death, Edith described their writing process: "Our work was done conversationally. One or the other—not infrequently both, simultaneously—would state a proposition. This would be argued, combatted perhaps, approved or modified; it would then be written down by the (wholly fortuitous) holder of the pen, would be scratched out, scribbled in again; before it found itself finally transferred into decorous Ms. would probably have suffered many things, but it would, at all events, have had the advantage of having been well aired." During the four-year period when the collaborators chafed at the frequent interruptions, they thought and rethought, talked and retalked their characters, playing with the dialect of their Anglo and Gaelic creations to achieve realistic representation and subtle ironies. Years later Edith referred to their work as bringing "forth a book" and to the book as "a first-born effort." This conversational gestation, then, so like that of *Castle Rackrent*, emphasizes the mutuality of the production and thus represents, in David Bakan's terms, communion. The women worked together to achieve a common goal rather than the individual, or agentic, goal traditionally associated with the author or creator of texts.[10]

The awareness of the agrarian situation that shadows *The Real Charlotte* reflects the authors' awareness of and ambivalence toward the political turmoil at home. Writing, for example, of the tenants' 1872 rejection of the landlord's—the Martin's—candidate, Violet noted, "One indefensible position had been replaced by another, feudal power by clerical." Edith's hostility to the land acts, even in 1917, was not overtly vented against her own class, who perhaps too eagerly accepted temporary respite in return for their livelihoods, but rather against those who fought the original injustice of landlords: "Parnell and his wolf-pack were out for blood, and the English government flung them, bit by bit, the property of the only men in Ireland who, faithful to the pitch of folly, had supported it since the days of the union."[11]

The Real Charlotte overtly attempts to portray the fine values of the aristocracy and the meanness of the forces that oppose it—the corrupt agent, Roddy Lambert; the upstart land grabber, Charlotte Mullen; and the almost savage tenantry, represented by the miserable inhabitants of Ferry Row. The quiet of Lismoyle is shattered when the poor but very pretty Francie Fitzpatrick visits her cousin Charlotte. All the local men—Christopher Dysart, the lethargic heir to Bruff; Gerald Hawkins, the dashing British officer; and Roddy Lambert, the husband of an ailing widow and secret passion of Charlotte—dance around Francie's flame. Throughout a summer of tennis parties and boating outings, Francie flirts with her pursuers, much to the concern of the local matrons—especially Lady Dysart, who has her own plans for Christopher. Charlotte schemes all the while to acquire the land and house for which she thirsts, a property occupied by the ill Julia Duffy and guaranteed her for life by the now senile Sir Benjamin Dysart. She also plots to raise herself socially through Francie's marriage to Christopher and to assuage her arid passion by her own marriage to Roddy, after she hastens the final exit of his first wife. Things go wrong when Gerald,

Francie's love, abandons her in the hopes of marrying an English girl and an English fortune. Angered by Francie's refusal of Christopher and enraged by her mocking of Charlotte's desire for Roddy, Charlotte puts Francie out of her house.

Ironically, by rendering Francie homeless, Charlotte places her in a position to accept reluctantly Roddy's proposal. Seeking revenge but feigning good will to the newlyweds, Charlotte in the role of chaperon plots to leave Francie alone with the returned and repentant Gerald. This precipitates the final tragedy, as Francie, torn between riding off with Gerald or riding to the comfort of her financially ruined husband, is thrown from her mare, which is frightened by Julia Duffy's funeral cortege. For Charlotte has succeeded in acquiring Julia's property, and Julia has gone rapidly from madness to death. Despite the ruthlessness of Charlotte and the dishonesty of Roddy, it is the weakness within the Big House—the senility of Sir Benjamin Dysart and the inertia of his son and heir—that makes the ascendancy easy prey. Recognizing this ambivalence, Thomas Flanagan sees Somerville and Ross as moved by "fierce though critical loyalty to the Big House and a harsh, often ungenerous opposition to its enemies. But," he notes, "they move steadily toward tragic knowledge, toward recognition of the fact that the Big House was not destroyed by the mutinous cabins but by its own weakness and capacity for self-deception."[12]

The response to their personal situation as daughters in the patriarchal family of the Big House is more wrenching: "Daughters," Edith wrote, "were at a discount, . . . permitted to eat of the crumbs that fell from their brothers' tables, and if no crumbs fell the daughters went unfed." Marriage also evoked Edith's ambivalence. Reminiscing about the great-grandparents she and Violet shared, the artist Edith voices regret at the Lord Chief Justice's "marital complacency" in averring that his artist/wife on her marriage "devoted herself to 'making originals instead of copies.'" The persistent conflicts between affection and justice that gnawed at Somerville and Ross throughout their lives emerge in *The Real Charlotte*—as do the parodic, qualifying, conflicting voices M.M. Bakhtin described in his analysis of novelization—in both the difficult narrational stance and in those

inassimilable passages that so frequently, in presenting a confusion of genders, emphasize the arbitrariness of gender-specific
roles.[13]

In this ignoble tragedy, whose subject is not so much the decline of the Big House as the destructive effects of these roles,
the two passages on "apostolic succession" invite interpretation,
for they point to what I call "narrational contamination," the
conflicts and ambivalence that infect the authors also infecting
both their characters and their narrators. Dividing Roman
Catholics from Protestants, the maid Eliza Hackett from Mrs.
Lambert and Charlotte, the doctrine of apostolic succession also
implies an unnatural generation that excludes women, much as
the law of primogeniture excludes the women who preserve the
estates from inheriting them. In this connection, the scenes
are replete with ironies. Lucy, the rich first wife of the spoiled
Roddy Lambert, complains to Charlotte of her maid's impudence
in attending mass and of her assertion "I consider the Irish
church [Protestant Church of Ireland] hasn't the Apostolic succession."[14] Charlotte's indignation at Eliza's doctrinal position—
"You don't tell me that fat-faced Eliza Hackett said that?"—reflects, of course, her contempt for servants and for what she sees
as the presumption of Roman Catholics. It may also, however,
reflect her unconscious or unverbalized indignation at all such
male preserves. Charlotte is herself excluded from the world of
business—the agentship of Bruff, for example—despite her
excellent qualifications, by another such unwritten, "men only"
law. (The Church of Ireland was also a male preserve, but only
the Roman Catholic church enunciated the doctrine of the Apos-
tles' male heirs so clearly.) But in the disintegrating, declining
world of Anglo-Ireland, despite the law of primogeniture,
women—Charlotte, Mrs. Lambert, and Julia Duffy—are the
sole survivors in their families and consequently do inherit property. Contrary to the apparent stability of church and property
laws, then, the text suggests the inherent instability and contradiction in any exclusively male system of dissemination and
generation.

The inherited male right, which apostolic succession decrees,
both to disseminate and to interpret the word of the law is connected to a paradigm of authorship. The nineteenth century, as

Sandra Gilbert and Susan Gubar show, envisioned the author as masculine, a reflection of the original Creator of the Word, "a father, a progenitor, a procreator, an aesthetic patriarch whose pen is an instrument of generative power like his penis."[15] Like apostolic succession, this authorship postulates an exclusively male, therefore unnatural, generation. Since his authority is semantically and metaphorically connected to that of the original Father, the male author, by implication, is not only omniscient and omnipotent, creator and judge of his creatures, but also just and objective, modeled on a just and objective God. Somerville and Ross undermine this paradigm of objectivity throughout *The Real Charlotte*, especially in scenes referring to the apostolic succession.

The conclusion of the first of these passages draws our attention to the Word and, by extension, to any word as text and to its potential subversion by a disruptive feminine discourse. Mrs. Lambert completes her complaint against Eliza, appealing: "I ask you Charlotte, what could I say to a woman like that, that could wrest the Scriptures to her own purposes?" The narrators are ironic at Mrs. Lambert's expense, for Eliza's Roman Catholic church would not allow personal interpretation or wresting of Scripture, whereas Mrs. Lambert's and Charlotte's Church of Ireland would. Although the phrase will not be repeated for some one hundred fifty pages, the dark side of the religious conflict surfaces repeatedly, alerting the reader when the phrase recurs. Charlotte, for example, cautions Julia Duffy, daughter of a drunken, Protestant father and a dairymaid, Catholic mother, that the "poor Archdeacon frets about" Father Heffernan's luring Julia "into his fold!"[16]

The phrase apostolic succession recurs as Francie, married by this time to the widower Roddy Lambert but still in love with the soldier Hawkins, strolls in the garden of Rosemount, attempting to avoid Hawkins and the temptation his visit would present. Eliza Hackett gathers spinach in a far corner of the garden, meditating, the narrators note, "with comfortable assurance on the legitimacy of Father Heffernan's apostolic succession, but outwardly the embodiment of solid household routine and respectability." The reader is jolted by the unexpected aside on a peripheral character, an aside which presents no new plot or character information but simply calls attention to the narrators. These narrators are not, or at least not consistently, the intrusive, guiding narrators of many nineteenth-century novels whose presence is always felt. We cannot predict the sympathies of the narrators of *The Real Charlotte*. In the descriptions of Lady Dysart's party, for example, they seem to depict objectively and journalistically, but they forsake this objectivity to comment unsympathetically on the unwashed denizens of Ferry Row, to plead finally for compassion for Charlotte, and to repeat the views of one of their creatures, the silly Mrs. Lambert. I would argue that this repetition is again an instance of the subtle emphasis Nancy Miller attributes to women writers in their delineation of their own stories, an emphasis which reinforces structural as well as thematic concerns in its underscoring of the sardonic, not to say prejudiced, narrating voice.[17]

Inviting the reader to witness the narrational contamination in this instance, the authors imply a partiality and lack of objectivity endemic to all authors. Given the context of apostolic succession and its association with the paradigm of male authorship, the passage can be read as questioning the legitimacy of the traditional authorial metaphor. Eliza is subversive, but her subversion consists in adhering to a model of male privilege and female exclusion, much indeed as Somerville and Ross themselves adhere to the Anglo-Irish world whose laws exclude them from inheritance. In place of a stable world with fixed truths, the authors of *The Real Charlotte* present an inchoate world dying and forming at the same time, a Bakhtinian world in which the voice of authority—apostolic, paternal, social, or authorial— is constantly undermined by the parodic voices of those not fully suppressed. In place of the voice, which—given the metaphor of authorial generation—must be a single one, the narrators stress their "we" duality and suggest the essentially compromised nature of their text, an offspring that by its genesis must embody the sometimes conflicting elements of its dual inheritance. The authors' names on the title page, the male-sounding E.OE. Somerville and Martin Ross, complicate, as does Edgeworth's male narrator, the narrational stance and allow us to read all the narrational insensitivities and acceptances of female victimization as the representation by two women authors of women's view of the contemporary male perspective.

Narrational bias and inconsistency are nowhere more evident than in the indulgence extended Lady Dysart (who closely resembles Edith's mother) and the aversion extended Charlotte Mullen, the weed (to use an image from the novel) in the garden of Anglo-Ireland. Charlotte is introduced in one of the novel's many inassimilable passages, a moment that also draws attention to the arbitrariness of gender-specific roles. The narrators interrupt Norry the Boat's midnight vigil by a sharp bell:

A woman's short thick figure appeared in the doorway.

"The mistress wants to see *Susan*," this person said in a rough whisper; "is *he* in the house?"

"I think he's below in the scullery," returned Norry; "but, my Law! Miss Charlotte, what does she want of him? Is it light in her head she is?"

"What's that to you? Go fetch him at once," replied Miss Charlotte, with a sudden fierceness. [my italics][18]

The reader suspects a misprint—who or what is he/Susan? Before our curiosity is satisfied, the narrators reveal Charlotte, a woman whose plainness and distasteful habits they constantly underscore. Brushing aside the dying woman's request to see her pretty niece Francie, Charlotte harshly insists that it was Susan the woman had asked for. But the dying voice reproves: "It isn't cats we should be thinking of now. God knows the cats are safe with you." Susan, we finally understand, is not Francie's female rival for the dying woman's attention but a tomcat, christened with the feminine nominative years before by the young Francie, who in so doing had disdained nominal gender conventions as she had also disdained behavioral conventions in tomboyishly leading the rampaging gang of children.[19]

The same neglect of Victorian restriction is tragic for Francie the woman, Somerville and Ross's beloved "wild bird." Francie's pursuit of Hawkins, who has awakened her love, meets with Lady Dysart's disapproval and leads directly to Francie's dismissal from Bruff, where she had been visiting, and indirectly to her marriage with Lambert. The problem in *The Real Char-*

lotte is not an absence of love—indeed almost all the characters
are "in love"—but rather it is the difficulty of achieving mutual
love. This difficulty is exacerbated for women by the restrictive
conventions: Pamela Dysart, for example, the model Anglo-Irish
Victorian woman, cannot reveal her affection to Captain Cur-
siter, who lacks the courage to speak his own. Francie, however,
is roundly condemned for her honesty. Pamela may thus be seen
as the positive, passive woman of the tradition Alicia Ostriker
condemns, and Francie, as a move toward the aggressive, negative figure. Somerville and Ross appear to adhere to convention
in depicting Pamela positively and Francie negatively, but the
picture is not so clear: Pamela, for example, is not rewarded with
marriage, and years later Edith wrote that of all the characters
she and Violet created Francie "was our most constant companion, . . . we were fondest of her." The conclusion of the Susan
scene suggests the pathos of suppressed love, as Charlotte
strokes and soothes the cat with unexpected, even quasi-erotic
tenderness: "Be quiet, my heart's love, . . . be quiet."[20]

The grotesqueness of the moment is heightened by the importance granted the female-named tomcat, a status bestowed
on all the cats in Tally-Ho Lodge but particularly emphasized in
Susan's case. Susan is the most important personage at Tally-
Ho, his position in Charlotte's house peculiarly akin to that of
Roddy Lambert, Charlotte's secret passion, in the house of the
rich widow, Lucy. As Lambert is humored and cosseted by his
wife, so Susan is by Charlotte. As Lambert expects the best,
most comfortable chair after his rich meal, so Susan expropriates
the best chair after a rich dish of cream. As Lambert, the independent, can walk off from dull Rosemount for entertainment
and privacy, so Susan departs from Tally-Ho when the bustle of
female activity infringes on his comfort and dignity. And finally,
as Lambert cheats his employers, Sir Benjamin and Christopher
Dysart, so Susan, the well-fed parasite, steals mackerel from
Norry's kitchen.[21]

Similarly the sexual rivalry of the eligible males—the heir,
Christopher Dysart; the agent, Roddy Lambert; and the soldier,
Gerald Hawkins—for Francie's favor is parodied by the hostility
with its implication of jealousy between Lambert and the cats.
On Charlotte's denying his visit to Francie, Lambert viciously

kicks Mrs. Bruff, grandniece and female surrogate of Susan, who is himself a surrogate of Lambert, into the bushes. The final play on the identification between Lambert and Susan occurs when Charlotte and Francie quarrel over Lambert's affections. Furious at Francie's mocking jibes, which are like salt to her private passion, Charlotte attempts to strike the younger woman. But Susan intervenes, jumps on Charlotte en route to his usual perch on her shoulder, and receives to his astonishment the blow meant for Francie.[22] The analogies between the human and animal behaviors serve to parody the former, and the confusion of Susan's gender calls attention to the arbitrariness, as irrational as Francie's childish naming of the cat, of gender-specific roles, roles that confer, among other privileges, the right, or at least the option, of pursuit to tomcats and men.

The tyranny of gender is again emphasized in the presentation of James Canavan, the one-time tutor of the Dysart family who is now tutor only to the young Garry and attendant to Sir Benjamin. Canavan has "from time immemorial been the leading lady in Garry's theatricals" and is thus given the part of Queen Elizabeth I in the presentation of *Kenilworth*. Having done his part to perfection, Canavan/Queen Elizabeth disappears from the stage as Leicester's love, Amy Robsart, is entombed. But to the surprise of the audience, the queen bounces back on stage with a cry of "discordant triumph." With Amy Robsart's white plume stuck in his crown, he jumps on the coffin flourishing the poker/scepter and continues his furious song and dance until he falls through, on top of the screaming Amy. Refusing to accept the part written for the queen by the male author, Canavan, the rejected queen, will not remain conveniently hidden but bounces on stage demanding that his pain be heeded. In effect, then, Canavan, by his persistent pursuit of his desire, Leicester, plays the role that male psychiatrists in the nineteenth and much of the twentieth centuries define as madness in women.[23]

But madness in a woman is sanity in a man: Canavan's persistent pursuit is endemic to all the males. Christopher courts Francie despite her disinterest, Lambert seeks her even in his first wife's lifetime, and Hawkins's pursuit after her marriage leads to Francie's death. Although marriage is the only "vocation" open to women, they can play no part in seeking happiness therein. Lady Dysart was compelled to marry the elderly Sir Benjamin, the lovely Pamela can only drift aimlessly, Francie's attempts to be with Hawkins before her marriage to Lambert meet with Lady Dysart's unmitigated contempt, and the plain Charlotte's efforts to engage Lambert are ignored or ridiculed.

Although the Kenilworth scene continues the gender play, James Canavan's origins rather than his gender may be the source of his madness. The tutor, Violet Martin noted, is modeled on James Tucker, a hedge schoolmaster who had helped in the Martins' school during the famine, remaining as the family tutor and, like Canavan, acting in the children's theatricals. The colonized Canavan, like Maria Edgeworth's Thady, is, to use Elizabeth Janeway's term and paradigm, one of the weak whose powerlessness and dependence align him situationally with all the nineteenth-century women, Anglo- or Gaelic-Irish. Canavan's original, however, played the role not of female but of male lover in Robert Martin's theatricals. Perhaps thematic resonances dictated the inversion. The day following the play, Francie Fitzpatrick meets Canavan and Garry, and in a scene that confirms his madness, Canavan kills a rat. The resentful Garry reports that had Lady Dysart not interfered, Canavan would have gone on jumping on Amy until he had killed her.[24] A victim of the patriarchal system herself, Lady Dysart, who had condemned Francie's attempt to elide the unfair rules of pursuit, again ends Canavan's mad attempt to destroy the system. Canavan's madness, depicted in his attempt to destroy his rival, Amy, parodies Charlotte's madness, which does in fact destroy her rival, Francie. Linked in *Castle Rackrent* by their dependence on the powerful, women and other colonized figures are linked in *The Real Charlotte* by the overt narrational perception of the madness in their pursuit of desire.

But madness, though continually repressed, is pervasive. The leaders of Lismoyle society, Sir Benjamin and Lady Dysart, are introduced in scenes that depict their imbecility. The narrators observe that the picture of Lady Dysart at work in the garden with her daughter, Pamela, might seem to be "worthy in its domestic simplicity of the Fairchild Family," but they add sardonically, a dachshund (that absurd parody of an animal) replaces the paterfamilias. And Lady Dysart, having mistaken the young chickweed in a seedling pan "for the asters that should have been there, was filling her bed symmetrically with the former, an imbecility that Mrs. Sherwood would never have permitted in a parent."[25]

Lady Dysart's imbecility is more than horticultural, though given the respect paid gardeners in Anglo-Ireland, this is grievous. Lady Dysart invites too many women to her parties. She is unaware, being English, of the dialectical nuances and parochial behavioral patterns that mark Charlotte as vulgar. Additionally she has no sympathy for Francie, whom she regards as a "man-hunter" and a threat to her plans for Christopher. Affection transcends narrational irritation, however, and Lady Dysart is allowed to emerge unscathed, reminding the reader of Edith's combined affection and exasperation with her mother, the model for Lady Dysart. Indeed Mrs. Somerville's comments on Francie's death could be Lady Dysart's: "Francie deserved to break her neck for her vulgarity," she wrote, "and the girls *had* to kill her to get the whole set of them out of the awful muddle they had got into!"[26]

Sir Benjamin is allowed to speak his own imbecility. Alone in the drawing room, Miss Evelyn Hope-Drummond, the English guest invited by Lady Dysart as a possible bride for Christopher, reaches to pick a rosebud.

"Ha—a—ah! I see ye, missy! Stop picking my flowers! Push, James Canavan, you devil, you! Push!"

A bath-chair, occupied by an old man in a tall hat, and pushed by a man also in a tall hat, had suddenly turned the corner of the house, and Miss Hope-Drummond drew back precipitately to avoid the uplifted walking-stick of Sir Benjamin Dysart.

"Oh, fie, for shame, Sir Benjamin!" exclaimed the man who had been addressed as James Canavan. "Pray, cull the rose, Miss," he continued, with a flourish of his hand; "sweets to the sweet!"

Sir Benjamin aimed a backward stroke with his oak stick at his attendant, a stroke in which long practice had failed to make him perfect, and in the exchange of further amenities the party passed out of sight.[27]

Failing to strike Miss Hope-Drummond with the phallic cane, a symbol now of his impotence, Sir Benjamin turns on Canavan. Dressing and speaking in Sir Benjamin's own mode, refusing to do his employer's bidding, and usurping the latter's power with his invitation to the English guest, Canavan symbolically fore-shadows the displacement to come that is suggested so vividly in the disturbing and frequent images of the barely repressed hordes of Ferry Row. Class and family converge in the head of Lismoyle society and the Dysart family only to be repudiated and rendered impotent by the dispossessed Canavan, the sur-rogate madwoman.

Sir Benjamin's viciousness to the English girl who might have been his son's bride is a reflection of the political schizophrenia of Anglo-Ireland, economically and politically aligned with England but emotionally tied to Ireland. What Somerville and Ross reveal is that this schizophrenia extended far beneath national politics to the family itself, the foundation, support, and model of the system. The hostility that Sir Benjamin exhibits to the guest from "across the water" is a pale, dulled reflection of the hostility he has cherished to his own English wife, Lady Dysart, who had been married in her youth "with a little judicious coercion" to this man, thirty years her senior, and who, "after a long and, on the whole, extremely unpleasant period of matrimony" was now freed from his companionship by the intervention of his stroke.[28] And the Anglo-Irish hostility to the English brides is also characteristic of Christopher, who evades not only Evelyn but all the women his optimistic but obtuse mother invites. The relative paucity of narrational comment on the victimization of Lady Dysart is itself ironic—again reminiscent of Maria Edge-worth's male narrator who accepts the fate of the Rackrent wives almost as a condition of nature, which, as such, requires no com-ment.

The confusion of gender in the cases of Canavan and Susan highlights the confusion and effects of Charlotte's gender in this ignoble tragedy. Both the narrators and the other characters ap-ply male adjectives or expectations to Charlotte. When she ar-rives at Lady Dysart's biannual party, for example, Charlotte is greeted by her hostess who bemoans the excessive number of women, treating Charlotte, as several critics note, as an hon-orary man. And Charlotte herself assumes the "brevet" rank throughout. Ignoring the "midge-bitten" rows of women, she joins a "fairly representative trio" of Anglo-Irish gentlemen who rail together about Irish politics and the pleasure it would give them "to pull the rope at the execution of a certain English statesman." Apparently equally upset by their land-leaguing tenants and by Gladstone's attempts to transfer land from the ascendancy to the tenants, the gentlemen seem incapable of anything but complaint. Declaring herself a better politician than any of them, Charlotte tells of the personal vengeance she extracted from her plumber, and Christopher Dysart acknowledges that "if anyone could understand the land Act," that person would be Charlotte. At the next party, the Beattie's, Charlotte, the narrators note, joins the "other heads of families" for a "gentlemanly glass of marsala." She creates, they tell us, a "gentleman's avenue" at her new home, Gorthnamuckla, does a man's job of repairing the potato loft, and acts like a "madman" in her altercation with Francie. It is surely no accident that one of her impoverished Ferry Row tenants, the most repressed group presented, addresses Charlotte as "Honoured Madman."[29]

In Somerville and Ross's disintegrating world the confusion of gender is not only a symptom of the overt political disease that threatens the society but also an indication of how the accident of gender determines one's life, creating another, more fundamental, political dis-ease at the core of the social order. Susan has been christened by the young, naive Francie; the problem of the cat's textual gender is therefore the result of an accident. Charlotte's gender too is the result of a purely fortuitous interaction of biological elements. Charlotte is not only an avid and intelligent reader, one who realizes Christopher's foolishness in reading Rossetti to Francie, but she is also more capable than any man in Lismoyle in the business reserved for men. Charlotte's father had been the agent for Bruff, and the intelligent woman apparently picked up the workings of the agent-tenant system from accompanying her father to his office. When Lambert became her father's pupil, Charlotte helped him to learn his work, lending him money whenever necessary. The implication is that Charlotte, more astute than Lambert, had frequently saved him from trouble—first with her father, then with his employer.[30] Yet as a woman Charlotte is not considered for the agentship of Bruff, whereas masculinity alone qualifies the mediocre Lambert.

The provisions of the land acts, which would eventually deprive Anglo-Ireland of much of its livelihood, are understood by
Charlotte who, greedy for house and land, rents to the poor and
buys for herself rather than selling to tenants as do her real-life
Anglo-Irish compatriots. Desiring Julia Duffy's home, Charlotte
is again the "master" of both Lambert and Christopher. All information is filed correctly and stored in her organized mind for
easy access and cross-reference. Thus when Julia Duffy's tenant
goes bankrupt, leaving Julia unable to pay her own rent to the
Dysart estate, Charlotte is able to take over the house she has
always wanted. Almost in the role of omniscient narrator, Charlotte understands Sir Benjamin's senility and inability to enforce
the verbal promise of lifetime tenantship he had given Julia,
Christopher's disinterest in and deplorable ignorance of his father's business that was soon to be his own, Julia's illness and
her inability to make her case to Christopher, and Lambert's
inability to force Julia out. Ethics aside, Charlotte's managerial
competency, energy, and resourcefulness are the the equivalents
of those women estate managers, Edith Somerville and Violet
Martin. Indeed we might see in Charlotte a bitter and perhaps
unconscious reflection of the authors' own status in their society,
Charlotte serving both as scapegoat and authorial representative. Charlotte's intelligence, decisiveness, knowledge of the
community and of human strengths and weaknesses, and her
eminent qualifications to perform the jobs reserved for the in-
competent males are ignored by her society and often by her
narrators.

Had Charlotte been content to accept her position as honorary
gentleman—feared by her servants and subordinates, avoided
by the genteel Christopher and Pamela Dysart, appreciated for
her humor (her vulgarity not understood) by the English Lady
Dysart, ignored and hardly considered a woman by the eligible
gentlemen, the soldiers, and by-times Lambert—she could have
lived an emotionally sterile but, despite the gender restrictions,
economically successful life. In other words, had Charlotte settled for the male individualism defined by Bakan as the manifestation of "self-protection, self-assertion, and self-expansion,"
she might have been happy. Ironically, however, Charlotte seeks
communion.[31]

Born plain, Charlotte is yet imbued with some of the values and desires of her age. Since the business world, the public world, was male, fulfillment for a woman could only lie in marriage. The pervasiveness of this social more need hardly be argued; the ranks of the hopeful Beattie and Baker girls, the hopes of Francie, her friends, and Lady Dysart are ample evidence of the marriage market, the business in which women must compete, though they cannot make the rules. And indeed Charlotte's desire is not simply an acceptance of convention. In return for her help in the old days, the young, handsome Roddy Lambert had expressed his gratitude in an "ardent manner—a manner that had seemed cheap enough to him, at the time, but that had been more costly to Charlotte than any other thing that had ever befallen her." Encouraged by this fleeting episode, Charlotte nourishes a fervid passion for Lambert even through his marriage to the rich widow, realizing, Lambert thinks, with her "eminent common sense" the necessity of such a marriage for a poor but ambitious man. Throughout the years, the narrators note, Charlotte evidences her desire by provocative glances to which, "unfair as it may be," Lambert, had he seen them, would not have responded.[32] In the epigraph to this chapter, the narrators consider Charlotte after she has won everything but that which is most important to her—Lambert. They note the ignoble tragedy to which the trivialities of appearance assign a plain woman in their beloved and vicious world. For Charlotte's is the tragedy of gender. Born female, she cannot employ her "male" talents; born plain, she cannot compete in the only business open to women. Charlotte is the weed, placed by cultural codes involuntarily—even insanely—in the bed of asters, helpless to transform her drab colors and bulky shape into the glowing shades and elegant forms of the asters yet condemned, nevertheless, for being as she is.

Somerville and Ross depict a society whose hideous injustices, both personal and political, they recognize, but one that, given paradoxical human nature, they nevertheless cherish. As women suffragists who worked tirelessly for the vote, writers whose work supported the Big Houses destined for their brothers rather than themselves, and human beings whose affections and emotions turned to their own rather than to the opposite sex,

Somerville and Ross stood in relation to their society as do their narrators to the society and text of *The Real Charlotte*. Critics have often noted the sympathy of the writers/narrators to the Dysart family, the effete and obtuse leaders of Lismoyle society. But the depth of that sympathy and its contamination of the narrators have not been observed. The code of good behavior, for example, which instinctively governs all the actions of the Dysart family, is constantly applied by the narrators also as a test of a character's appeal. Lambert's pretension to middle-class respectability and his consequent awareness of Charlotte's vulgarity is mocked, whereas Lady Dysart's unawareness is treated indulgently. Christopher's and Pamela's instinctive recoil from vulgarity receives narrational approval, even when such recoil renders Christopher impotent. Charlotte's obvious vulgarities of manner provoke both characters and narrators, and the latter join the Dysarts in observing and ridiculing the signs of Charlotte's ill-breeding, the "electroplated teaspoons" and the "grocer's cake." Indeed *vulgarity*, a word that constantly recurs, seems to be more than surface deep. Its presence in Francie's case, we understand, has not only limited her sensitivity and obscured and distorted her world view, but it also has, like a smothering parasite, stunted her moral development.[33]

More important, however, are the implicit alignments. In the comic scene when the first Mrs. Lambert complains to Charlotte of Eliza's attending Catholic mass, the narrators note that one of Charlotte's "most genuine feelings was a detestation of Roman Catholics." This narrational assessment not only contributes to the humor of the occasion but also exposes the dark side of Charlotte's bigotry. Elsewhere the narrators note that Charlotte "affected a vigorous brogue, not perhaps being aware that her own accent scarcely admitted of being strengthened"; again they note the "guttural at the end of the word that no Saxon gullet could hope to produce." Sneering at her manner of dressing, they suggest she has the "Irish peasant's" habits. Finally, the narrators comment that "there was a strain of superstition in her that, like her love of land, showed how strongly the blood of the Irish peasant ran in her veins."[34]

In ridiculing Charlotte thus, in aligning her with Celtic rather than Saxon gullets, peasants rather than landlords, the narrators simultaneously distance her from English and Protestant, or ascendancy, origins and link her to the Gaelic Catholic hordes she despises. Ironically, however, in thus aligning Charlotte, in thus ridiculing her origins, the narrators themselves share the religious prejudice of which they accuse her. Although the code that governs the Dysarts' behavior is insufficient (witness Lady Dysart's destructive obtuseness, Christopher's effete posturing and his almost inhuman detachment, and Pamela's complete loss of self in her role as angel-in-the-house), the narrators make no secret of their personal bias toward these sympathetic, charming, though perhaps useless relics of a past age.

The idea of art as mimesis is destroyed by Somerville and Ross's deliberate involvement with their characters. There can be no distinction between the object reflected in the glass and the glass itself. The properties of the glass and the skill of its makers (narrators and authors) determine, as they always have, the reflection. The assumption of objectivity that reflection implies is discarded, the vested interest and prejudice of every author and her fictional narrational representative being recognized in its place. *The Real Charlotte*, an ignoble tragedy of gender-specific roles, attacks by this narrative strategy the traditional assumptions of patriarchal texts. The notion of a male intelligence that can transcend its affections and prejudices, so palpably untrue in the social and political arenas, and that can fairly represent its own society is undermined by the intrusive biases of the narrators of *The Real Charlotte*, biases which often reflect those of the authors. The ideal of art Somerville and Ross offer seems diminished, but it is also more honest than that of traditional narrative. The biased narrational stance may have been deliberately conceived, but at times the authors, like Charlotte and like the narrators, may have been driven by subconscious impulses, by the subversive, parodic voices, to say more than they knew.

The appropriateness of the narrational stance is evident in any case from a reading of *The Real Charlotte*, whose very richness is in great part the result of the thematic recognition and the superb structural representation of the wayward, often tragic patterns of human affections. A passage near the end of the work summarizes Somerville and Ross's attitude to their own society:

"Civilization at Bruff had marched away from the turf quay. The ruts of the cart track were green from long disuse and the willows had been allowed to grow across it, as a last sign of superannuation. In old days every fire at Bruff had been landed at the turf quay from the bogs at the other side of the lake; but now, since the railway had come to Lismoyle, coal had taken its place. It was in vain that Thady the turf cutter had urged that turf was a far handsomer thing about a gentleman's place than coal. The last voyage of the turf boat had been made, and she now lay, grey from rottenness and want of paint, in the corner of the miniature dock."[35]

Like Thady, the narrators of *The Real Charlotte* urge that their society, the society of the Anglo-Irish ascendancy, is far handsomer than the emerging society of the Gaelic-Irish peasantry, and like Thady too the narrators have a vested interest in the preservation of this society. Overtly asserting this interest and surrendering the pose of authorial objectivity, *The Real Charlotte*, a tragedy in which women are defined and valued by their appearance, becomes itself the weed, the bristling chickweed, in the artificial aster garden of Anglo-Irish literature.

4. Elizabeth Bowen
Out of Eden

It is not only our fate but our business to lose innocence and once we have lost that it is futile to attempt a picnic in Eden.
—Elizabeth Bowen, "Out of a Book"

BORN IN 1899, Elizabeth Bowen grew up in a Europe losing its innocence in World War I and in an Ireland engaged in wrenching a sense of national identity from the Anglo-Irish. The political turmoil of Bowen's youth is reflected in much of her writing, in which orphaned heroines wander homeless and countryless through indifferent or unsympathetic environments. This representation of dislocation and dispossession as a natural condition of life is unsurprising, given Bowen's history and sensitivity to place and surroundings. What is shocking is the narrational ambivalence toward the condition: the heroine's position is not seen as tragic. It is difficult, yes, but preferable in fact to the comfortable serenity of her peers, whose complacence, Bowen suggests, springs from ignorance, not knowledge, from a naive acceptance of the doctrines and illusions of their particular Edens.

Bowen's reflections on her life and writing, especially *Bowen's Court*, the history of the home she loved in Cork, help us understand something of her sense of place and the consequent irony of her ambivalence toward the wandering heroine. Elizabeth Bowen's first seven winters were spent in Dublin, her summers in Cork; the child thus imbued Bowen's Court with magic from an early age, believing "that winter lived always in Dublin, while summer always lived in County Cork." In 1906 the pattern of life itself seemed broken when Elizabeth and her mother, Florence, left Ireland for England, initially to visit. But they were soon to live there. Although she enjoyed England, Elizabeth "was exceedingly anxious to go home," and the "triumphant return" in 1912, when the "sun baked the steps and streamed in at the windows," when she woke early on her thirteenth birthday to run "barefoot all over the house," reads like a ceremony of reclamation. "Florence loved Bowen's Court," Bowen wrote of her mother. "Its large light strong plainness touched her sense of the noble." Bowen's own love for her home need never be stated explicitly: she remembered the "distinct shock" she felt upon hearing her third governess pronounce it "an ugly house." She later likened this governess to a witch.[1]

After decades of sheltering Bowens, the house was quickened by the abandonment of the heir, Henry Bowen, Elizabeth's father. Forced to fight for its existence, "Bowen's Court," Bowen said, "met and conquered . . . the assaults of nature." To those "first phases of emptiness," however, she traced "the start of the house's strong *own* life." And the house became a touchstone by which the child could judge events. Unable to read the neighbors' faces as they bade farewell to the ill Florence Bowen and prayed that she might return to them, Elizabeth turned to Bowen's Court. Less able to mask its grief, the house in its "indomitable loneliness" revealed that her "mother would not come back." So close was Elizabeth's relationship with Bowen's Court that, as one friend put it, "it became, indelibly, part of the memories of many friends, too, for Elizabeth and Bowen's Court seemed for many people to be a single entity."[2]

The identification with Bowen's Court, the home built on the lands Cromwell awarded his soldier, Henry Bowen, Henry I, is complicated by Bowen's sympathy with the aspirations of Gaelic Ireland. *Bowen's Court* can perhaps be seen as an apologia as well as a celebration of the Bowen family. Bowen, like Maria Edgeworth and Somerville and Ross, felt the need to defend her ancestors. But Bowen could not accept the status quo that seemed natural to Maria Edgeworth and whose loss Somerville and Ross deplored. The ambivalence Somerville and Ross expressed is toward their own place as women in family and society, but the ambivalence Bowen experienced sprang initially from unease at the relationship between Anglo- and Gaelic-Ireland— the division between the two was always a source of great sadness. Bowen imagined the seeds of division as sown by the early plantations and watered by centuries of unthinking English prejudice. This destructive prejudice was especially tormenting, for, like most Anglo-Irish writers, Bowen looked to England not simply as the source of power and privilege but also as the source of civilization, of much loved traditions. It was difficult for her to accept the blindness, not to say injustice, of this gifted parent. Consequently when Bowen's father, Henry Bowen, the last male heir of the Bowen family, threw himself enthusiastically into working for the Land Commission, the organization engaged in implementing the reforms Somerville and Ross opposed, his daughter applauded his action.

In the final chapter of *Bowen's Court*, Bowen makes her sympathies apparent. "Home Rule," the goal of most Irish politicians, is presented as a reasonable and just desire. Although Britain has promised many times to accede to Irish demands and requests, the Irish Ulster members resist, fearing a change in their predominantly Protestant stronghold. One of the most farcical scenes of twentieth-century politics ensues: Ulster arms itself to forcibly resist Britain's withdrawal—the infant fights its own birth. Rather than confront the offspring's perfidy, England ignores the illegal arming. Bowen condemns this ostrichlike behavior. Ulster's action and England's oversight are the inevitable catalysts to southern rebellion. "This mobilization of Ulster could not fail—was it intended to fail?—to provoke the South." England's prejudice is reinforced for Bowen in 1914: when Germany marched into Belgium, she notes, the south offered its unarmed volunteers to join with Ulster's in the defense of Ireland, a defense that would free British soldiers for service elsewhere. This united action might have contributed, as the Irish leader John Redmond hoped, both to the empire and to "the future welfare and integrity of the Irish nation." But, Bowen notes despairingly, Lord Kitchener was not willing "either to arm or to recognize the willingness of the Irish Volunteers." She cries, "Must an undivided Ireland be always a shadow? Must anything else be always too much to hope?"[3]

To come back to Bowen's family and their part in the divided country, I turn to a 1950 essay, "The Big House": "After an era of greed, roughness and panic, after an era of camping in charred or desolate ruins (as my Cromwellian ancestors did certainly) these new settlers who had been imposed on Ireland began to wish to add something to life. The security that they had, by the eighteenth century, however ignobly gained, they did not use quite ignobly." This is the general tone of Bowen's examination of her family's role in Irish history—an attempt to explain, to gain understanding and sympathy for ancestors of whose injustice she is always aware. Again, in a 1963 afterword to *Bowen's Court*, after the lovely house was demolished by the new owner, Bowen implies that, despite the justification tendered in the first pages, she had never felt that the original sin, the "affair of origin," had been expiated: "The stretches of the past I have had to cover have been, on the whole, painful: my family got their position and drew their power from a situation that shows an inherent wrong." Narrational ambivalence toward the wanderings of the heroine springs from the knowledge of this "inherent wrong," an understanding of which is also essential to analysis of the role and fate of Danielstown, the Big House in *The Last September* (1929). This is the only Bowen novel analyzed here; although Bowen's poetic style—her ability to suggest complex chains of events and emotions in a few brief and lovely words— developed over the course of her career, neither the style nor her perspective changed dramatically. The best novels then, of which *The Last September* is one, are representative. Also, the focus as well as the setting of *The Last September* is Irish; *A World of Love* (1955), while also set in Ireland, lacks the focus and energy of the earlier novel. Loving attention to house and place, as suggested by the title of the family history alone, is a trademark of most of Bowen's work, but nowhere does she explore the "Big House" theme as fully as in *The Last September*, the novel closest to her heart.[4]

"I *am* the daughter of the house from which Danielstown was drawn," Bowen writes in the 1952 preface, asserting her interpretative authority. The word *Daughter* implies an inheritance both physical and emotional. It is as if Bowen's Court preserves the traits, the passions, and the emotions of generations of Bowens, and, growing within its walls, the heir, the daughter, imbibes and absorbs their essence. "I recognize that I am," she writes, "and was bound to be, a writer intensely subject to scene and time: both do more than figure, they play their parts in my plots."[5] Bowen's Court is the scene that plays its part in *The*

Last September, a part that we can read as determined by Elizabeth Bowen's personal experience as the daughter of the house.
The abrupt break with the pattern of life and the ensuing loss
of Bowen's Court in 1906 are part of this experience. The break
would in the first place invest the house with a nostalgic attraction.

But the effect goes deeper than that. The trauma of her father's illness and the subsequent repression of anxiety are associated with this early loss of Bowen's Court and may be
synonymous with it. When Henry Bowen became ill, his doctors
advised that the presence of his wife and daughter was detri-
mental. Florence thus took Elizabeth away to England on a visit
which stretched to six years. During this period, Bowen notes,
"my mother hoped I would notice nothing, and I did not notice
much." The "campaign of not noticing" was aided by the determined cheerfulness of her mother's relatives. Despite the apparent success of the venture, however, Bowen concludes the
paragraph by noting, "I was exceedingly anxious to go home."
The attitude of not noticing, which initially seems positive in this
connection, occurs elsewhere in Bowen as a negative, immature
approach to difficult situations. Britain, as we have just seen,
ignores, will not notice, the arming of Ulster at the beginning
of the twentieth century—a lapse that brings years of struggle
and death in its wake. And the Anglo-Irish in *The Last September*, we shall see, refuse to notice the activities of fomenting
Gaelic-Ireland, a refusal which also costs dearly. Loss of home
and father—exile from Eden—may indeed have been the more
searing because it was not noticed. The belligerence that Bowen
identifies as her Irish trait emerges most strongly at this time;
this muted rebellion may have been the child's venting of the
repressed problem.[6] The traumatic experience of suppression
may also have played an important part in determining the way
the future adult, Elizabeth Bowen, would perceive human behavior.

At this time, too, a second force helped shape the imagination
of the future writer. Elizabeth Bowen learned to read. Reading
on her own was not, however, as satisfying as being read to.
The governess who taught the child was the Welsh woman who
had pronounced Bowen's Court ugly; she it was who expelled the

magic, the "enchanted readings-aloud" of less demanding gov-
ernesses. Learning to read was thus the beginning of another
loss, one associated in time with the move to England. Though
Elizabeth made new friends, the absence of her early childhood
companions may have played some part in the child's becoming
an avid reader. The personal debt to fiction is emphasized in "Out
of a Book." The adult narrator who responds to the vicissitudes
of history is mothered, Bowen tells us, by the child who responded to the magic of fiction. "I know," she writes, "that I
have in my make-up layers of synthetic experience, and that the
most powerful of my memories are only half true." The child,
and the woman in later years, may be unaware of the invasive
presences in the imagination. "Reduced to the minimum, to the
what did happen, my life would be unrecognizable by me. Those
layers of fictitious memory densify as they go deeper down."
Laid down over decades, these deposits shape perception itself.
"Books made me see everything that I saw either as a symbol
or as having its place in a mythology—in fact reading gave bias
to my observations of everything in the between-times when I
was not reading." Not only did the child live in the book, "but
just as much the book lives in the child." Thus Bowen concludes,
"The imagination, which may appear to bear such individual
fruit, is rooted in a compost of forgotten books."[7]

The patterns traced by the forgotten books lie, as Bowen implied, in the deepest and least questioned layers of the mind.
And from these depths, too, the imaginative, intuitive writer
draws her themes. Bowen identified herself as such a writer, one
whose "loyalties are involuntary and inborn" for whom "environment is the most lasting" and "deepest" influence." Theme, she
writes in a general consideration of the elements in the novel,
"is something of which you will feel the effects and which works
strongly for the novelist but which is down so deep that you may
have to analyze the story to find what it actually is." Given the
close relationship between theme and the patterns of fiction in
the imaginative mind, we can expect to find established fictional
patterns defining the behavior of Bowen heroines and intersect-
ing the themes of Bowen novels. A recognition of these patterns
is essential if the Bowen heroine is to become a fully indivi-

duated, thinking human being. "All susceptibility belongs to the age of magic, the Eden where fact and fiction were the same," Bowen concludes her essay "Out of a Book." But it is the adult's duty to separate the fact from the fiction, to lose the innocence, to question and perhaps even to exorcise the very paradigms inherited from the child through the forgotten books that have affected or infected her mind.[8]

The paradigm that underlies *The Last September* takes the novel far beyond the Irish political situation to the roots of Christianity and of English myth. Bowen emphasizes, both in her preface and in the first few pages of the novel, the pastness of the events: " 'All this,' I willed the reader to know, 'is over.' " Further, "the reader must look—and more, must be aware of looking—backward, down a perspective cut through the years." This perspective is important if we are to identify the paradigms controlling the novel: an adult narrator, an artist, identifies these patterns. The heroine, the young Lois Farquahar, does come to reject conditioned behavior, the result of unquestioned acceptance of pattern, but she is not initially capable of such recognition. The Ireland identified by this narrator is a golden, privileged world, the Eden of the innocent, of the Anglo-Irish. This Eden is irrevocably lost once they recognize their original sin. Into this world wanders the new Eve, an innocent grasping at the shadows of myth. The Naylors, the Big House family, attempt to ignore the activities of the Irish rebels—and of the British army sent to suppress them—and to continue their lives of tennis parties, houseguests, and civilized behavior. Aimless and vaguely dissatisfied, Lois hopes for drama and perhaps romance from the advent of the houseguest Hugo Montmorency, the friend of her long-dead mother. Lacking purpose, she thinks of marrying Gerald Lesworth, one of the British officers charged with suppressing the rebels, one who loves her. Miltonic echoes abound, and Lois's struggle with her "old conceptions" may be understood as a wrestling with these echoes.[9] In the apocalyptic world of Ireland in 1920, Lois clings to the Edenic myth, but the Miltonic paradigm, the Eve figure conceived in Genesis and made flesh in *Paradise Lost*, is, Bowen suggests, pernicious in a fallen world. Refusing to be the creature, the fiction, of myth and his-

tory, Lois must grasp the gifts of curiosity and intelligence inherited from, though ultimately rejected by, that fictional mother
and employ them to create herself.

   In the novel of Lois's awakening, Danielstown is presented at
one level as the symbol of the Anglo-Irish in the long war waged
between the Big House and the cabins.[10] The opposition between
the house and the Irish countryside is established early; Lois is
first aware of this opposition as she looks down on the house from
the vantage point of the surrounding hills.

To the south, below them, the demesne trees of Danielstown made a
dark formal square like a rug on the green country. In their heart like
a dropped pin the grey glazed roof reflecting the sky lightly glinted. Looking down, it seemed to Lois they lived in a forest; space of lawns blotted
out in the pressure and dusk of trees. She wondered they were not
smothered; then wondered still more that they were not afraid. Far from
here, too, their isolation became apparent. The house seemed to be
pressing down low in apprehension, hiding its face, as though it had her
vision of where it was. It seemed to huddle its trees close in fright and
amazement at the wide light lovely unloving country, the unwilling
bosom whereon it was set.[11]

Representing the older Ireland, the hills are part of all that opposes the house of Anglo-Ireland, so it is appropriate that Lois
first becomes aware of the division when she shares their perspective. Hiding in the hills, too, Lois knows, is the rebel, Peter
Connor, a member of the illegal army that seeks to overthrown
the British army, the defenders of Anglo-Irish ascendancy. The
house, "a very reservoir of obscurity," the narrator suggests as
if explaining the characters' obtuseness, blinds its inhabitants,
"as though the fountain of darkness were in one's own perception." The practice of seeing the conquered country as female
goes back to the early Gaelic poetry, to the perception of Ireland
as "Mother Ireland," "Dark Rosaleen," or the most insidious image, "Cathleen Ni Houlihan," the old woman restored by the
warrior to youthful beauty. England, the conqueror, is always
male in this paradigm. The image of rape, the "pin" in the heart
and the pressure on the "unwilling bosom," anticipates Seamus
Heaney's "Act of Union." The act, Heaney suggests, engendered

a "fifth column," one which, in resisting the father, tears the "stretchmarked body" of the mother.[12]

But at another level the house and nature are engaged in a much older, more fundamental struggle. Representing the conqueror, the house symbolizes the new order that defeated and then established itself on the body of the older order, a usurpation that reenacts the overthrow of female deities by patriarchal religions. Studies of the civilizations of the Near East suggest that the beginnings of religion were associated with ancestor worship. This took the form of female worship, since the male role in conception was not understood. The original creator was, logically it seemed, a woman, a great mother, a fertility symbol. The Indo-European invasions of the East, however, succeeded in initially assimilating the female deity and in later repressing her entirely. Whether these invaders brought with them a patriarchal god or whether they simply devised one to supplant the female deities and the matrilineal customs is uncertain. Certainly women's power, attested to in early records, decreased with the advent of the patriarchal god: Hebrew women were among the most repressed, and the Hebrew god was among the most unquestionably patriarchal.[13]

Many myths of creation reenact the victory of the male over the female god. The Mesopotamian myth, for example, the *Enuma Elish*, tells the story of the murder of the goddess Tiamat (cognate with the Hebrew *Tehom*—the deep) by Marduk, the son of the sun, championed by the invaders, and of Marduk's remaking of the world from Tiamat's corpse. The Bible is less explicit. Chapter 1 of Genesis, which presents the simultaneous creation of Adam and Eve, reveals even as it attempts to conceal its revision of an earlier myth. "Darkness was upon the face of the deep; and the spirit of God moved over the waters," writes the poet. The deep replaces Tiamat, and the spirit of God, Marduk. Genesis 2 further represses the goddess: the deep and the maternal waters disappear and Adam partakes with God in the creation of Eve. Genesis 2, which supplied the justification for the church fathers' silencing of women, also supplied the seed, or rib, from which Milton shaped his Eve. In *The Last September*, Danielstown, imposed on the unwilling bosom of mother nature represents the patriarchal order of the Judeo-Christian

tradition and, specifically, of Anglo-Ireland, erected on the older
body of the great mother and of the Gaelic Irish people, the
Tuatha de Danann, the people of the goddess Dana.[14]

The opening sentence of the novel subtly establishes the dichotomy between house and nature. "About six o'clock the sound
of a motor, collected out of the wide country and narrowed under
the trees of the avenue, brought the household out in excitement
on to the steps." The "excitement" suggests an ambiguous danger in the "wide country" through which the houseguests, Francie and Hugo Montmorency, have traveled and which, in gaining
the patriarchal establishment of Danielstown, they have escaped.
The guests' comments on Danielstown and Lady Naylor's reply
reinforce the opposition. Francie notes that Danielstown looks
lovely, and she asks if some trees have been cleared. These trees
are part of the Danielstown estate. "The wind had three of the
ashes," Lady Naylor replies, and, as if reminded of their own
danger by the threat of nature toward the estate, she asks, "You
came quite safe? No trouble?"[15]

Constantly personified, Danielstown is identified with its
owner, Sir Richard Naylor, the uncle and guardian of the orphan
Lois. Reacting to events as Sir Richard would, the house, the
narrator implies, shares his responsibilities and privileges. Dis-
approving, like Sir Richard, of the activities of both the Irish
rebels whom nature shelters and of the British army, Danielstown reveals its displeasure. As Lois runs back from her "almost
encounter" with the Irish rebel, the narrator notes the competing forces: "The crowd of trees straining up from the passive
disputed earth, each sucking up and exhaling the country's essence—swallowed him [the rebel] finally," while "below, the
house waited." The adult artist/narrator, not Lois, draws the
reader's attention to the adversaries. When Marda, the trou-
blesome guest who upsets the Naylors, leaves and when Lois
stands desolate in her room, the narrator notes that "the vacancy
of sky" and the wind enter the house through the "defenseless
windows" of the room. Although she has partially awakened
Lois, Marda has abandoned her own fight for autonomy and has
opted instead for a quintessentially patriarchal marriage, one in
which she will no longer consider economic and, more important,
moral issues but will simply be guided by her husband—becom-

ing a perfect Eve. But, the narrator implies, nature itself remains as teacher/exemplum to Lois—an exemplum the house is powerless to exclude. On Lois's return from the dance at the British army barracks, the dance which Sir Richard disapproved her attending, the narrator again notes the presence of the frowning spectator: "Twenty dark windows stared over the fields aloofly out of the pale grey face of the house." Indeed the house so "loomed, and stared so darkly and oddly" at Gerald Lesworth, the British army officer whom Sir Richard finds an unacceptable partner for Lois, that Gerald "showed a disposition—respectful rather than timorous—to move away from the front of it." But Daventry, the career soldier, shell-shocked in World War I and verging on madness because of the nature of his duty in Ireland, "superciliously" returns "the stare of the house," as if to blame it as much as the rebels for the death of his friend Gerald.[16]

As Adam's successor in the fallen Eden of Anglo-Ireland, Sir Richard assumes the Adamic power of naming, of defining, assumes the control of discourse that Tony Tanner identifies with the control of economic and social life. Although the novel opens with the discreet questioning of the Montmorencys, the Naylors determinedly suppress any further consideration of the political situation. When Francie questions the safety of sitting out after dark, Sir Richard laughs off her concern; but when Laurence, Hugo, and Lois would discuss the situation, Lady Naylor cautions silence. She indicates her concern that the servants will overhear, but her own reluctance to face the issue would seem to be the real reason. Irrepressible, Lois tells Francie the story told her by one of her uncle's servants of strangers' digging and burying something in the grounds of Danielstown. At this Sir Richard explodes: "I will not have the men talking, and at all accounts I won't have them listened to." But Lois protests a right to knowledge: "I feel that one ought to dig. If there is nothing there I can confound Michael for the good of his soul, and if there should be guns, Uncle Richard, just think of finding them! And surely we ought to know." Just so Milton's Eve, alive with curiosity, explores the tree and, wishing, as she says, to "grow mature / In knowledge, as the Gods who all things know," eats the fruit.[17]

But Adam-like, Sir Richard questions: "And why would we

want to know? . . . This country is altogether too full of soldiers
with nothing to do but dance and poke old women out of their
beds to look for guns. It's unsettling the people, naturally." Will-
fully Sir Richard misinterprets the situation and denies the exploration necessary in a fallen world; the native Irish, he implies,
would be "loyal" if it were not for the disturbing activities of the
British army. Sir Richard and Lady Naylor seem to believe, as
did Bowen's mother, that discussion would aggravate the situation. As the Black and Tan trucks tear the fabric of conversation,
as barriers against travel are erected throughout the country,
as soldiers are ambushed and rebels are captured, and as Big
Houses like Danielstown burn, the Naylors refuse the forbidden
knowledge and trust in their Eden, declaring that "the whole
thing's nonsense."[18]

The forbidden knowledge in *The Last September*, like that in
Genesis and *Paradise Lost*, is sexual as well as political. Lady
Naylor links the two semantically. When Francie suggests that
people speak of Lois and Gerald together, Lady Naylor responds:
"One cannot help what people say, though it is always annoying.
Not that I ever do know what they say. I make a point of not
knowing. You know that I've always turned my face against gos-
sip, especially these days: it's annoying to find it everywhere,
even at one's own parties. It's a very great danger, I think, to
the life of this country." Lady Naylor's attitude here replicates
her attitude to politics. When Sir Richard attempted to suppress
the political talk at the opening dinner, Lady Naylor effectively
concluded that topic and determinedly turned the conversation
to parties. "From all the talk, you might think almost anything
was going to happen, but we never listen. I have made it a rule
not to talk, either," she said in that instance. The language of
suppression is almost identical in both cases. As Francie insists
of the Lois/Gerald conversation, "Oh, but really, you couldn't say
this was political," the adult narrator emphasizes the connection
with a martial metaphor: "Lady Naylor was forced into open
country." Aware, as Lois is not, of Lois's emerging sexuality and
of its power, Lady Naylor extracts a promise from Gerald not
to kiss Lois when he engages her in a "frank conversation" about
their relationship. Being both romantic and honorable, Gerald

keeps his promise, and Lois realizes that a kiss would have compelled her to agree to marriage.[19]

Clinging to the contribution they have indeed made since the eighteenth century, the Naylors thus attempt to ignore the original sin, "the affair of origin" whose expiation is demanded by the avenging goddess, Gaelic-Ireland. Their refusal to recognize the serious political discontent that surrounds them is presented as a deliberate screening-out, similar to that of England and of Bowen herself in the passages quoted earlier. The outsiders, Marda and Lady Naylor's nephew Laurence, remark this pattern. Perhaps because they are not emotionally involved, they can trace the predictable design. Discussing the situation with Hugo Montmorency, Laurence notes that he would like to be present when Danielstown burns. Shocked by the harsh intrusion of the actual, Hugo attempts to dispel the notion, but Laurence holds fast: "Of course it will, though. And we shall all be so careful not to notice." Marda echoes Laurence and again to Hugo: "Will there ever be anything we can all do except not notice?"[20]

Most forcefully, Hugo resists this knowledge. Married to a woman who makes herself an invalid, Hugo constantly plans for himself a career, a home, and a country. But Francie's "illness" protects him from action: "There was never a time when I had not other people to think about," he replies to Laurence's insistence on the reality they ignore. The phrase "unstoring the furniture," a reference to the Montmorencys' dream of building their own home and ending their peripatetic lifestyle, recurs often, underscoring the limit of Hugo and Francie's goal. Even this, however, they will not accomplish. As Lady Naylor notes, the house the Montmorencys so frequently planned was "just an idea," and Mrs. Trent concludes, "They won't unstore the furniture? . . . It's a pity he never did go to Canada." Hopelessly romantic, Hugo divorces himself "equally from fact and from probability," yet, as Laurence shrewdly recognizes, he feels "positive hatred" for the artificial barriers with which he has surrounded and limited himself.[21]

This, of course, is the problem with Eden. The paradoxes and contradictions will not stay suppressed indefinitely. Despite his romanticizing, Hugo recognizes that the barrier is self-created.

Despite their best efforts, the Naylors will be forced to recognize
the serpent: their visitor will be shot, their home burned. The
romantic symbiosis, the mutuality of interests that the Naylors
imagine between themselves and Gaelic-Ireland, is false. Such
a symbiosis might spring from an alliance of equality or even
from the weaker member's need for nourishment—the basis
Hugo claims for his own lassitude. But the relationship between
Anglo- and Gaelic-Irish is one of forcible possession, an enslavement of the weaker by the physically stronger, a possession paradoxically dictated by a sense of vulnerability and inadequacy in
the stronger member. In *Paradise Lost*, too, one can argue that
Adam's dream of symbiosis, resting on the myth of Eve's dependency, is false. Although initially daunted by Eve's autonomy—"So absolute she seems / And in herself complete"—
Adam argues that Eve should stay with him always, under his
protection.[22]

> Leave not the faithful side
> That gave thee being, still shades thee and protects.
> The wife, where danger or dishonor lurks,
> Safest and seemliest by her Husband stays,
> Who guards her, or with her the worst endures.[23]

Like Hugo, Adam suggests Eve's dependency. When Eve explains the suspicion of her frailty inherent in Adam's concern,
he advances another reason. It is not that he fears Eve will fall,
he says, but "to avoid / Th'attempt itself, . . . / For hee who
tempts, though in vain, at least asperses / The tempted with
dishonor foul." Again Eve explains that "th'attempt" repulsed
can only bring her praise, not dishonor. And when Adam finally
invokes their mutual dependency—he feels stronger when Eve
is with him and asks why she should not feel the same—Eve
replies that she would not suspect "the Maker wise" of creating
so imperfect a creature, for what, she asks "is Faith, Love, Virtue unassay'd / Alone, without exterior help sustain'd?" Adam
has gone the full circle from asserting Eve's dependency to con-
fessing his own. In a provocative essay on *Paradise Lost*, Christine Froula argues that the repression of the mother is the
genesis of Genesis and that Adam's dream, his "fancy" of crea-

tion, is the original expression of "womb-envy." "Through the
dream of the rib Adam both enacts a parody of birth and gains
possession of the womb by claiming credit for woman herself."
It is Adam, not Eve, who feels vulnerable, his insecurity, like
Hugo's, masked as protection of the "weaker" partner.[24]
· Eve-like, Lois refuses to ignore the flaws in Sir Richard's rea-
soning. A typical Bowen heroine just released from school and
not fully accepted into the adult world, Lois balances on the walls
of Eden, capable of looking either back toward innocence or forward into the unknown. At this point she opts for the future.
Everything she observes—the intent man she sees hurrying
through Danielstown grounds, the trucks that tear the fabric of
the night, the convoys from which the girls hide, the rebel hidden
and later arrested in the Connor house—indicates to Lois the
nonsense in Sir Richard's word.

Despite her questioning of specifics, however, Lois does not
question the underlying pattern but in seeking to fit in, to be
secure, follows in Eve's footsteps. Eve, though initially attracted
to her own reflection in the water, is enticed by a disembodied
voice to another image. This image she thinks "fair indeed and
tall" but yet "less amiably mild, / Than that smooth wat'ry image." Hence she wishes to return to the water. But the voice
reproaches, "Whom fli'st thou? whom thou fli'st, of him thou art."
Eve yields, henceforth acknowledging, "How beauty is excell'd
by manly grace." Froula argues that in thus turning, Eve rejects
"the authority of her own experience," allows patriarchal discourse to "speak her" as " 'shadow' or image that has and can
have no value except for what patriarchal authority attaches to
her. Eve's value is created by the patriarchy whose discourse
she becomes. Her narrative proves the 'triumph' of her education
or colonization; she has received the imprimatur of the realm,
has *become* its text, image, and token of value."[25]

Centuries later Lois awaits the same validation. Impatient
"for the curtain to rise" on her life, she longs constantly for romance and marriage as the only definite destiny she can imagine
for a woman. Her culture and her schooling have taught her to
see marriage as completion. Even the awful Livvy seems privileged by her engagement, which Lois associates with "a pass-
port," a male-conferred diploma (or imprimatur) that permits the

female to leave the training ground of childhood and enter adulthood. But like Eve, Lois is not attracted to the available male,
Gerald: "She would have loved to love him; she felt some kind
of wistfulness, some deprivation." And again like Eve, Lois finds
Gerald's dependence, his need to be constantly with her, smothering: "If he would not love her so, give her air to grow in, not
stifle her imagination." And although she too catches glimpses of
an alternate life, a "wat'ry image," she retreats in moments of
crisis to the deeply laid script, reassuring herself each time that
she will marry Gerald.[26]

Lois's immaturity and her desire to be shaped by others surfaces as she shows Marda her drawings. On the frontispiece of
the book, Lois has transcribed the passage from Browning's
"Pippa Passes," beginning "I am a painter who cannot paint,"
and ending "But do one thing at least I can / Love a man or hate
a man / Supremely." "But can you really?" Marda asks, and Lois
replies, "I don't see why not," revealing both to Marda and to
the reader her readiness to be defined by the male poet. Further,
Lois's belief in woman's intuitive ability to love a man (Lois has
not, as she knows, loved yet) suggests her absorption of the paradigm that depicts woman's natural role as being that of loving
man. The paintings give Lois "the kind of surprised assurance
one might expect from motherhood," the reproduction (of painting traditions and of children) being a validation, the only validation Lois believes possible. Recognizing the imitative quality
in the work and indeed in the desire, Marda suggests that Lois
write, create her own life. But frightened of unknown scripts,
Lois cries: "I like to be in a pattern. . . . I like to be related; to
have to be what I am. Just to *be* is so intransitive, so lonely."
The assigned place in the pattern does bestow a security, as
Marda knows, one that in turn justifies remaining in one's place.
"It's a good thing we can always be women," she notes dryly,
acknowledging the easy option. "I hate women," Lois replies,
"But I can't think how to begin to be anything else."[27]

Like Adam, Gerald, though unsure of his own autonomy,
imagines that he can validate Lois. When Lois attempts to explain what she sees as her unconscionable emotional distance
from the war, Gerald refuses, or is unable, to discuss the situation. Instead he assures her of "her wonderful power of feeling,"

provoking an angry response, which intuitively links the political and the gender situations: "When *we* do nothing it is out of politeness, but England is so moral, so dreadfully keen on not losing her temper, or being for half a moment not a great deal more noble than anyone else. Can you wonder this country gets irritated? It's as bad for it as being a woman. I never can see why women shouldn't be hit, or should be saved from wrecks when everybody is complaining they're so superfluous." Unable to grasp the link, Gerald is nonplussed. There are some things he doesn't expect a woman, at least *his* woman, to understand: "A fellow did not expect to be to a girl what a girl was to a fellow— this wasn't modesty, specially, it was an affair of function—so that the girl must be excused for a possible failure in harmony, a sometimes discordant irreverence. When he said: 'You will never know what you mean to me,' he made plain his belief in her perfectness as a woman. She wasn't made to know, she was not fit for it. She was his integrity, of which he might speak to strangers but of which to her he would never speak."[28]

Gerald, too, sees the role of woman as conferred, a given. Maturity is not something a woman achieves as a man does but something that is biologically inevitable. Aligned with the father in the belief that woman was not "made to know," Gerald, like Adam, suggests that he should protect Lois but also needs Lois to be his integrity.

The integrity that Lois's acceptance will create for Gerald is the integrity of the British empire and of his role as colonizing soldier. Laurence, the cousin from Oxford, probes the inarticulate Gerald, forcing him to reveal hidden layers of colonizing hubris. Responding to the probing, Gerald asserts:

Well . . . the situation's rotten. But right *is* right.
Why? [asks Laurence]
Well . . . from the point of view of civilization.
What do you mean by the point of view of civilization?
Oh—ours.

Laurence smiles, but Gerald continues, "We *do* seem the only people. . . . And we are giving them what they really want." Sensing the contradiction, Gerald thinks he "would have wished

to explain that no one could have a sounder respect than himself
and his country for the whole principle of nationality, and that
it was with some awareness of misdirection, even of paradox,
that he was out here to hunt and shoot the Irish." This misdirection is expelled when Lois agrees to marry Gerald. Now that
she is "all mine," he can write: "What I am doing this morning
[attempting to put down the rebels] seems so important—although it keeps me away from you—because I am doing it *for*
you."[29] Lois's eagerness to marry Gerald, to be his Eve, to embrace his rule as England wished Ireland to embrace English
rule, allows him to see as worthy a civilization that colonizes
women and nations.

The pivotal mill scene, which links sexual and political violence, awakens Lois simultaneously to her own sexuality and to
the language of her female personality. In a complex, sensitive
interpretation that identifies Bowen as a Christian Jungian, Harriet Blodgett reads entry into the mill as entry into the "deep
well of personality." Blodgett sees the Irish rebel hidden therein
as the "archetypal image of man in the depths of the psyche."
Associating this male level of the psyche with Lois's artistic abilities, Blodgett thus views Lois's awakening as an awakening to
the male in herself. Although recognizing the myth Bowen re-
creates as a fall, Blodgett identifies the archetypes with Greek
mythological figures and Lois's "fall" as that of the young woman
who by denying the god Apollo/Gerald denies her mature (het-
ero-)sexuality and her creative abilities. The struggle in Lois,
she suggests, is that between the lure of Marda, which is pernicious, and that of Gerald, which is salutary.[30]

I would agree that the mill scene echoes into deep layers of
the unconscious, but I read it as rebounding more from Chris-
tian/Miltonic than Jungian images. The conflict is that between
Lois's old romantic conceptions and the frightening realization
of the real nature of those ideas. It results in a partial acceptance
of female autonomy and sorority. Like Danielstown, the mill is
personified, and thus it acts as a displaced representation of the
patriarchal order of Anglo-Ireland. In its decaying state, however, the mill is a frightening reminder of the fragility of the
new artificial order imposed on the body of nature. Hugo, made
nervous by this evidence of instability, draws Marda's and Lois's

attention to the indecent corpse: "Another . . . of our national grievances. English law strangled the————." But Lois will not listen—Hugo's account is in line with Sir Richard's. Both blame England rather than Anglo-Ireland for the unrest and poverty in the country—a position that justifies inaction, but one which is by 1920 both irrelevant and useless. Again it is the narrator who draws our attention to the place of the mill, and by extension to that of Anglo-Ireland, in the country's history. "Banal enough in life to have closed this valley to the imagination," the mill, she tells us, is transfigured in death, taking "on all of a past to which it had given nothing." Lois identifies the mill as her night-mare. The narrator, linking the buildings through personifica-tion, provides the reason for Lois's fears: this other Big House does not stare insolently like Danielstown, but rather these "brit-tle, staring ruins" grin "with vacancy: corpse of an idiot."[31] This is Lois's nightmare because, like the fools in Shakespeare, this idiot speaks the truth—the transitory nature of the orders of men, specifically of the patriarchal Anglo-Irish order, in whose stability and permanence Lois has trusted. Nightmare, because it suggests that Lois's goal, the design in which she wants to have to be, is illusion.

"Deliciously" enticed, Lois goes "as near as she dared" but does not want to enter. She plays, in effect, the tease. Marda, however, will not tolerate the immaturity:

Marda put an arm round her waist, and in an ecstasy at this compulsion Lois entered the mill. Fear heightened her gratification; she welcomed its inrush, letting her look climb the scabby and livid walls to the fright-ful stare of the sky. . . .
    "Hate it?" said Marda.
    "You'd make me do anything."[32]

The fear and gratification suggest the novice's sexual initiation, but this is not an initiation of heterosexual love or of the male in her own psyche but a rite of shared female experience. Hidden in the deep recesses of the mill, of the displaced Big House, the rebel is the political dis-ease, Heaney's "fifth column," or "bat-tering ram," which threatens the stability of the very structure that houses him. When the rebel awakes, warning the women to stay in Danielstown "while y'have it," Lois in panic reverts to a child. "I must marry Gerald," she thinks, retreating from the reality of temporality to the Edenic illusion, the dream of stability, and linking, again without thought, her political and sexual situations. The awakening is not a linear progression but a series of stops and starts. The accidental physical violence of the rebel's gun going off and the bullet's striking Marda coincides with Lois's realization of the violence of sexual passion as Hugo betrays himself in his urgent shout for Marda. The narrator, the adult looking back "down the perspective of time," notes that on hearing Hugo, "Lois, as though the mill were falling, went white, then crimson."[33] The mill, the displaced Big House, is falling for Lois, and with it the whole patriarchal system on which it is founded. Coinciding with the pistol shot, Hugo's call acts as a revelation, jolting Lois into a recognition of the violence endemic in both political and sexual situations.

Asserting her sexual and political independence simultaneously, Lois bars Hugo's entrance to the mill. In preserving the women's and the Irish rebel's secret, Lois symbolically asserts the mutuality of women's and rebels' interests. Recognizing "the stronghold" of their sex, the women turn away from Hugo. The bandaging of Marda's hand, when "Providence" herself seems to have provided Lois with a clean handkerchief, is an intimate sororal ceremony of adulthood. Marda asks if Lois is sorry they went into the mill, sorry to have seen the heart of her nightmare. But Lois is not: Hugo's shout, she explains, revealed to her the "awful" nature—for Marda—of his romanticizing and consequently freed Lois from her old notion that Hugo could have been her father and her own romantic initiator. Leaning her head on Lois's shoulder, Marda acknowledges Lois's honesty and imagination. Having discarded the old conceptions, Lois discovers that she has also lost her old fear; illusion and fear are truly symbiotic. "All this," she tells Marda, "has quite stopped any excitement for me about the mill. It's a loss, really, I don't think I'll come down this part of the river again."[34]

"Appreciation of literature is the end of magic," Bowen writes. Maturity, too, is the end of the magic illusions; understanding the reality of sexual relationships means abandoning the dreams that had nourished the imagination. As if to mark the ending of the old life, Lois asks Marda where she will be next day at this time, at "half-past six." On the train, Marda replies; Lois finds it difficult to imagine what she, the new person she has become, will be doing.[35] In generously accepting the company of the middle-aged Hugo Montmorency on the walk home, however, Lois reveals the new humanity implicit in her maturity.

In Marda's absence, as suggested earlier, nature itself intervenes to alert Lois to the danger of being drowned in an inappropriate marriage. After the ball at which she agreed to marry Gerald, Lois tries to suppress her anxieties as she reads of Gerald's happiness that she is all his: "If this is so perfect to anyone, can one be wrong?" But the narrator points to the observer Lois offends: "An escape of sunlight, penetrating the pale sky in the southwest, altered the room like a revelation. Noiselessly, a sweetpea moulted its petals on to the writing table, leaving a bare pistil. The pink butterfly flowers, transparently balancing, were shadowed faintly with blue as by an intuition of death. Lois bowed forward her forehead against the edge of the table." This revelation evokes the earlier one, for the reader and now also for Lois. Then Lois knew that Hugo was awful to Marda. The association suggests Lois's realization of the death in both old conceptions—in an affair with the romanticized lover of her mother or in marriage with the romantic representative of indulgent patriarchy. But pushing aside her doubts, Lois assumes "a placidness, a sense of being located" as she pictures her marriage to Gerald. Similarly Marda, at the end of the mill scene, imagined her own formation in marriage to her English fiancé, Leslie. "So much of herself that was fluid must, too, be moulded by his idea of her. Essentials were fixed and localised by her being with him—to become as the bricks and wallpaper of a home." Marda might be Eve here, speaking the original patriarchal discourse, accepting Adam's fancy of molding her.[36]

Lois, in desiring the definite something of marriage with Gerald, reveals the hidden Miltonic pattern that shapes her perspective. But when Gerald, in his surprise at Marda's engagement, implies his own belief in this pattern—"She was all herself. Doesn't love finish off people . . . with something that isn't them, in a way you can feel?"—Lois recoils. "She understood him, but did not know how to agree. What must one be

for him?" She worries, "Was Gerald, sublimely, the instrument
of some large imposture?" Again nature seems to warn Lois:
Gerald says, "You are everything. I want so much of you." Then
he kisses "her with frightened violence." This time Lois rather
than the narrator senses the disharmony: "The laurels creaked
as, in his arms, she bent back into them. His singleness bore,
confusing, upon her panic of thoughts[.] [H]er physical apprehension of him was confused by the slipping, cold leaves."[37] Sensitive to the disharmony, Lois breaks off the scene, arresting
another of the kisses that might have compelled her agreement.

In the final interview with Gerald, the memory of Marda, or
rather the memory of Marda's decision, will not allow Lois to
agree with Gerald, though she agonizes to do so. Entry into the
mill was effected, we recall, only through Lois's "ecstasy" at
Marda's "compulsion," only through surrender to a sexual force.
As Gerald pleads that Lois is everything and asks if she understands, Lois replies, "You sometimes make me." And "She
wanted to add: 'Touch me now'; it was the only way across. In
her impotence, her desolation—among the severe trees—at not
being compelled, she made a beseeching movement."[38] But, although sexual experience is maturing, marriage based on sexual
compulsion is not a mature decision. The six o'clock bells ring,
evoking for Lois "a train curving past in a rush," recalling the
earlier mill scene. And as Gerald presses for a commitment, Lois
comprehends all the connections.

A light ran almost visibly up inside him. She saw now where they were,
why he had come today.
    She thought of going, hesitating with delight, to the edge of an un-
known high up terrace, of Marda, of getting into a train. "No," she cried,
terrified.[39]

The "hesitating with delight" and the "high up terrace" verbally
echo the entry to the mill, awakening Lois for the first time to
a full consciousness of the power of sexual passion. The mill scene
also reminds her of the realities of male passion, Gerald's in this
instance, and the price this passion entails for women. "Getting
into a train" is synonymous with Marda's marrying Leslie, abandoning her quest for autonomy. Juxtaposing these realities for

the first time, Lois finally understands that the sexual fulfillment and security offered in romantic marriage are balanced by a woman's loss of autonomy. A terrified no is her response.

Gerald's death, as Bowen notes in the preface, is not Lois's tragedy, for Lois has matured beyond Gerald, and it would now be impossible to picnic in Eden. It is the innocent Gerald who "falls" in Bowen's tale: as Daventry tells Lois of Gerald's death, the narrator notes, "they both saw the amazed white road and dust, displaced by the fall, slowly settling."[40]

The sacrifice of Gerald acts rather like that of Septimus Smith in Virginia Woolf's *Mrs. Dalloway*—it allows Lois to experience both life and death vicariously and, for the first time, to consciously connect colonization with the paradigms of patriarchal marriage. "She went into the house and up to the top to find what was waiting. Life, seen whole for a moment, was one act of apprehension, the apprehension of death." Lois has not eaten of the fruit herself but experiences, through Gerald's death, mortality. She experiences it, appropriately, where it waits at the top of the father's house. The last picture of Lois is that of a mature woman, one who understands the forbidden knowledge. Indeed Lois appears to be the only person in Danielstown capable of comprehending the disaster: Francie plays the tragic heroine; Sir Richard "slipped away quietly—he was an old man, really," the narrator notes, "outside all this"; Lady Naylor busies herself to avoid Lois; and Laurence "walking about the grounds unguardedly, was exposed to what they all dreaded—Lois." But the dreaded emotional scene does not occur; Lois contains her knowledge. And Laurence, becoming "almost personal," attempts condolence: "I expect—I don't know—one probably gets past things." It is not, however, Gerald's death alone that Lois apprehends: "But look here," she answers Laurence, "there are things that one can't—(She meant: He loved me, he believed in the British Empire.) 'At least, I don't want to.' "[41] The extraordinary parenthetical interruption of Lois's response emphasizes the narrator's conclusion that Lois has established the necessary connection. Lois's own conclusion emphasizes her will to remember, to notice. Significantly we do not see Lois again, but we hear from Lady Naylor that she left Ireland, refusing to be accompanied, or protected, by her male cousin.

The love Gerald wished to give Lois—the protective, insu-
lating, defining, limiting love, the Adamic inheritance—is associated, is indeed indigenous, with love of empire. "We are
giving them what they really want," Gerald suggested, though
he was uneasily aware of the paradox of shooting the Irish to
give them what they wanted. Asserting on the one hand the
autonomy of nations but insisting on the other on England's primary, or paternal, role in guiding those nations, English representatives address Ireland as Adam does Eve: "Not then
mistrust, but tender love enjoins, / That I should mind thee oft,
and mind thou me."[42] The magic of Eden, the romance and security, is dispelled once Lois comprehends the illusion. Maturity
demands not getting over this knowledge, and the novel of awakening appropriately concludes at this point.

Eden for the imaginative child, Elizabeth Bowen told us, consists in accepting books, in accepting the word, usually of the
father, as fact. Again we recall that maturity is not achieved
without loss: "The young person is then thrown out of Eden; for
evermore his brain is to stand posted between his self and the
story. Appreciation of literature is the end of magic."[43] Hence
the young woman like the young reader tries to deny her reason
and linger in the father's house. Lois's realization that paternal
colonization and paternal marriage both involve the suppression
of female creativity points the reader to the artist/narrator and
ultimately to Elizabeth Bowen herself, who in the preface drew
our attention to her own role. The Miltonic echoes and displace-
ments also suggest the narrator's passage to maturity through
her refusal to accept any longer the word and paradigms of those
forgotten books that infected the child. Like her friend Virginia
Woolf, Bowen realized the extent to which Milton's great epic
had influenced both literary and religious presentations of women,
and like Maria Edgeworth, Bowen also realized the extent to
which women had internalized these representations.

But Milton has an even more personal connection to Bowen's
family and to Bowen's Court, the "house from which Danielstown
was drawn." As the Puritan Milton dictated his great "argument" to his dutiful daughter in England, another Puritan,
Oliver Cromwell, subdued Ireland, forcing the country to become Eve-like, the reluctant consort, creation and creature of

England. And with that other Puritan came Elizabeth Bowen's ancestors, those "new settlers" whose imposition betrayed an "inherent wrong." Indeed I would suggest that the burning of Danielstown in *The Last September* might be read as Bowen's symbolic expiation of the original sin. In a night of Miltonic apocalypse, Danielstown, the personified, personally loved house of the fathers, is "executed": "It seemed that an extra day, unreckoned, had come to abortive birth that these things might happen. . . . The roads in unnatural dusk ran dark with movement, secretive or terrified; not a tree, brushed pale by wind from the flames, not a cabin pressed in despair to the bosom of night, not a gate too starkly visible but had its place in the design of order and panic."[44]

As the executioners leave, even the sounds of their cars are "demolished" in "the open and empty country"—the same wide country from which the Montmorencys escaped to the shelter of Danielstown in Bowen's opening page. And nature, the dispossessed mother, (re)claims her own: "The first wave of a silence that was to be ultimate flowed back confidently to the steps. The door stood open hospitably upon a furnace." As Lois's abandonment of her dual illusions involves a recognition that both illusions inhere in and are integral parts of the same paradigm, so Bowen's abandonment of the father's word (Milton's in this instance) involves her recognition of the relationship between Milton's ethics and the patriarchal foundation of Bowen's Court. In the Eden of Anglo-Ireland, Lois experiences the effects of the relationship Bowen recognizes, but in her novel of "destruction unto reconstruction" Bowen herself celebrates the triumph of the repressed country, the "unwilling bosom," maternal Ireland.[45]

5. Kate O'Brien
Family in the New Nation

And be the judge of your own soul; but never for a second, I
implore you, set up as the judge of another. Commentator,
annotator, if you like, but never judge.
  —Mother Superior to Anna in *The Land of Spices*

ONE OF THE first Irish women to focus on and write from personal knowledge of the Irish Catholic middle classes, Kate
O'Brien should, on this count alone, be considered in any analysis
of Irish women's writing. More important, however, she continues her predecessors' exploration of women's position, examining
education and religious sentiment as well as the ties of love and
marriage. But O'Brien's exploration is subtle, and her literary
techniques must have seemed intensely traditional, even old-
fashioned, in the experimental climate of the 1920s and the early
1930s. Both facts probably contribute to the current neglect of
her work, so that critics focusing on the overt concerns with
family and religion neglect the more subtle insight into the condition of women in the new political entity—the Irish Free State.

Acknowledging the dual sources of the traditions she inherits,
O'Brien embraces her heritage as rich rather than divided. A
comment by an Oxbridge don on the paucity of Irish writing in
English sparked her essay on the Irish literary tradition, "Imaginative Prose by the Irish, 1820-1970." O'Brien recalls how the
don's remark silenced her momentarily, but then a "vast cata-
logue" of Irish writers streamed from her lips. The surprise, she
asserts, is not that there are few, but that there are many. Wea-
rily she acknowledges the old saw that Irish literature in the
nineteenth century and earlier was the product of the Protestant
ascendancy. This is unsurprising, given the repression of language and the denial of educational, religious, and economic liberty to Catholics prior to emancipation in 1829.[1]

But Irish literature, O'Brien suggests, is no more divisible into Anglo-Irish and Gaelic-Irish camps than is the Irish population at large. The jagged boundaries of such divisions are clear in a sketch of the O'Brien family origins, origins surprisingly similar to Elizabeth Bowen's:

In the 1650's, a soldier of Cromwell's army named Thornhill, having fought at the sieges of Limerick and Clonmel, was garrisoned awhile at Kilmallock, and at the allocation of the lands of the conquered decided to take his share and settle down on the western face of Ardpatrick. He married a girl of the neighbourhood, and almost certainly, if to his surprise, became a Papist. Or if he did not, his children, without doubt, were Papists to a man. And three hundred years later to the very decade, my grandfather, Patrick Thornhill, then only a boy, was having to fight with guile and energy—in common with uncles, brothers, cousins—to hold on to the same lands which the original conqueror had given to their Plantation ancestor.[2]

O'Brien has cause to be proud of these ancestors, who "throughout the crazily difficult and tragic nineteenth century . . . kept on farming and raising good cattle stock with intelligence and success; so that they were able to hold to their lands, meet the fantastic extortions of agent and absentee landlord, keep the trust and respect of their own class and kind, and put money in the bank."[3]

Happily O'Brien does not identify her literary ancestors by either religion or politics but claims Maria Edgeworth as the first of modern Irish fiction writers. What particularly pleases O'Brien in Edgeworth's work is the earlier writer's ability to hear and speak the muted voice of repressed Ireland. "She heard how we spoke, and she knew what we were talking about; us, the ordinary people of Ireland. She broke through, most amazingly at that time, from all the artificiality of novelists." O'Brien lists all the nineteenth-century names as her ancestors. Somerville and Ross perturb her conscience, though she admits that they wrote "one really good novel—alarming in a way"; these women, she says, never laugh quite fairly, or quite truly. But again O'Brien admires the ability of her ancestors to hear the muted voices, to understand and represent the silenced segment: "But God knows those ladies had an ear for our rural idiom."[4]

The amusement at and tendency to caricature the Irish Catholic peasant, to which O'Brien objects, is indigenous to the *R.M.* series—fictional, exaggerated accounts of Irish life, written to amuse the English audience of a popular magazine. In *The Real Charlotte*, however, Somerville and Ross's concern with gender roles anticipates O'Brien's, but O'Brien extends the study to small-town Irish Catholic middle-class society.

To appreciate this extension, one need but glance at the subjects of British and Irish nineteenth- and early twentieth-century literature. Dickens and Hardy roused England to concern for the plight of the urban and rural poor. The middle classes had been sympathetically portrayed by Eliot, Trollope, and Galsworthy. But these middle-classes were in the main both educated and somewhat removed from the trade of an embryonic middle class. They were not the sons or grandsons of working-class but of middle-class parents. Bennett and Wells did move closer to a newly forming middle class, one whose goal was membership in this class. The Catholic middle class that emerged in Ireland at the end of the nineteenth and the beginning of the twentieth century was also such a group. Members of this new class were the direct descendants of working-class and peasant parents, nearer to the soil and to trade than were the industrialists which Galsworthy, for example, celebrated. Nineteenth-century Irish writers generally explored the Protestant ascendancy, though Somerville and Ross did introduce the Protestant middle class. The endurance of Catholic peasants was recorded by the Banim brothers and William Carleton; the romance of historical figures, by Lady Morgan; and the stifling and sometimes rich life of the slum-dwellers, by Sean O'Casey in the twentieth century.

Noting her literary ancestors, O'Brien recalls Yeats, who was "growing into a great poet, round Coole." O'Brien, however, could hardly sympathize with Yeats's vision of Ireland. For Yeats, as Seamus Deane notes, was almost single-handedly responsible for the myth "of the greasy philistinism of the Catholic bourgeoisie and of the intellectual fragrance of the aristocratic Protestant tradition." But O'Brien continues, "A more difficult thing was happening" in Dublin—Joyce. In taking a Catholic small-town, shopkeeping family as the subject of her first novel, *Without My Cloak*, O'Brien, like Joyce, asserts the possibility of human interest and sensitivity in a generally unexplored or grossly caricatured class. Indeed, as is clear in Lorna Reynolds's recent biography, both the family backgrounds and the experiences of many of her characters correspond to O'Brien's own.[5] In the last Mellick novel, *The Land of Spices*, O'Brien not only analyzes the same segment of Irish society as Joyce, but she also presents a female bildungsromane that carefully parallels Joyce's *Portrait of the Artist as a Young Man*, asserting at the same time the increased difficulty for the artist as a young woman and positing an alternative paradigm for all would-be artists.

In exploring O'Brien's significance in a female tradition, I consider three of her Mellick novels—*Without My Cloak* (1931), *The Anteroom* (1934), and *The Land of Spices* (1941)—because these early works announce all the O'Brien themes more subtly, and thus more artistically, than other texts. *Mary Lavelle* (1936), for example, and *As Music and Splendour* (1958) emphasize the conflict between love and liberty that often confronts women, a theme introduced in *Without My Cloak*. Focusing on the narrowness and prejudice of Irish society, *Pray for the Wanderer* (1938) and *The Last of Summer* (1943) extend the critique in *The Land of Spices* but lack the delicacy of the earlier text. *The Flower of May* (1953) continues to stress the necessity of female education already illustrated in *The Land of Spices*. *That Lady* (1946), the story of Ana Mendoza's suffering at the hands of Philip II of Spain, is perhaps O'Brien's foremost example of the problem of love and liberty for women. Further, as Lorna Reynolds argues, *That Lady*, like all O'Brien's work, is a "chronicle of her time" in the undrawn but clear parallel between the despotism of Philip II and the German threat that shadowed the world when O'Brien first conceived the idea of the novel in 1940.[6] I exclude this text to focus on O'Brien's critique of women's place in the new political entity of Gaelic Catholic Ireland, but obviously, as *That Lady* suggests, the critique extends to all countries where women's freedom is suppressed. Finally, these three novels are selected because they reveal O'Brien's technical skill, her willingness to experiment with different forms (a practice rarely considered by her critics), and her implied critique of particular form.

O'Brien has been misread as the matriarch who celebrates the

"supreme matriarchy" of the Catholic church and the family modeled on it, beside which "all else is of little passing significance."[7]
Certainly she focuses on both family and church, but celebrate
she does not. The origin of the Irish Catholic middle-class family
is the subject of *Without My Cloak*, an origin analogous to that
of the modern state. The exigencies of a Catholic conscience are
examined in *The Anteroom*, but these very exigencies are by-
passed; they are not finally the ultimate basis on which decisions
are made. And *The Land of Spices*, while again centered on
family and religion, suggests more the gender injustices inherent
in patriarchal families than anything else. The picture of the matriarch has unfortunately prevailed, blanketing in its voluminous
folds the fine distinctions and qualifications O'Brien so carefully
painted.

In the first novel, *Without My Cloak*, O'Brien employs epic
techniques to present three generations of an Irish Catholic
family from its founding in 1789 to the peak of its economic success in 1877. Arriving in Mellick, O'Brien's fictional western
town, during the last days of the severe penal restrictions, Anthony Considine succeeds in establishing himself. His descendants consolidate their position through tireless striving and a
ruthless will to suppress all that threatens them. Economic success achieved, marital alliances which increase the family's respectability, power, and prestige are pursued. Although Caroline
Considine is unhappy in her marriage, her brothers will not countenance her escape, which they see as a reflection on their good
name. When young Denis Considine, son of the namesake of the
first Anthony, becomes infatuated with the poor, lovely, but illegitimate Christina, the economic and religious power of the
Considine family (represented by Father Tom Considine) effects
Christina's immediate departure for New York. Although he
eventually follows and finds Christina, Denis fails to read the
girl's enduring and heroic love in her dismissal of him. No longer
in love himself, the relieved Denis returns to the fold of his
family, but he resents his father's smothering love and his desire
to have Denis join the Considine business in Mellick. As he
moves to confront his father, Denis—in a most unlikely ending—
meets and falls in love with the beautiful Anna Hennessy, a member of an even more respectable family than the Considines, who

is destined to make him happy in his father's business. In its panoramic sweep and depiction of the simultaneous rise of family and nation, this novel suggests a tale of origins.

In this connection, M.M. Bakhtin's remarks on epic devices may help us to understand O'Brien's technique. The epic-maker, in contrast to the novelist, Bakhtin argued, sought to direct, limit, and unite the perspective of audience and narrator. Establishing distance, he suggests, is essential to this task. The past of which the epic-singer speaks must be inaccessible to both speaker and hearers. This inaccessibility allows no point of view but that of the speaker, who usually celebrates the heroic clan and their traditions, valorizing them with reverential language, effectually isolating the heroes and their world—its meaning, values, and content—from contemporary times. Total character description is another device of the epic-singer. The establishment and preservation of the values and traditions the epic celebrates necessitate the reader's exclusion from independent judgment and evaluation of character and incident. Hence the hero or protagonist can only be what the speaker says he is. The male protagonist is his essence. Everything he is is seen by both himself and his peers and passed on to the listener, leaving no surplus to spill over into the present, no loose ends for the contemporary reader to extend. The deus ex machina, providing a contrived and unexpected ending, is the final unrealistic device.[8] Celebrating courage and patriotism, the epic is closely tied to myths of origin that venerate the founding father's bravery and his loyalty to a particular country. The *Aeneid*, for example, may be seen primarily as a myth of origin. In this respect, epic devices are appropriate in O'Brien's novel; the fiction is close enough to the "fiction" of O'Brien's own family and of many Irish Catholic families to serve as their myth of origin.

The opening description of the arrival of Anthony Considine, the founding father, at the site of his future home rings with the echoes of other legendary arrivals. "The light of the October day was dropping from afternoon clarity to softness when Anthony Considine led his limping horse round the last curve of the Gap of Storm and halted there to behold the Vale of Honey." The man's beauty is "nature's heedless quality," while that of his stolen horse is the "work of art . . . [brought] to the threshold of degeneracy." Not a natural creature, the horse is the highly trained, delicately bred product of a leisured class. The peasant's appropriation of the horse, that symbol of Anglo-Ireland, thus suggests the rightful accession of the new, natural man over a decadent civilization. Considine has come from the "treeless, lovely west," and he surveys the whole fruitful vale sheltered by hills "from the Atlantic-salted wind" and watered by "a great river." Despite the "grey smudge of a town," the picture is one of an untouched, new land, a rich, warm, and beautiful natural shelter. The elevated language bespeaks the epic distance, a distance preserved in the epithetical naming of the characters: Honest John, the horse thief, and John Aloysius Hennessy, the Grand Old Man of Mellick, are named and drawn as types rather than as individuals. Distance is further suggested by the narrator's insistence on the pastness of these events, not only the horse thief's arrival but also the final dance of Denis Considine and Anna Hennessy, which the narrator notes was the "discreet waltz of their day." Epic distance is also emphasized by the storyteller's ability to see, as the characters cannot, a future consequent on the recorded action, a future which is itself history at the time of the narration.[9]

These distancing devices are repeated in *The Anteroom*, O'Brien's continuation of the Considine story. Here again the narrator reminds the reader of the pastness of the events: the manners of 1880 are not, she notes, those of today. The fictional nature of the narrative is stressed by the narrator's picking-up of one character's thought to reveal another character. Thus the omniscient narrator reflects on Dr. Curran's unexpressed opinion of his rival, Vincent O'Regan, and uses this reflection herself to definitively establish Vincent's character.[10] The deliberate narrational interjection recalls the contamination of apostolic succession in *The Real Charlotte*, but the device is not disturbing in O'Brien because the reader is always kept aware of narrational omniscience, is—the technique suggests—expected to trust rather than to question, is indeed placed in the position of a child being told the story of her origins.

O'Brien also encloses and isolates her heroes by resorting to total character description. John Aloysius Hennessy, the Grand

Old Man of Mellick, is, she tells us, the same age as the century and

> a fair example of the qualities and achievements that the majority of its important people stood for. But he inherited all their proud blood that had known power and pride in other centuries, and was tinged with their traditions, a blood in which the attributes of soldier and priest and fanatic and worldling and wit ran with the attributes of a successful merchant. He stood for the autocracy of wealth and the supremacy of the bourgeoisie, but he was in spirit, faintly and deprecatingly as he might suggest it, an aristocrat. He cared little for the distinctions of rank, which seemed to him to settle themselves arbitrarily in the womb, but he cared much for the traditions of fine behaviour and fine breeding in the Hennessys.[11]

Finally, the contrived deus ex machina epic ending also concludes *Without My Cloak*. The story lines are all neatly tied as in a nineteenth-century novel, but the meeting of Denis and Anna in the final scenes recalls the endings of fairy tales or epics rather than realistic novels. Magic is evoked by the strangeness of the scene: Denis, weary of family pressures, dusty and a little drunk, crosses the moonlit garden on his way, he thinks, to say goodbye to his father. More particularly, he plans to say goodbye to his father's plans for the Considine clan and to his own place in those plans forever. Beautiful Anna Hennessy, the expected fiancée of Denis's cousin Victor, waylays and enchants Denis. *La Belle Dame* calls Denis, and he, "drowning," has no other choice. The representation of Anna and Denis as transfigured lovers whose brilliance escapes and blinds the ordinary human points to the artificial ending.[12] In this origin myth of the Catholic middle class, O'Brien asserts a belief in that class's own qualities, in its members' ability to create worth from their own stock. Therefore Denis does not marry the illegitimate, beautiful Christina, daughter of an Irish peasant and an English aristocrat, as the hero of romance or of the pioneering novels of the New World might have done, but a girl approved by both his clan and his religion. And this Belle Dame does not cause her knight to wander but to stay home.

Such an arrangement is not simply the material of myths of

origin: Levi-Strauss has argued that the social, political, and economic binding of families in marriage, symbolized by the giving of the important gift of the daughter, is the basis of human civilization, the reality on which myths of origin are constructed. More recent theorists, however, as we saw in chapter 1, argue that what Levi-Strauss has shown is that the dominant male civilization has erected itself on the bodies and the unpaid labor of women, not that such an erection was the only path to civilization. Denis's early despairing cry to Christina—"If we were only just ourselves, not bits and pieces in a scheme of someone else's"—suggests his tortured but passive acceptance of the Levi-Strauss theory. But appearing as if by magic, Anna is the impetus and reward for Denis's assumption of the place reserved for him in the Considine scheme.[13]

Although epic devices may have seemed dull in the early twentieth century, O'Brien's use of these techniques, which traditionally celebrate patriarchal dominance of nation and family, is ironic in her study of the "new" society. For O'Brien's text presents a subtle but devastating critique of the toll these systems of civilization take on women. If on the one hand the Irish Catholic middle class had been deprived of what philosophers, historians, and democratically inclined people would see as that class's rightful place in their country and in their literature, this rightful place also carried with it a repression of women that philosophers, historians, and democratically inclined people have been slow to recognize. O'Brien has been read as the spokeswoman for marriage and for the matriarchal Roman Catholic church, since, some critics have found, her writing suggests the "relative unimportance of revolution."[14] But the revolution O'Brien dreams of is far more radical than the transfer of political power from one patriarchal government to another. At best O'Brien's approval of traditional marriage is qualified: the imbalance in the relationship is always evident.

Lorna Reynolds's recent literary biography attempts to rectify the accepted reading of O'Brien. Liberty and love always struggle within O'Brien marriages, she notes, and "the women of the Considine family do not fare very well in this respect, any more than women in other novels of the time or in real life fared." This is an understatement. The reifying of the family, be it na-

tional or personal, is presented in *Without My Cloak* as a burden
that falls much heavier on women than on men. The lovely Molly
dies bearing yet another heir for the Considine dynasty. Christina, the inappropriate one, is abandoned to loneliness in New
York while her fickle lover is rewarded with magical love in Ireland (the Almighty Father in league with the earthly one?). And
Caroline's flight from her insensitive husband provokes the united
action and fury of her brothers. Her misery is dismissed: "The
pitiful antics of a woman not far from her dangerous time"; she
is important only as a threat to the Considine name and to the
marriage alliance, that powerful economic, social, and political
bond, sought by the Considines with the Hennessys. Her despair,
if it could have been imagined, would have been ignored. Epic
omniscience allows the narrator to draw the complete brotherly
response and at the same time to undermine—in a nonepic fashion—the reader response her epic structure implies. "It would
occur to neither of them [Anthony or Tom]," she notes wryly,
"to set his sister Caroline above his surname." Angrily the brothers ask who is responsible, what man is to blame; their imaginations are incapable of comprehending any other reason for a
woman to leave her husband. Their sister Teresa, long married
herself, laughs: "If she's been so mad . . . as to run away from
one man after twenty years of it for no better reason than to go
straight to another." This makes the brothers suspect that Teresa
as well as Caroline may be mad! But the narrator always knows
more than her characters: "It was beyond the span of Considine
thought that a wife should leave a husband. A husband might
conceivably desert a wife—but—oh, well, what was the good of
raving?"[15]

As if responding to the belief of the male Considines in the
naturalness of their being the center of women's lives, O'Brien
writes in *The Anteroom* of the sorority that could prompt a
woman to reject not simply marriage but union with the beloved.
The three-day sequence of this action corresponds, as Lorna
Reynolds explains, to the three acts of a classical play, in which
"the unities of time, place and action are rigorously observed."[16]
This structure furnishes us with another variety of O'Brien's
technical skill. As Teresa Mulqueen lies dying, her daughter
Agnes fights her desire for Vincent de Courcy Regan, husband

to her beloved sister, Marie-Rose. Agnes has never spoken this love, but she is concerned that she may be unable to hide it while the family is together for Teresa's death. In the emotionally charged atmosphere Vincent and Agnes do declare their love, a love they both believe strong enough to endure exile from home and family. Thinking of Marie-Rose, however, Agnes refuses to flee with Vincent, and Vincent commits suicide.

On another front, Teresa fights, or attempts to delay, death until she can arrange for the marriage and care of her syphilitic son, Reggie. O'Brien portrays Teresa's excessive love for her wayward son beautifully and sensitively; indeed she returns to this common Irish phenomenon with Hannah Kernahan in *The Last of Summer*. Teresa Mulqueen, the Teresa who scoffed at the idea of Caroline's running away to another man in *Without My Cloak*, Caroline of that novel, and Hannah all have their frustration in common. Teresa feels no love for her silly but kind husband, and Caroline feels cheated by hers. By the end of *Without My Cloak*, Caroline has become an embittered woman who begrudges anyone, Denis specifically, happiness. Hannah ruthlessly shapes her children's lives. Caroline and Hannah are not so much examples of the tradition discussed in chapter 1, that of the aggressive woman as negative and destructive, but rather of John Stuart Mill's prediction that "An active and energetic mind, if denied liberty, will seek for power."[17]

To return to Agnes in *The Anteroom*: the heroine's minute examination of her conscience before Vincent's arrival is, as Benedict Kiely says, as detailed as that of any "zealous Jesuit." O'Brien's detail here, her effort to register every movement, resembles more the realism of Henry James or Edith Wharton than the poetic bareness of an Elizabeth Bowen portrayal. Unfashionable even at the time of writing, realism, O'Brien believed, was a natural English talent: "English genius is rooted in realism and derives from the least common multiple of every day, and of things understandable by the least of us." Agnes's options are very limited, and her painstaking exploration of her conduct demands the reader's concentrated attention. The detailed struggle with conscience causes one critic to misread Agnes as finding "religious belief as natural and as difficult to sacrifice as passion."[18] The original struggle is not with passion,

however, but with Agnes's own fantasies, for at this point she
has not experienced passion and is unaware that Vincent returns
her love.

When she does realize the power of her love for Vincent and
his for her, it is not religion that forbids acceptance nor is it the
fact that Vincent is married to her own sister, Marie-Rose. But
sorority with this sister/friend will not countenance betrayal.
Wanting Vincent more than anything except life, Agnes tells him
that she could never forget that it was Marie-Rose she hurt, that
if Vincent were capable of making her forget, then she would
hate him for it. The bond of loyalty goes back to her first year
at school when her older sister, Marie-Rose, publicly and quix-
otically, Agnes thinks, maintained Agnes's beauty in defiance of
the "popular vote" that she was "the plainest girl in the school."
Agnes remembers this scene early in the novel, and the friendship and loyalty engendered in the past are manifested by both
women throughout. The friendship itself determines the final action. Recognizing the sisters' mutual devotion, Vincent attempts
to persuade Agnes by insisting that Marie-Rose "would be hap-
pier if I went—in the end." "Perhaps," Agnes answers, "But not
if I did."[19] It is not depriving Marie-Rose of Vincent that pre-
vents Agnes from accepting his love, but the consequent depriving Marie-Rose of the friendship with Agnes.

The story of Diana and Actaeon, which can be read as a tale
of sorority in the nymphs' shielding of Diana from Actaeon's
view, shadows that of Agnes and Vincent. References to the
gods, to Greece, and to moonlight, symbol of the chastity of
which Diana is goddess, cluster around Agnes and Vincent.
When she first met Vincent, Agnes thought him "Hellenic in his
perfect balance of gaiety, intelligence, and beauty"; Dr. Curran
sees him as a "God in marble"; and Sir Geoffrey views him as
a "cold and glorious-seeming god." Agnes's virginity is emphasized not as the naive, ignorant, perhaps romantic condition of
a young girl but as the considered position of a mature woman.
Vincent hunts (though he targets snipe rather than deer) prior
to his encounter with Agnes. Deciding to confront Vincent and
kill their mutual hopes of loving each other, Agnes halts as a line
from Scripture assails her: "He that loveth the danger shall per-
ish in it." But challenging the male god she addresses emphati-

cally as "You," Agnes determines to go and prays to another
Diana figure, the Virgin Mary, for protection. As prologue to the
climactic garden scene, Vincent thinks he is caught in an anteroom "to truth, or fate, or any of those awful abstracts. And she
was all of them, entangled in their moonshine, making both sense
and nonsense of their echoes."[20]

The truth Agnes reveals is also their fate—that she and Vincent love each other as they can no other; that Agnes is incapable
of betraying her friend; and that Vincent, though he desires such
betrayal, could not love her were she so capable. Vincent, whom
the narrator sees as an emotionally stunted, failed artist, fails
to read his own and Agnes's fate until such reading is too late.
Actaeon-like, he has rambled "without any especial object," until
espying Marie-Rose he felt compelled to possess her.[21] Unlike
the passive Pamela Dysart in *The Real Charlotte*, Agnes is forbidden to speak her love for Vincent, not by the convention of
the hunt but by her love for her sister; later O'Brien heroines
(Mary in *Mary Lavelle*, and Rose and Clare in *As Music and
Splendour*) will forthrightly select their own lovers.

The moonlight serves to separate and shield Agnes from Vincent. Having questioned her own motives in "running out into
the moonlight with a message of purity," Agnes seeks and apparently receives the Virgin's protection. As Vincent accuses her
of loving Marie-Rose more than him, a charge she does not refute, and as Agnes suddenly swerves away from him, the narrator draws the reader's attention to the moonlight, which "made
a dividing stream between them." Separated from Vincent as
the nymphs separated Diana from Actaeon, Agnes can think of
her options. Vincent for his part seems powerless to cross the
stream and can only study Agnes, apparently without understanding. But when Agnes crosses the stream to impart "a caress
of resignation" which she hoped would "set them free," she sunders Diana's protective shield and is punished by an intense
awareness that "she could not do without what she must never
have."[22]

In the next Mellick novel, *The Land of Spices*, O'Brien charts
middle-class Irish Catholic society's attempts to model a young
girl into an appropriate wife for the new Ireland. Daughter of
a drunken father and a mother dominated by her own mother,

Anna Murphy grows up in the convent of Sainte Famille from 1904 to 1914, developing ideas of intellectual and gender liberty in large part as a result of her education. Important too is Anna's exposure to the English mother superior who, in spite of clerical opposition and demands for purely Irish education, introduces and maintains a wide, liberal curriculum. In a contrapuntal textual movement, Mother Superior's spiritual refreshment parallels Anna's growth as, seeing herself in the young child, the nun reappraises her own youthful judgment and treatment of her father as cruel and unfair. We too witness Anna's emotional and intellectual growth, primarily through the nurturing education but also through her love for her simple and decent brother Charlie and the healing that follows the terrible wound of his death. We also see Anna grow through her friendship with the English suffragist, Miss Robertson, her admiration for Miss Robertson's courage and goals, and finally through her discretion, courage, and maturity when faced with the hostility of the bishop and her grandmother toward her political and personal ambitions. Although Mother Superior is unable to repair her own intolerance of her dead father, she balances it to some extent as she uses her power to help Anna achieve the liberty of a college education and gifts her with her own new breadth of accepting vision.

Anticipating Simone de Beauvoir's work on the traditional distortion and re-creation of compliant women from resistant girls, O'Brien also presents a nontraditional Irish Catholic female bildungsromane. (*Bildungsroman* refers to novels of male development in this study; *bildungsromane*, to novels of female development.) In his classic study, Jerome Buckley enumerates the characteristics of what he calls the "typical" bildungsroman. Buckley suggests that the child of the bildungsroman is one of "some sensibility" who grows up in an environment hostile to his imagination, whose father, in particular, impedes his progress. Schooling is inadequate or frustrating, and the real education begins when the child leaves school and home to explore his social environment. This education involves at least two love affairs, "one debasing, one exalting, and demands that in this respect and others the hero reappraise his values." The end of the bildung, Buckley suggests, is the hero's recognition of who he is and the integration of this individual into society, values intact.[23] Integration may take place within a society other than that in which the hero matured: Joyce's Stephen Dedalus, for example, leaves Ireland in search of a society less inimical to what he sees as his needs.

As this definition makes clear, Buckley's depiction is resolutely androcentric. The psychological development he charts, stress the editors of *The Voyage In*, a volume of fictions of female development, is not human, but male. Recent psychoanalytical theorists noted in chapter 1 as well as analyses of bildungsromane with female protagonists suggest an alternate—different rather than inferior—pattern of female development, one that valorizes relatedness rather than separation. Exploration of environment and lovers was, of course, denied young women in the nineteenth and early twentieth centuries. Other differences cited by the editors of *The Voyage In* will be considered in later chapters, particularly chapter 7, the analysis of Molly Keane's ironic bildungsromane. Suffice it here to say that while employing many of the elements of bildungsroman Buckley identifies, O'Brien's story of a young girl's development and a powerful mother's nurturing mirrors in a parodic female fashion Joyce's *Portrait of the Artist as a Young Man*.[24]

There is in *Portrait* and again in *Ulysses* a moment when Stephen Dedalus almost transcends his self-interest, a brief occasion when the reader almost likes the hero. This occurs in *Portrait* as Stephen returns to the dirty, poor shelter that houses his impoverished brothers and sisters. Seeing the poverty, Stephen realizes that "all that had been denied them had been freely given to him, the eldest; but the quiet glow of evening showed him in their faces no sign of rancour." Not wealthy but financially viable and intellectually nurtured with his university education, the Stephen of *Ulysses* comes across his shabby sister buying a secondhand copy of a French primer for one penny. Aware that he himself may have stirred her mind with his tales of Paris, Stephen, momentarily remorseful, asks, "I suppose all my books are gone." "Some," his sister says, "We had to." Moving quickly away from pity, Stephen warns himself: "She is drowning. Agenbite. Save her. Agenbite. All against us. She will drown me with her, eyes and hair." In *The Land of Spices*, Kate O'Brien takes up her pen to write, in effect, the sister's story—not, as Virginia

Woolf did, the tragic story of Shakespeare's sister, nor even the pathetic tale of the poor Dilly Dedalus whom Stephen abandoned. Harking back to Charlotte Brontë's *Jane Eyre*, O'Brien prescribes for her heroine, Anna, an alternate family, one that would nurture the God-given curiosity that Stephen had simply titillated, one that would train Dedalus's sister according to a model based not on patriarchal concepts of utility but rather on that of the relationship between an individual soul and its creator, one that would train her, in other words, primarily for her own sake.[25]

Before considering the differences between the male bildungsroman and the female bildungsromane, I want to briefly note the parallels that suggest O'Brien's deliberately revisionist treatment of Joyce. O'Brien follows Anna from her arrival at boarding school at the tender age of six—like Stephen, Anna is the youngest child at the school—to her realization that a beautiful girl could be "a motive in art." Anna goes through the same stages of experimenting and playing with words. She too is the subject of a grave injustice at school; she also must learn not only academic lessons but the more difficult lessons of class distinctions. The world of adults is also to Anna a world of giants. Like Stephen, she must use "cunning," and her sexual education is also distorted and oblique. Anna's mother is ineffective, her father is a drunkard, and the entire family is deprived so that Anna's oldest brother, Harry, can, like Stephen, attend Clongowes Wood College. O'Brien verbally echoes Joyce in several scenes: for example, the child Anna likes her mother's embrace better than her father's, just as the child Stephen prefers the smell of his mother. Also, the suggestion of German spying in *Portrait* is echoed in *Land of Spices*. The larger thematic concern with language and intrusive national politics is evident in both works. Finally, Anna's story opens in 1904 and concludes in 1914, a date which is emphasized. This span parallels Joyce's final double dates: "Dublin 1904, Trieste 1914." Difficult as life was for the artistic Stephens, it was twice as difficult for the girls trained only to be Irish Catholic wives.[26]

In O'Brien's story of "Stephen's sister," the family as institution is of primary importance not only because it first trains the young child but also because it acts as model for national, religious, and educational institutions. O'Brien's perception in this respect links her to Maria Edgeworth, Somerville and Ross, and Elizabeth Bowen. With an English mother superior, a French foundress, and an Irish setting, the school young Anna Murphy attends acts as a unique example of the tolerance, fairness, and equality absent from national, religious, and domestic families. Appropriately the order of nuns is that of the Sainte Famille, the Holy Family. Domestic, national, religious, and international strife overshadow all the families. In early 1914 Mother General writes from Belgium to the English mother superior that Germany seems intent on breaking the Entente Cordiale by invading smaller, weaker Belgium.[27] England, we understand, will go to war to protect the rights of small nations, of the weaker international family members. In Ireland, however, both priests and politicians have requested and struggled in vain for their independence from England, for their rights as a small nation. As the international patriarch, England sets standards for others, standards from which England itself deviates. Within the national family, too, O'Brien reminds us of the capricious enforcement of standards of fairness and equality: the English suffragist in the Irish town is a reminder of domestic domestic repression, which is analogous to the repression of the weaker countries by the more powerful.

Across the water the Irish men, the priests O'Brien presents, model their behavior on that of England. As noted in chapter 1, contemporary psychologists remark that the absence of fathers from routine domestic life means that male children tended by mothers or female care-givers must model themselves on a role rather than a person, while female children have the opportunity to model themselves on a person as well as a role. O'Brien's bishop, in fretting that the French convent of Sainte Famille is free of his pastoral control, demonstrates his identification with English colonial patterns. The independence of a group of women is suspect, since indeed this exploited, overworked area is the site of potential instability. The family must be exclusionary to be safe; hence both the bishop and Father Conroy suspect the English mother superior. Everything must serve the cause of a new Ireland, which they perceive to be synonymous with Gaelic Catholicism. Education, then, must train girls in nationalism and the Irish language, not train them to develop their talents and widen their horizons but, corresponding both to the political model of family adopted from England and to the model of civilization outlined by Levi-Strauss, train them to be appropriate wives for Irish men. To this end, both the relatively enlightened bishop and the presumptuous priest would force-feed Irish children with nationalism and the Gaelic language, much as England force-fed the resistant women.[28]

Those who see the job of education to be the shaping of wives naturally see no reason for young women to attend universities. As the eldest son in the Dedalus family, Stephen expects a university education. Anna's brother Harry has the same expectations. Anna's hopes of expanding intellectually are slim, however, for control in the Murphy family has passed from the drunken, idle father to the monied grandmother, Mrs. Condon. If Stephen were dependent on scholarships because of his father's background, then O'Brien reveals that Anna, who has won one, cannot even rely on this. Enforcing the dictum that both society and church seemed to endorse, Mrs. Condon insists that Anna become a bank clerk, education "being wasted on girls." (Mrs. Condon misreads here, for the bishop, though insistent on nationalism and the Gaelic language, supports higher education for women.) Intellectual and political liberty are connected as Anna replies to this judgment, noting that Miss Robertson, the suffragist, does not think this way. As her mother and grandmother dismiss Miss Robertson, Anna realizes the need for cunning and silence: "If a girl sees liberty as the greatest of all desirables, she will have to spin it out of herself." Anna must not only win scholarships but she must also, as Mother Superior makes clear, insist on her rights in opposition to her powerful grandmother. Fully aware that her honesty may cost her years of "cruelty and unforgiveness," Anna resists the grandmother and sides with "her rash champion," Mother Superior.[29]

Through Mother Superior O'Brien images an alternate model of education, one that is nurturing rather than utilitarian, detached rather than biased, maternal rather than paternal. When Mrs. Murphy fails to defend Anna's legitimate aspirations, Mother Superior assumes the mantle of a surrogate mother. The duty of the educator, she asserts, is to take care of her children, and Mother Superior resists any attempts, however powerful, to undermine this duty. In the interests of her children she introduces a broad range of subjects, including European culture and "optional Irish language." "Indifferent alike to the needs of Gaelic Leaguer or British officer," the narrator notes, "she still thought it necessary to train girls, for their own sakes and for the glory of God, to be Christians and to be civilized." Indeed Anna is first awakened to conscious solidarity with Mother Superior when she hears the bishop criticize to Miss Robertson the nun's educational practices. Given the anomaly of the overwhelmingly Catholic nation, Ireland, governed by a country whose monarch is head of a different church, the bishop believes that Sainte Famille is "too European for present-day Irish requirements. Its detachment of spirit seems to me to stand in the way of nationalism." The fear that intellectual and gender liberty will clash with political liberty underlies his comment and underscores the nationalistic belief in the preeminence of national independence above all other liberties. Sensing the bishop's prejudice, Anna feels "compelled to speak more accurately for her school." She attempts in fact to illustrate the advantages of that preeminent quality in educators, detachment of spirit. Focusing the issue so clearly, the bishop allows Anna to realize her own admiration for Mother Superior, and, in a gesture that also links gender and intellectual freedom, Anna asks Miss Robertson for a piece of the green, white, and purple suffragist ribbon Miss Robertson wears. The bishop, the shepherd of the flock, frets in this instance because this convent, unlike its Irish counterparts, is French and thus not under his control.[30] Ironically then, O'Brien's Holy Family, her alternate school, is, like the original, one in which the father's role is more formal than practical.

In *A Portrait of the Artist as a Young Man*, Joyce presents Stephen as identifying with that most absent of fathers, Dedalus, in his artistic ambition, identifying with the role of artist and with the hubristic goal of Dedalus. Although the boy responds to words from his earliest days and although the language of Simon Dedalus and indeed of the Roman Catholic church is colorful, no living artistic model is presented, so Stephen identifies with a literary fiction. O'Brien, on the other hand, allows her heroine to respond to the careful molding and to the personality of Mother Superior. Anna's interest in words is encouraged; Mother Superior selects the finest poetry for the small child to memorize. Anna is not limited to poetry, however, but devours all kinds of writing. We are shown Anna's realization of the necessity for cunning and allowed to see Mother Superior use that same weapon of the weak in dealing with Mrs. Condon. We see Anna close in on herself so that teachers and peers declare her cold after the death of Charlie, the only person with whom she had had a warm emotional relationship. In the contrapuntal movement of Mother Superior's life, we see Mother Superior, too, close in on herself and deny human relationships after her father "dies" to her, when she discovers his homosexual relationship with his student.

Reading Anna's need correctly, Mother Superior protects her "at long range" from the "assaults" of well-meaning intruders. Aware of the needs of the developing woman, Mother Superior does not decide what is best for Anna but is "confident that a soul, left to itself, has good chances of recovering in some measure from any sickness—whereas rash manipulation may establish a deformity." And Anna does turn to Mother Superior when her soul recovers. To her surprise she discovers that she "likes" this nun, and she finally sees that all the "magical" things this mother has done for her in the year after her brother's death— the healing of her soul and the battling to allow her to follow her destiny—"were after all only sudden strong lights, flashed and gone, on something that was always there and might never be seen fully or appreciated."[31] Anna has in fact responded in this miniature mother-daughter relationship in the ways Nancy Chodorow identifies as consistent with female development: she has absorbed into her own personality both the Reverend Mother's lessons and her traits of detached sympathy, fairness, and courage.

In *The Land of Spices*, O'Brien depicts the individual's full personal development despite many obstacles. Anna develops because her potential was nurtured by a wise (god)mother. Although the personal family betrays Anna, the family of Sainte Famille act as true mothers. Reverend Mother herself understands Anna "as hysterically perhaps as if she were the child's mother," and Letitia, *Mère* Martine, and Molly Redmond defend their "daughter"—a service that Anna returns for Molly. The biological tie does not of itself constitute maternal sorority: even old Sister Simeon discovers that the incubator makes a better "foster mother" than the mother hens and begins "to despise the natural ways of hens."[32]

The question of nationalism and language overshadows both *Portrait* and *Land of Spices*, as it does so much of Irish literature in English. Irish writers, whether of Gaelic or English ancestry, consciously wrote for a predominantly English audience. Thus feeling themselves to be outsiders, they explain or attempt to justify their perceptions, sometimes in addenda, sometimes in the text itself. In the epilogue to *Castle Rackrent*, for example, Maria Edgeworth notes that she places her text "before the English reader as a specimen of manners and characters, which are perhaps unknown in England. Indeed the domestic habits of no nation in Europe were less known to the English than those of their sister country, till within these few years." The parallel between the Irish writer's problems of presentation and acceptance and the feminist critics' attempts—almost two hundred years later—to include women writers in the canon is startling. Somerville and Ross's irritation with their overshadowing neighbor is frequently expressed in *Irish Memories* and is dramatized in *The Real Charlotte* in the caricaturing of Miss Hope-Drummond, the English visitor. Elizabeth Bowen's Lady Naylor asserts the superior intelligence and wit of the Irish country person over her English counterpart. Bowen also dramatizes Somerville and Ross's irritation with the tendency of English visitors (in the persons of the English officers' wives) to know all about Irish problems and how best to solve them.[33]

In her early work O'Brien too uses the English visitor to point up both the prejudices and condescension she believes inherent in the British view of Ireland. The narrator of *The Anteroom* mocks Sir Geoffrey's vision of a barefooted, wild colleen whom he will delight with easy imitation of her lilting brogue. Unlike Edgeworth and Somerville and Ross, Sir Geoffrey, we may assume, had no ear to hear how or what the people spoke. Faced with the reality of the graciousness of his hosts, the elegance of the home, and the sophistication of the women, Sir Geoffrey is mute.[34] Revealing as it is of the writers' sensitivities and their ability to speak at least doubly, to and about the English reader, this concern has happily disappeared in *The Land of Spices* and in contemporary writing.

In *A Portrait of the Artist as a Young Man*, Joyce carefully charts Stephen's growth through his relationship with language. We first see the young child's response to the creative magic of words, then his growing awareness of and experimentation with language, and ultimately his resentment at his outsider status with his native language, English. Like Dedalus, then, or like the tragic heroes who attempt the impossible, Stephen finally determines to employ that foreign tongue to "forge" the "conscience" of his nation.[35] Stephen's final assertion, in its epic difficulty and grandeur, is a will to control; both the foreign language and the consciousness of the Irish people are to be forged/forced into a shape determined by the artist/smith. Although arguably different in effect, this desire is similar in its hubris to the English urge to control the weaker island, to the political, religious, and familial patriarchal desire to dominate and shape the entity of which it is only a part.

Foregoing the defensive need exemplified in *The Anteroom*, a need not dissimilar to Stephen's, the narrator of *The Land of Spices*, on the other hand, welcomes a diversity of languages. French is the first language of many of the Sainte Famille nuns, one which becomes an easy second language to all the girls. Anna's enjoyment of the German "Wallensteins Tod" at the Chaplain's Concert suggests an appreciation of the language as well as the drama. But the young Jesuit novice, the guest the girls flatter, though a teacher of Greek, cannot understand their delight at the obvious disconnection—the fat priest's "hellish noises" as he sings "Dark Rosaleen." Perplexed at the girls' responses, the young man wonders, "Was there something which escaped him in the singing? Was it perhaps what was called traditional? Was it some offshoot of the Gaelic Revival, and should one be able to admire it?"[36]

In contrast, ease with several languages and with the nuances of language characterize the atmosphere of Sainte Famille. Mother Superior introduces the Irish language, that of her potential oppressors, but will not make it compulsory, as the nationalists in O'Brien's novel seem to wish. Indeed the Irish nationalists did make the language compulsory, contributing to generations of distressed Irish students. Anna's appreciation of the shape, color, and balance of words begins, however, with the lovely poetry of Vaughan which the six year old memorizes from a Christmas card, an appreciation which is encouraged by Mother Superior and by Anna's later explorations into foreign languages. Neither the narrator nor the principal characters exhibit any discomfort with the English language. Indeed such discomfort in *Land of Spices* is defensive, as with the bishop and priest, and at a more serious level suggests imbalance or even madness. When the German exiles sing "Die Lorelei" in the Irish seaside town, for example, one of the locals invariably loses "his control," expressing his hatred by roaring and kicking at the band.[37] Such mad transference of anger from the acts of nations to language itself ultimately deprives the attacker. Analogous to the Anglo-Irish writers O'Brien admires, her English mother superior might be said to hear and speak other languages.

The healing moment comes to Anna through a blending of both the words of "Lycidas" and the beauty of Pilar, the lovely, foolish girl whom Anna helps to read the poem. In this, Anna's moment is similar to Stephen's epiphany in the climactic scene of the wading girl in *Portrait*: "So Anna beheld her; something that life can be about, something with power to make life compose around it." Anna realizes that "this moment was a long-awaited, blessed gift." She also realizes that "she was encountering, alone and in terms of her secret need, a passage of beauty as revelatory and true as any verse of the great elegy." Peace comes to both Anna and Stephen, peace and a sense that life can be art. But Stephen's moment is transitory, romantic. His bildungsroman moves from vision to the squalor of self, family, and home—to the rejection of "nationality, language, religion," to the rejection of life for art, to the intellectual hubris of Dedalus forging "the uncreated conscience" of his race.[38]

Anna's bildungsromane moves to the *Te deum*, to the understanding of all that "school"—the shorthand for the family Mother Superior provided—has meant, and to the expression of the debt to this "mother." In direct opposition to Stephen's goal, Reverend Mother's last words call for familial acceptance, not rejection. "And be the judge of your own soul," she tells Anna.

"But never for a second, I implore you, set up as judge of another." Soul, as O'Brien makes clear here, can be read as text: concluding, Reverend Mother advises Anna to be the "commentator, annotator, if you like, but never judge." We recall that this (god)mother has read Anna's soul correctly, has refused to force the text, but has waited patiently for the text to reveal itself. And Anna, too, as we've seen, has read Mother Superior's soul by the light of her deeds. This mutual reading is, like Denis's, an intellectual expression and acceptance of the psychological intuition. But Denis's cry "If we were only just ourselves, not bits and pieces in a scheme of someone else's" is one of despair, as he senses his own impotence to be anything but the cog in the Levi-Strauss, "new" Gaelic-Irish society. Denis, in fact, eschews the creative power, which Bakhtin identifies with the novel, for the archaic values of country and name enshrined in epic. Mother Superior suggests no such surrender: her ability to read is a positive force, which, as her successful championing of Anna's rights suggests, will not mire the character in the status quo but will, with due respect to others' rights, allow the individual, for her own sake and her God's, to develop and to be civilized.[39] Denis abandons the fight that a new fiction, a new myth of origin, demands. O'Brien, however, in reading back through her mothers and her fathers preserves and appreciates their forms but at the same time understands and expresses the need for a new fiction.

Summarizing one vision of Kate O'Brien, Margaret Lawrence, as I noted in the beginning of this chapter, reads her as the matriarchal conscience that sees revolution as unimportant, the author who sees that "wars come and go. . . . But one thing remains unchanging—that human beings must be born of two parents—a man and a woman, which constitutes family, and that they must worship God with dignity, which constitutes the place of the Church in life." Recognizing in O'Brien's work the presence of the human conflict between societal and individual goals ("The soul must go alone on its great adventure."), Lawrence argues that O'Brien resolves the conflict by siding with the demands of society.[40]

I suggest instead that O'Brien deplores the contemporary world's tendency to privilege the institution over the individual.

The fact that she depicts such victories does not suggest she condones them. Indeed, as I have tried to show, her texts constantly underscore the terrible destruction of the individual soul sacrificed for the good of the community. Her point is surely the simple one that the whole is no more than the sum of its parts, that the health of the whole organism can only be maintained by attention to the health of the individual elements. If the domestic family is the model for the international family, O'Brien asks that we apply the same standards to its members that we apply to the individual nations in the international family. An Ireland that violently sunders its unequal relationship with England must accord all the members of its domestic family the same status that it seeks for itself in the international family. Only this regard for individual members will produce healthy domestic and international families. Lawrence is certainly correct in suggesting that Kate O'Brien sees revolution as unimportant—unimportant, that is, if all it entails is the passing of the reins from one unjust, pragmatic government to another. The revolution O'Brien looks to—the dignity accorded equally to each human soul or text within the whole body of the family or of literature—is of course more radical and still more distant than that to which Irish nationalists aspired and aspire.

6. Mary Lavin
Textual Gardens

What was it worth—a happiness bought that dearly?
   Mother had never questioned it. And once she told us how
on a wintry day she had brought her own mother a snowdrop.
It was the first one of the year—a bleak bud that had come
up stunted before its time. "I meant it for a sign. But do you
know what your grandmother said? 'What good are snow-
drops to me *now*?' Such a thing to say! What good is a snowdrop at all if it doesn't hold its value always, and never lose
it! Isn't that the whole point of a snowdrop? And that is the
whole point of happiness, too! What good would it be if it
could be erased without trace? Take me and those daffodils!"
Stooping, she buried her face in a bunch that lay on the table
waiting to be put in vases. "If they didn't hold their beauty
absolute and inviolable, do you think I could bear the sight of
them after what happened when your father was in the hospital?"
                     —Mary Lavin, "Happiness" [my italics]

THE CONFIDENT assertion and celebration of life in this passage,
the botanical metaphor, and the mother-daughter situations are
familiar to the reader of Mary Lavin. The same affirmation of
life rings through all Lavin's work, from the first stories published in 1942 to the most recent volume, published in 1985.[1]
Despite the long span of time and the variety of subjects, Lavin's
stories almost always reflect, structurally and thematically, a
sense of the interdependence of all life—spiritual as well as material. Individual texts are richly yet tightly woven; the removal
of even one thread is destructive to the entire pattern. The body
of texts itself is woven to and from Lavin's life in a similar organic manner: as if learning from the insights they uncover, stories grow and move away from earlier ones, often repeating the
growth and movement of the author's life.
   Although most, if not all, writers draw material from their

own lives, Lavin interweaves the two more closely than most do. Indeed the blending is part of her creed, an important element in the underlying philosophy that shapes artistic perspective. A description of the writer's process by Elizabeth Peavoy, the oldest of Lavin's three daughters, suggests the relationship: "As mother's writing is so intrinsic to her life, it always seemed to me that there were no visible distinctions between the time she gave to writing her stories and the time she gave to us. Her duties to her family, her writing, the making of her lovely garden and a considerable amount of hard work on the farm are so closely knit that they could not be disentangled. She almost always wrote in our company as we played and chattered around her, evidently not feeling the need to shut herself away in another part of the house."[2]

Widowed like the characters in many of her stories, the young Mary Lavin raised her three daughters on her own, while running a farm in Meath (about thirty miles from Dublin) as well as a small home in Dublin so the girls could attend school. Although she published her first stories before her first husband's death, writing did not offer quick recompense, and finances were always a problem. Finding both the time and necessary money to continue writing and consequently to make a living for her family was a constant source of anxiety.[3] Many writers, male as well as female, are, of course, only too familiar with financial pressures. Somerville and Ross come to mind immediately. And women writers in particular have had to fight for "a room of their own" in which to work—I think not of the coiner of this phrase, Virginia Woolf, but of Jane Austen, Maria Edgeworth, and Somerville and Ross again. Elizabeth Bowen and Kate O'Brien, like an increasing number of women writers in the mid–twentieth century, had rooms of their own. But Mary Lavin differs from all these women in being a mother; further, she was a widowed mother, poor and totally responsible for three small children. This fact, one would think, might make sensitive, detailed work well-nigh impossible. But again Lavin differs. Unlike Somerville and Ross who understandably resented the intrusions on their limited writing time, Lavin welcomed and continues to welcome all the people and the interruptions that make up her life. Her children, she asserts, were never a distraction.

Neither apparently are presumptuous interviewers: despite an illness that required hospitalization in 1985, Mary Lavin talked with me at length by phone and allowed me to visit during her convalescence. Friends and grandchildren called during my visit; all were heartily welcomed and asked to return. Describing herself as a "one-armed writer," one hand stirring the pot, the other steering the pen, Lavin sees her extraliterary duties as enrichment rather than sacrifice and blesses the mothering, gardening, farming, and even management that, while nourishing her writing, at the same time prevent her from publishing more than she "ought to." By this Lavin means more than she has crafted to her own standards of "artistic economy."[4]

That motherhood was for Lavin both a personal decision and a rewarding experience may account for the difference between her response to her responsibilities and the responses of many other women writers, a difference that became in turn a difference not only in theme but also in structure. Discussing women writers, Margaret Lawrence is one of several critics who relate women's genres to their maternal duties: the necessity of breaking off a children's story to attend to some household duty, she believes, led to a casual, episodic style, suitable for serialization.[5] Tillie Olsen's *Tell Me a Riddle* comes to mind. The to-and-fro pattern of work suggested by Lawrence's remark appears as pattern of thought, conversation, and text in Lavin's writing, but this pattern is incorporated into a broad framework in which the apparent digressions are both stages of progression, duplicating the organic process itself, and individual elements that retain their own value and integrity.

Several short stories written over a twenty-year period and illustrating the writer's style and changing interests are the focus of this chapter. Although she wrote two novels, these, unlike the stories, receive little critical acclaim, and Lavin herself dismisses them as "two bad novels."[6] Perhaps style is more important in a short story than in a long novel, or perhaps the short story or novella lends itself better than the novel to an analysis of style. Whatever the case, Lavin's condensed and allusive prose merits attention both for its own sake and as an example of the philosophy that shapes her perspective. Hence I wish to examine briefly a few of the images in the epigraphic passage from "Happiness" and trace their growth and transformation throughout the story before turning to the development of Lavin's subjects.

In this passage, the narrator recalls how her mother explained her vision of happiness as something unaffected by the tragedies and accidents of life. Despite the early losses of her beloved husband and her treasured father and the ensuing life of hard work and economic pressures, the mother still claimed to possess and be infused by happiness. Happiness, she asserted, exists independently, like the value of a snowdrop. The snowdrop is a familiar symbol of resurrection, for in braving snow and ice to penetrate the frozen January clay, the fragile flower suggests the apparently impossible victory of life over death and the cyclical, transforming power of a world where life dwells in death. The snowdrop strand seems to be abandoned, but a later resurrection image, another manifestation of this thread, suggests the organic nature of a world or a text in which nothing can simply disappear. Ardently defending her vision of life, the mother, as the daughter/narrator recalls, explained to her friend Father Hugh, "I don't think you realize the onslaughts that were made upon our happiness! The minute Robert died, they came down on me—cohorts of relatives, friends, even strangers, all draped in black, opening their arms like bats to let me pass into their company. . . . They weren't living in a real world at all; they belonged to a ghostly world where life was easy: all one had to do was sit and weep. It takes effort to push back the stone from the mouth of the tomb and walk out."[7] Life, the text suggests, demands the constant effort of resurrection, the pushing back of the huge stones, the uneven struggle of the snowdrop.

The image of the stone acts as the textual revelation of the growth of the idea—the effort of the snowdrop, of life, is unseen through most of the text but is growing nevertheless, until such effort is identified with that of Christ. Similarly the grandmother in the opening passage is transformed into the image of the resurrection-deniers in the later passage. The simple *now* in the early passage, like so many simple words in Lavin, like the snowdrop itself, works very hard. On the one hand, the grandmother suggests that the snowdrop has lost its meaning because her own husband is dead. Thus she asserts her right to sit weeping at the mouth of the tomb, dispiriting her daughter and grand-daughters constantly with the reminder of her widowed status and her dead husband. Refusing all effort, she, like the heavy clay, leans on her daughter, expecting frequent, twice-daily attention from the busy, tired, widowed mother of three. But the *now* is itself dishonest: the narrator reports her grandfather's failure to provide the grandmother with happiness, and all indications point to her ceaselessly demanding, unsatisfied nature.[8] *Provide*, of course, is a telltale word, for happiness cannot be provided: the stones must be rolled back from the inside. The snowdrop must push its own way through the earth. The grandmother may seem pathetic and harmless in the opening passage, but in refusing growth and denying happiness, she is the embodiment of the batlike creatures, the blind ones who, unlike the women who proclaimed the Resurrection, deny the reclaimed life.

The final image in the epigraphic passage, that of the daffodils, is also well woven into the whole text. Connecting the reader to the death of the narrator's father, the daffodils also take us further back, to the "happiness bought" so "dearly." All these images—the happiness, the father's death, and this passage of explanation itself—will be gathered together in the final daffodil image at the mother's death. Despite her weariness and loneliness, the mother has always insisted that she had a "lion's share" of happiness, but the narrator has to strain hard to account for this assertion. "Perhaps," she says, weaving her own text, "there were times when she had had a surplus of it—when she was young, say, with her redoubtable father, whose love blazed circles around her, making winter into summer and ice into fire. Perhaps she did have a brimming measure in her early married years. . . . Our father, while he lived, had cast a magic over everything, for us as well as for her."[9]

The narrator has not understood her mother's point, that her happiness was inviolable, indestructible. In recalling the memory, however, she confirms for the reader the mother's memory of a glowing past. The "dearly" refers to the awful vigils the narrator and her sister sustained following their father's death, when, terrified lest their mother should commit suicide, the girls awaited her return from solitary swims. The basis for such a fear, apart from the children's understanding of their mother's loss, is sown earlier in the story. Remembering another instance of their mother's telling of her happiness, the narrator notes that one of the dreams her mother had entertained as a young girl was that of swimming the channel. "Did you swim *that* well?" the girls ask. "Oh, not really—just the breast stroke. . . . And then only by the aid of two pig bladders blown up by my father and tied around my middle."[10] The children's fear, then, was based on knowledge that, though unexamined, continues as does the snowdrop to resonate in their lives and in the text.

Confirming for the reader the narrator's distant memory of the great happiness her parents had shared and leading us to the father's death, a second daffodil image also introduces another manifestation of the figure of denial. As Robert lay in a city hospital, dying, though neither he, his wife, nor his children knew this, the mother left him briefly to visit the children at the farm in the country. There the sight of the daffodils blooming "in the woods, under the trees, and along the sides of the avenue" saddened her as she thought of her husband's missing this loveliness. So gathering a "great bunch" to delight him, she rushed back to the hospital. As she approached the room, however, a nun pounced on her, grabbing the flowers and causing many to fall and be crushed underfoot. " 'Where are you going with those foolish flowers, you foolish woman?' she said. 'Don't you know your husband is dying? Your prayers are all you can give him now!' "[11] This event occurred before the first image in the fiction, but because Lavin places it later in the text, we necessarily read it as a second image. Perhaps she changed the chronology here to present a progression of figures of denial: grandmother, nun, and cohorts at the tomb. Clothed in the black garb of denial, then, the figure achieves textual maturity at the tombside.

Despite the mental association of daffodils with this harsh awakening to her husband's imminent death, the flowers hold their intrinsic value for the mother. "Stooping," the narrator notes, "she buried her face in a bunch." Unlike the weeping women at the tomb and the grandmother who now has no use for the snowdrop, this mother understands that the daffodils are always the symbols of spring and beauty, of life and the effort of life. Rather than burying herself with the past, she embraces beauty, happiness, and the future. As she lies dying herself, she worries, incoherently both narrator and reader think, "What will be done with them?" Apparently upset, she asks that they "be put in water," and "peremptorily" she says, "Don't let that nun take them; she'll only put them on the altar. And God doesn't want them! He made them for *us*—not for Himself!"[12]

It is skeptical Bea, the middle daughter, who finally understands that her mother is now back with her father. Time has collapsed for her, and she has regained what she had temporarily lost. Although the mother had not condemned the nun in her earlier explanation to her daughters, she definitively associates her here with the figures of denial. Bea reassures her mother, apparently suddenly inheriting—or intuiting—the mother's apprehension of the inviolability of happiness, the inviolability of her mother and father's love. Not comprehending, the narrator explains what she sees: "Over her [Bea's] face came the light that had so often blazed over Mother's. . . . 'It's all right, Mother. You don't *have* to face it! It's over! . . . You've finished with this world, Mother,' she said, and, confident that her tidings were joyous, her voice was strong."[13]

At this point, the narrator notes, "Mother made the last effort of her life and grasped at Bea's meaning, . . . her head sank so deep into the pillow that it would have been dented had it been a pillow of stone." The mother's effort gathers into itself the many narrational remembrances of efforts that constituted happiness. For happiness is the dominant unifying image, and the mother's final effort of understanding, of living, brings her to the knowledge of death and of having earned the right to die. That this is knowledge of the organic and interdependent nature of all things is suggested by the "pillow of stone," which imagistically unites the dying woman with the Christ figure. In evoking the pillow on which Christ lay, the text, one reader suggests, implies not death but the renewed life Christ claimed, the Resurrection that by extension all living creatures can claim.[14]

This tight weaving results, of course, not from the hurried and casual writing of a woman preoccupied with other duties but from the painstaking efforts of a demanding stylist—hence Lavin's remark on not writing more than she ought. Neither are the biographical details that Lavin chooses exact reflections of events. Indeed such reflections would be neither artistic nor organic, for it is the mutual nurturing and blending of life and art that is important in an interdependent world. Peavoy's conclusion that there are no visible distinctions between Lavin's life as mother and as author, between the text of the life and the life of the text, suggests the inadequacy of a mimetic theory in Lavin's, as in Somerville and Ross's, art. Lavin reports that she responds to an intuitive sense of "that happens." She means that a certain effect or event is not an isolated, anomalous incident but a recurring human situation. Janet Dunleavy has explored the writer's process in the making of "A Memory" and of "Happiness," and she notes: "The real-life images and incidents that were coloured by the author's memory, embroidered by her creative imagination, and molded by her to fit 'Happiness' were introduced into the story only after the author had the idea of it clear in her mind; they were not the source of the idea itself." What happens in one part of Lavin's cosmos can happen in any other part, for it is all a unity. This interplay of art and a woman's life enriches and distinguishes the texts and gives Lavin's work the "sensual richness" that, one critic suggests, leaves the Irish man even more at a loss than a foreigner in an alien plot.[15]

Indeed Lavin's first collection of short stories, *Tales from Bective Bridge*, did seem, despite Lord Dunsany's appreciative introduction, such a foreign plot when published in 1942. The disappearance of the Irish revolution and of what had come to be seen as Irish symbolism and its substitution by the foreign materials of women's experience seemed not so much an expansion as an implied criticism, even a betrayal. Perhaps the advocates of the young country can be pardoned for their insularity and defensiveness; those whom critics saw and see as the luminaries of Irish literature, from George Moore to Liam O'Flaherty, did indeed deserve high aesthetic praise, and their work, which reproduced undeniably Irish problems in Irish settings, was structured on identifiable and hence valued literary patterns. Indeed even Elizabeth Bowen's *The Last September* could be read as a view, albeit from "the other side," of contemporary Irish history, and Kate O'Brien, as I have suggested, was also misread as the unquestioning spokeswoman for the Irish Catholic family on which was modeled the embryonic state. Small wonder then that as late as 1963 Frank O'Connor, despite his dislike for Lavin's one political story, feels at home here, "on familiar ground, the [male plot] ground of O'Flaherty and O'Casey," whereas he remains an alien in most of Lavin's work.[16]

If Lavin's writing process enacts in its development and its appropriation of materials the process of nature, the resulting style also suggests nature's economy. Lavin's descriptions of the long gestation period of her work reminds us of the long processes Edgeworth and Somerville and Ross also described. During this gestation, the work often swells to novel size as Lavin becomes familiar with her characters and their situations. Then the "editorial conscience" takes over, shapes and prunes the huge work into an elegant short story. The gardening metaphor, in another instance of the blurring of distinctions, serves both to describe the writer's process and to image life's process in much of the work. As Janet Dunleavy notes of the blossoming and pruning of Lavin texts: "For her, craft is artistic economy. To be able to suggest what is stated or explained, to replace with a single right word the ten previously used to describe an object or situation, to substitute gesture for action; these, to her, are the skills of a literary artist."[17] This condensation accounts for much of the richness.

Early Lavin stories deal with young love, stories such as "Happiness" from the middle period of her life often explore the problems of widows, and the later ones examine the even more complex relations of mothers, daughters, and granddaughters. In many of these stories, Augustus Martin notes, "the indestructibility of human love given generously, is a constant energizing principle." Frank O'Connor found this concern "old-fashioned" in 1963; he suggested that for Lavin's women, failure of love in a romantic relationship meant failure in life, whereas a man would not so judge his life. While it is true that many of Lavin's characters have love tested in romantic heterosexual relationships, their failure in these affairs is not simply a failure with men, but a failure with love itself. The marriages of the Bedelias in "The Little Prince" and "Frail Vessel" and of the mother in "A Cup of Tea" are failures, but these are also continuations in patterns of failed love.[18] The mistake is to think one can isolate and separate oneself and a chosen one from the web of life.

Indeed, as A.A. Kelly notes, the failure of men in love is also viewed by Lavin as failure in life: James in "A Memory" and Matthew in the early story "Love Is for Lovers" are as incomplete and as barren as any of Lavin's unloving women. Seamus Deane rightly sees Lavin as a "social writer" who considers not "singular individual relationships with the mediocre world" but "the closely meshed nexus of feelings in which the protagonists are bound." Love is her subject, Deane argues, and "love demands relation."[19] I would go further: life demands relation in a Lavin story. Underlying all her work, this intuitive apprehension may spring from Lavin's personal situation as a widowed mother/writer who welcomed and saw as healthy the integration of all the elements of her own life. That love should be the superior binding and nurturing force in an organic world is not surprising; Lavin's difference is her celebration of love as indestructible, of the preservation and transformation of both material and spiritual in a wholly organic cosmos.

The belief that love survives death is nowhere more clearly enacted than in the figure of the widow, a character whose experiences often correspond to Lavin's own. The survival of both love and the dead lover is more than a survival of memory; though, as the widow makes clear in several stories, she must also battle to save her image of her dead husband from the distortion of the pious (the figures at the mouth of the tomb) who would canonize the dead. But Lavin's characters imply that the dead and love itself exist in a space other than that of memory: Mary, for example, in "In a Cafe" finally understands that she need not struggle to hold on to her picture of her dead husband, Richard, but "she had a sense of having all the time in the world to look and look at him." And the widow in "In the Middle of the Fields" assures another character that he is not responsible for his actions but that the dead girl he loved so passionately is punishing him for his attempt to forget her.[20]

As she extends her vision in these later stories, Lavin again intertwines life and art, revealing in the process the anomalous condition of the widow in modern society. The preservation of love and of nonmaterial elements is mysterious. Lavin does not attempt to explain: her characters' responses imply the presence of what critics have called Lavin's "extended dimension" or "double vision," the reality which can only be dimly sensed through the veil of life. In the seamless life to which Elizabeth Peavoy attests, the experience of widowhood becomes transmuted into art only after many years' gestation. "Villa Violetta," for example, published in 1972, many years after the death of Lavin's first husband, William Walsh, dramatizes the confusion and anxieties that confront a young widow who brings her three daughters to Italy for the summer. Lavin did make such trips after her husband's death with her own children.[21] "In a Cafe," the first widow story examined, was written in 1960, seven years after Walsh's death, and explores the problems of a new widow who must rebuild her individual identity. The story in which the widow figure dies, "Happiness," was written in 1969, the year the widow Mary Lavin metaphorically died through Lavin's marriage to her longtime friend Michael MacDonald Scott. I wish also to look briefly at two intervening stories, "The Cuckoo-Spit" and "In the Middle of the Fields," considering how the widow in these texts both sees herself and is apparently seen by society as a deviant, marginal element, and how finally it is both her own assertion of identity and the indestructibility of the love she has enjoyed that sustain her in this humiliating situation.

Anthropologists' examination of the condition of women in general and of widows in early societies helps us understand this marginalization. Excluded from the male-ordered system or culture, women were/are seen in some societies as anomalies, as necessary but disruptive to "the formal articulation of social order." In other societies, women in conventional roles, that is, in roles in which their status is assigned by their relation to men— as mother, wife, sister—are not threatening. As widows, however, women are removed from the relational paradigm and become marginal figures, potentially disruptive to the cultural choreography, hence the terrible mourning rituals prescribed for widows from India to New Guinea.[22] The Western response to widows may be more subtle, but it is also, as Lavin shows, more insidious. The very subtlety of the widow's situation is part of the problem—how can one counteract that which is not overtly articulated? The problem for society, however, is the same as that encountered in the early Lavin work—the necessity of accepting all life into the one organic whole, the necessity of realizing the value of each organism as an independent entity as well as part of some sanctioned partnership. The widow must attempt to reshape herself into an independent form in face of a society that denies, ridicules, or ignores her need to do so.

The necessity to create a new identity is both psychological and physical, Lavin suggests. Cut off from unity with Richard, Mary, the widow of "In a Cafe," is separated both from her premarital independence and from the totality she and Richard once made. Her attention caught by some paintings, Mary thinks she knows what Richard would say about them, but "she and Richard were no longer one. So what would she say about them? She would say—She would say." She cannot say. No longer at one with Richard, Mary has neither identity nor opinion because, the text suggests, she has internalized the negation and the subtle ridicule accorded the widow in Western society. Awaiting her friend Maudie, for example, Mary cringes: the "incongruity of their both being widowed came forcibly upon her. Would Maudie, too, be in black with touches of white? Two widows! It was like two magpies: one for sorrow, two for joy." Married to Richard, Mary was accorded some status; she and he, she thinks, would never have come to this rather shabby, arty cafe. "Say what you liked, there was something faintly snobby about a farm in Meath, and together she and Richard would have been out of place here. But it was a different matter to come here alone. There could be nothing—oh, nothing—snobby about a widow."[23] This Mary thinks, despite still retaining the farm, the overt emblem of snobbishness. The truth is that as a widow, a marginal, displaced woman, Mary can have no reason for pride. Her panic is the result of internalizing the absurdity that isolates her from society.

But single status alone is not the problem. Mary has come to the cafe to meet another widow, Maudie, rich, young, and pretty. "Looking at her [Maudie], it seemed quite inaccurate to say that she had lost her husband: it was Michael who had lost her, fallen out, as it were, while she perforce went outward. She didn't even look like a widow. There was nothing about her to suggest that she was in any way bereft or maimed." Intuitively realizing the implications of Maudie's situation, Mary reassures the younger woman impulsively: "You'll marry again, Maudie." This is an assurance that Maudie, recognizing the economics, "could not violently refute."[24] Maudie can resume a position within society because rich, young, and beautiful, she is still a valuable object of exchange in a culture that defines women in relation to men in, in fact, the old Levi-Strauss pattern that Kate O'Brien criticized in *Land of Spices*. Without these attractions, on the other hand, Mary is seen and sees herself as "bereft or maimed." Her anomalous condition is as obvious in her society as that of the physically maimed New Guinea girls whom Rosaldo cites.

The pervasiveness and behavioral molding of these social mores can be seen in Maudie's responses. As Mary turns for her friend's opinion on the work of the young artist with whom she converses, she recognizes Maudie's reaction: "Maudie was waiting to be introduced! To be *introduced*, as if she, Mary, did not need any conventional preliminaries. As if it was all right that she, Mary, should begin an unprefaced conversation with a strange man in a cafe because . . . it was all right for a woman of *her* age to strike up a conversation like that, but that it wouldn't have done for a younger woman."[25] Recognizing her own market value and seeing herself primarily as an object on this market, Maudie plays by the rules. She will not engage the artist as a human being whose concerns range beyond marital economics. Such engagement might be seen as presumptuous or overeager. And in placing Mary in the limbo, the margin where such conventions no longer obtain, Maudie implies her own acceptance of Mary's lack of value in this market, since value for a women is dependent on her youth and beauty. Ironically, of course, though such marginalization isolates, it also frees Mary from the inhibiting, binding rules of the game.

Ironically, too, successful marriage is partially responsible for the limitation of women. The imagery Lavin uses to describe this restriction is similar to that of Charlotte Brontë's Shirley as she complains that Milton has blocked God's clear light from women, an image that must have crossed Virginia Woolf's mind also when she in her turn smarted under "Milton's bogey." Lavin's imagery, however, is more ambiguous, less explicitly negative in its connotations. The husband is at once lovable and

impeding: Mary recalls that she knew Richard was dead when
she heard a bird call sweet and clear outside his hospital window,
"because not for years had she really heard bird-song or bird-
call, so loud was the noise of their love in her ears." The widow
Vera in "The Cuckoo-Spit" has a similar experience. Looking
over the beautiful countryside, she is filled with longings. As a
girl she remembers having these feelings but never during her
married life, for "always, no matter what the day or the night,
there was him blocking out all else." Successful marriages, like
grafting, entail in the relatedness Seamus Deane notes, the in-
terdependency of those joined. While positive in the total unity,
these marriages necessarily deprive each partner of a measure
of individual development. Widowhood (and the consequent financial strains) forces a woman—if she is to continue growing
and living—to refill this measure, but society, rather than as-
sisting, regards her effort as strange.[26]

Restoration of identity, the texts suggest, is both mysterious,
related to the perception of all life as organic, and, as in "Happiness," the result of individual assertion. The widows struggle
to stem the "fall" of the past, but the harder they try to regain
the memory of the dead one the more it escapes them. Absorption in such recall and in the past is, of course, in Lavin's terms
a weeping at the mouth of the tomb and a stunting of the individual growth now necessary. Aching because she cannot recall
Richard completely and repressed by social convention, Mary
finds personal expression and action difficult. Concerned that the
impoverished artist may, as convention decrees, pay the small
coffee bill, Mary determines to pay it herself. Her concern and
the necessity of calling up all her spiritual resources to accomplish the minor task underscore her fragile position and the great
effort involved in asserting the individual life in defiance of society, in defiance of the deadly, weeping figures. This act is Mary's
first reassertion of her individuality, a step toward shaping her
own environment rather than acquiescing in tradition.

A second act of assertion awakens the widow to the fact that
she is lonely not, as she has believed, maimed. Seeking company,
Mary knocks on the door of the artist's studio. But when a voice
asks who is there, she panics again. Without an opinion earlier
when confronted with the pictures, Mary is now without voice

and identity: "But where was she to find a voice with which to reply? And who was she to say what she was? Who—to this stranger—was she?" Flying from this nightmare, Mary catches sight of her own reflection in a mirror. "That face steadied her. How absurd to think that anyone would sinisterly follow this middle-aged woman?" Into her head ironically comes the answer to the artist's query: "I'm lonely." In voicing, she identifies her plight and asserts an identity. She is a full person, not the maimed or blighted creature her society suggests but a human being in pain. Thus awakened to her own condition, Mary, who has been unable for two years to recall Richard's face, is distracted by a sudden awareness of the integrated life of the busy people, the trees in the park and the birds in the trees. Involuntarily she remembers that this was the time she usually met Richard: " 'Oh Richard!' " she cries, 'it's you I want.' And as she cried out, her mind presented him to her." Now Mary realizes that it is not what Richard gave her she needs—not simply marriage, the stamp or mark that distinguishes and validates women—but Richard himself. Whole in her knowledge despite her pain, Mary becomes herself again. Her becoming is signaled by her instinctive appropriation of the driver's seat of the car, not the passenger's which she has "stupidly" sought since Richard's death. She has, she thinks to herself, "got back her rights."[27]

In "The Cuckoo-Spit," social forces attempt to displace the widow's perception of her relationship with her dead husband and, in substituting a deception, necessarily deprive her too of her identity. The widow Vera in this story tells Fergus, the nephew of her neighbor, of her panic following Richard's death that his relatives would obliterate his memory under the "whitewash" they indiscriminately applied to all the dead. Richard did not need their euphemisms. This panic was dispelled one wet evening when, puncturing a tire on a lonely dark stretch of the road, Vera, true to her real relationship with Richard, turned on the dead presence and berated him for abandoning her "in this mess." Fergus supplies the ending: "I know what happened next. . . . You had him back again—just as he always was—unchanged, amused at you."[28] In a world both material and nonmaterial, these healings, though explicable in psychological terms, also suggest mysterious preservation, interference from the sensate cosmos in which all life partakes.

In "The Cuckoo-Spit" and "In the Middle of the Fields," Lavin combines water imagery with the gardening metaphor to illustrate the mystery. The protean quality of water suggests the changing face of life, and the blurring of distinctions therein, the melding in the primeval oceans. The image works, of course, not only within the fictional context but also within the wider context of the life that is woven into the art, the art that is woven into the life. The ambiguous nature of the fields introduces "The Cuckoo-Spit": "Drenched with light under the midsummer moon, the fields were as large as the fields of the sky. Hedges and ditches dissolved in mist, and down by the river the thorn bushes floated loose like severed branches. Tall trees in the middle of the fields streamed on the air, rooted by long, dragging shadows." Moved by the beauty of the night, Vera ventures outside her house but turns back "unnerved." For on this night "the unreal alone had shape"; the existence of the cattle and of the house was indicated more definitively by their shadows than by their physical presences.[29]

Finding walking in the grass like "wading through water," Fergus asks if it never gets "eaten down." And, suggesting life, richness, and endurance, Vera replies: "It would take all the cattle in Ireland to graze it down at this time of the year." The same protean quality is suggested in "In the Middle of the Fields": "Like a rock in the sea, she was islanded by fields, the heavy grass washing about her house, and the cattle wading in it as in water."[30] The distinctions between physical objects disappear in the water, but the objects themselves do not disappear. Similarly, the texts suggest, the nonmaterial is not only preserved, but at certain times it, like the shadows, dominates the physical.

In "In the Middle of the Fields" Bartley Crossen, whose mundane qualities are emphasized, returns to the fields where long ago he began the brief and passionate relationship with his first wife. His young wife dead and Bartley himself long since contentedly remarried, his memories are awakened by the sight of "the small string of stunted thorns that grew along the riverbank, their branches leaning so heavily out over the water that their roots were almost dragged clear of the clay." The thorn trees, like the tall trees in "The Cuckoo-Spit," seem ready to move from one element into another. Similarly Bridie's wild love, for which Bartley had in the past abandoned material ambition, almost dragged him clear of his physical rootings. Later that night when the unnamed widow, the owner of the fields, is dressed for bed, Bartley returns to ask, unfairly, for permission to postpone the work he was hired to perform. Seeing the widow in her nightclothes with her hair down, Bartley, again loosed from his moorings, dragged from his element, acts totally out of character and attempts to kiss her. Rebuffed, he is instantly ashamed of his actions and berates himself, unable to understand how he could have betrayed himself so. In a flash the widow is inspired: " 'It's got nothing to do with any of us—with you, or me, or the woman at home waiting for you. It was the other one! That girl—your first wife—Bridie! It was her! Blame her. She's the one did it!' The words had broken from her. For a moment, she thought she was hysterical and that she could not stop. 'You thought you could forget her,' she said, 'but see what she did to you when she got the chance!' "[31]

As Catherine Murphy notes, "Passion is not a force within the human spirit but beyond it. . . . The dead who had in life yielded to this force, . . . become one with that force, influencing the imaginations of those whom they have loved." The passionate dead girl, existing in the "extended dimension," has the power to affect Bartley when the shadows dominate. In the great macrocosm, Bridie and the wild love of Bartley and Bridie are preserved, and in the microcosm of Bartley's life, that love can still compel. In "The Cuckoo-Spit," Fergus has a similar realization, as he tells Vera, "There is a kind of happiness that is indestructible; it lives on no matter what comes after." And like the widow in "In the Middle of the Fields," Vera concludes: "I sometimes think love has nothing to do with people at all. . . . It's like the weather!"[32] Whether we're cognizant of it or not, the weather *is*, and sometimes it makes its presence forcibly felt. Similarly the past and the love of the past exist: influenced by that which seems to have disappeared, Bartley acts again as he did in its visible presence.

The blending of life with art, of matter with spirit, of sky with land, of rock with water, of past with present becomes in Lavin's

later, most complex and sensitive stories a blending of person-
alities of mothers and their daughters. The mutual readings of
mothers and daughters, the intuitive responses to each other's
emotions, even indeed the experiencing of the other's pain, suggest the blurring of ego boundaries that Nancy Chodorow identifies as typical in female personality formation. The relationship
of Anna and the Reverend Mother in Kate O'Brien's *Land of
Spices* is at once a more conscious, more overt, and less intense
manifestation of this type of relationship. The humiliating "accidents," the bed-wettings, that beset Ada, Laura's mother in
Lavin's "Senility," are the source of Ada's unvoiced concern for
her own sanity and of Laura's concern for her mother's physical
condition.[33] Although the story is told primarily from Ada's view
(and thus the agony of aging is emphasized) and although Ada
stresses her own ability to read Laura thoroughly, the reader
also understands Laura's ability to read her mother.

Sensing her mother's sadness, Laura acts to please and to
dispel the sadness by deferring to her mother's gardening expertise and by employing the superlative of her childhood.
"Those masses of pinks [that her mother had planted] were the
bestest thing I've ever seen in any garden" has the desired effect, and Ada regains her balance momentarily. What the adult
Laura has done in effect is to give her mother back the past—
the past of Laura's childhood, the past of her dependency and
admiration for Ada, the past of Ada's competency and care for
Laura. The boundaries between mother and daughter are so thin
that each not simply senses but feels within herself the other's
pain. Thus some time later Ada, having won her argument, is
not happy, "not at all happy," at her favorite work in the garden,
not only because she is oppressed with the sense of her own
mortality but also because she aches from the pain she has deliberately caused Laura. Laura's response to her mother's
depression reaches, in this instance, both backward and forward:
"Laura chattered away uncharacteristically and almost incon-
sequentially," which suggests both the behavior of the young
child and of the mother who humors the child.[34]

The conflict as Ada sees it emerges from Laura's insensitivity
to Ada's concerns about placing her own mother (now dead) in
a nursing home, and from Laura's overattention to Ada's acci-

dents. Tormenting herself about the possible humiliations her own mother suffered in the hospital in which she died, Ada dwells on one particular scene, suggesting that in that and perhaps other instances the nurses had made fun of her mother. "Laura said nothing for a moment. Then she put her hand on Ada's and stroked it gently. 'Don't you think, Mummy, that a bit of fun might have been a welcome change in that ward—for all concerned?' " Her grandmother, Laura reminds Ada when she persists in the dispiriting memories, always enjoyed a joke and might "have cackled at the good of it" had she heard Laura describe her as senile. The first response is a successful reaching across ego boundaries, another return to the past, as Ada's reaction shows: "It was so sweet to have her daughter stroke her hand, Ada was prepared to compromise."[35] The second is both a verbal energizer, a refusal to weep at the mouth of the tomb, and actually a distancing of Ada and consequently Ada's fear from Laura's grandmother. The very fact that Laura can joke about her grandmother's senility suggests the distance she has established between that grandmother's condition and her mother's. The implication is there for Ada to receive; Laura would not joke about senility were Ada in that condition. Laura's concern is not for Ada's mental but for her physical condition. Her behavior is a more than verbal expression of support for her mother.

In a beautiful dream passage, we see Ada's fear of age as a fear of exposure, of the invasion of privacy, a fear grounded in what she sees as Laura's "disloyalty" in discussing with her husband, Ada's problem. But both women fear for Ada's health: Ada's casual dismissal and Laura's voiced concern are simply different responses to their mutual anxiety. Although she wishes her mother to see a doctor, Laura, because she identifies so much with her mother, cannot distance herself sufficiently to consider her mother's death. Whereas John, Laura's husband, can be gracious about Ada's desire to leave them "some token of . . . love and gratitude" when she dies, Laura rejects it gruffly: "By the time you die, Mummy, your nest-egg will seem very small to John and me."[36] The implication of course is that Ada will not die for a long time. Laura's rejection parallels Ada's casual dismissal of her accidents; both women verbally dispel the omens, as if verbal control could exorcise the fast-approaching threat. Laura's rejection, then, attempts to distance—not herself from her mother—but both mother and daughter from the unthinkable.

Later stories continue to develop the mutual interreadings of mothers and daughters and to highlight the almost compulsive repetition of response and action. "A Family Likeness," for example, overtly focuses on the physical resemblance between grandmother and granddaughter, while sensitively exploring the more striking personality resemblance between mother and daughter. Again Ada is the mother, Laura the daughter, and this time Laura is also the new mother of Daff. Feeling tired on a spring walk to collect wildflowers, Ada suggests first that they carry Daff and then that the primroses they have come to pick grow rather closer than she had anticipated. Correctly reading Ada's tiredness, Laura suggests that her mother rest with Daff while she goes further. And Ada too understands Laura's perception: "Fine as the prick of the smallest needle ever made, one with an eye so narrow it was quite impossible to thread, Ada's heart was pierced with sadness. Had her daughter seen that she was failing?"[37]

The mutual readings in this instance are conscious, but the mutual responses to similar situations are instinctive. When Ada worries again about tiring Daff, the tired and irritable Laura speaks savagely of her daughter: "All to the good. Maybe after this she might sleep through the night for a change." As Ada carefully shows her granddaughter how to pick primroses properly, giving her the attention Laura is too tired to give, Laura snaps at her mother. "For goodness' sake, Mother. They're only wild flowers. Let her enjoy them." It is as if forcing her mother to be indulgent with Daff compensates for Laura's own irritation. In an attempt to reestablish harmony, Ada turns the conversation to her own mother. But refusing the comfort, Laura attempts to wound Ada: "Poor Grandmother. I used to feel so sad when you were mean to her."[38]

What Laura has in effect done this time, not as a result of mental calculation but of savage instinct, is to force Ada to experience the pain of her own tired injustice. The passage also reveals, of course, the model of the Ada/Laura behavior. Ada too has been irritable with her mother. Ada too has been under stress to perform her many household tasks and has been unaware until this conversation that her own mother and her daughter had a close relationship. "We had such fun," Laura says, her memory of the "unending store" of stories her grandmother had shared with her and of the grandmother's brushing of her hair suggesting an attention similar to that we see between Ada and Daff. As if feeling unfairly left out of the fun, Ada responds to Laura's memory as Laura responded to Ada's fun with Daff: she too snaps at her daughter.[39] Mother and daughter each recognizes the other's personality traits and responses but ironically fails to recognize that they themselves repeat the deeply laid patterns.

Perhaps "Happiness" might be seen as the culmination of Lavin's organic vision, in that the protagonist's death is integrated into the whole indestructible picture. But culmination itself is a misnomer, for how can an organic, indestructible world culminate? So appropriately Lavin moved on after "Happiness," continued to integrate the physical and artistic world in her three-generation stories with their emphasis on another form of preservation. That the widow in "Happiness" dies in 1969, the year in which the widow Mary Lavin died by remarrying, contributes to the suggestion of the story that death, like remarriage, is transformation, not conclusion. The vision that the widow of this story constantly attempts to explain to her three daughters closely resembles the concept of the organic world of matter and nonmatter developed in the corpus of Lavin's work. Happiness, the textual widow suggests, has nothing to do with laughter or health, sorrow or pain, but with the acceptance of the indestructibility of all: "What good is a snowdrop at all, if it doesn't hold its value always, and never lose it!" Love is not wiped out by the death of the loved one but is still inviolate. Neither is memory, "dry longing," the locus of this preservation, for one's own death is also a part of the organic vision, and if death is the end of memory, then memory cannot be the residence of the spiritual.

We recall that as Vera lies dying, beset by temporal worries, the face of her second daughter, Bea, suddenly becomes irradiated with the light the narrator has often seen on her mother's face. Like the earlier intuitive understandings, Bea's also is mysterious. And Bea's understanding and that of all the widows noted mirrors the dissolution of ego boundaries between mothers and daughters, mirrors the blending of boundaries that takes place in nature, mirrors the dissolution that the moon effects between the fields of the earth and the "fields of the sky," mirrors the dissolution of the boundary between the riverbank and the sky.[40] Similarly, Bea now understands, death is but the movement from one state to another.

The unity of Lavin's craft and subject is remarkable. Working for over forty years toward an expression of her organic vision, she unerringly selected and developed the metaphor of gardening to demonstrate the human need for love. Pushing beyond the material, however, she incorporates her belief in the permanence of the spiritual as well as the temporal with images of primeval seas. Nurtured by her gardening, mothering, scholarship, marriages, and friendships, Lavin's work structurally reenacts as well as expresses this constant theme, from the tentative murmur or hope of early characters to Vera's and Bea's confident assertions. The organic nature of the life she celebrates is restaged in her work; each part of each story is dependent on others, and later stories develop ideas uncovered earlier. Though stylistically close to Bowen, Lavin's concentration upon the whole, upon the relationship between elements rather than the individual, places her closer to Kate O'Brien. Once again, this perspective could spring from the relational world in which girls develop personality, as Nancy Chodorow suggests, and/or from the world of the Catholic church which also emphasizes communion. This is an intuitive rather than a cultivated perspective, then, and one which eventually affects theme. But again there is a distinction to be remarked: although focusing on the community, O'Brien emphasizes the sacrifice of the individual for the community, whereas Lavin emphasizes the value of the community. That Lavin's subject is not grounded in Irish politics is, in fact, praise rather than criticism. Focusing on women and on human concerns, Lavin's work is firmly and importantly grounded in the particulars of Ireland but rises above purely national—hence ultimately confining—interests to the sphere of universal humanity.

7. Molly Keane
Bildungsromane Quenelles

You are a woman if you have had a lover in your bed.
—Aroon in *Good Behaviour*

MOLLY KEANE's writing career began in the late 1920s with the first of the pseudonymous M.J. Farrell's series of popular and risqué novels. Keane, an inveterate storyteller, suggests that she wrote only as she needed pin money, and that the ambiguous pen name (male or female, Anglo- or Gaelic-Irish?) was essential in the horsey world of Anglo-Ireland: "For a woman to read a book, let alone write one was viewed with alarm, I would have been banned from every respectable house in County Carlow." In any case, when a Keane book made the bestsellers' list, the author met Elizabeth Bowen. Initially unsympathetic to literary people, Keane soon saw Bowen as her greatest friend and delighted in Bowen's Court as she does in all beautiful, gracious houses even now—years after Bowen's Court's demise.[1] Thus, although Molly Keane draws Anglo-Ireland in hilarious, philistine garb, she is and was aware of the existence of the cultivated Anglo-Ireland of Elizabeth Bowen, to be depicted from yet another perspective in the 1970s by Jennifer Johnston.

Despite her pleasure in caricaturing, Keane does reflect her own background in her work. The daughter of landed, and therefore relatively wealthy, Anglo-Irish parents, Keane remembers the "dreadful neglect" of her childhood: her mother, the poet Moira O'Neill, dwelt in a nineteenth-century world, and her father seemed to care only for horses and hunting. "You can't think how neglected we were, by our parents. I mean they didn't do anything with us at all, they simply didn't bother. They were utterly reclusive." Perhaps naturally then, horses and riding became the most important things in the children's lives: "I really disapproved of people who didn't ride, it was the only thing that counted." Of her mother, she notes: "I fought her every inch of the way. She really didn't know how to treat us."[2]

Keane's world opened out when the Perry family invited her to live with them in Tipperary. In their gracious home Keane encountered and responded to elegance, civilization, and the fringe of London literary society. This was the milieu that developed the wry, humorous, sometimes scandalous M.J. Farrell. Although these early novels combine wit, alert intelligence, and willingness to broach controversial issues (lesbianism, for example, in the 1934 *Devoted Ladies*), I wish to concentrate here on Keane's masterpiece, *Good Behaviour*, the novel she published in 1981 after more than thirty years' silence. The texts that followed *Good Behaviour*, *Time After Time* (1983) and *Loving and Giving* (1988), prove that the earlier novel was not simply a brilliant, never-to-be-repeated flash. Equally clever, probing, and rich, these novels are not examined here because *Good Behaviour* is a representative text presenting the same kinds of excellencies and because readers should experience first-hand Keane's shocking and surprising conclusions. The 1981 *Good Behaviour* almost bridges the century as it enacts the development of a young woman in the Ireland of 1900-1920, the years of Molly Keane's own childhood and adolescence, and should become, in the words of one reviewer, "a classic among English novels."[3]

Let us briefly consider the kinship of *Good Behaviour* to the novels already discussed. The shocking and grotesque occurrences in this text take us back to *Castle Rackrent* and, to a lesser extent, to *The Real Charlotte*. All three novels present an apparently casual recording, without authorial comment, of gross cruelties to women and to servants. We recall Thady's calm acknowledgment that neither he nor any of the other servants either saw or spoke to Jessica for seven years and his more sympathetic but equally passive acknowledgment of the tenants' poverty. Somerville and Ross's text suggests that eccentric, vicious behavior is a commonplace whether the protagonist be lord of the manor, a member of the middle class, or a servant. In Keane's novel, the protagonist Aroon St. Charles, deprived and eager for any display of affection, is treated by her homosexual brother, Hubert, and his lover Richard as a spectacle.[4] In turn,

Aroon is brutal and dismissive of the needs and rights of others.
Keane differs from the earlier writers in depicting Aroon's character and behavior as the logical, if not inevitable, consequences
of her childhood training.

Keane's next two novels, *Time After Time* and *Loving and
Giving*, continue to present destructive and murderous behavior,
not as deliberate evil but as the almost casual, natural result of
membership in a particular family or society. J.G. Farrell, who
was not Irish but lived in and wrote of Ireland, especially of
Anglo-Ireland, comes closest to this sangfroid in the twentieth
century; Julia O'Faolain's grotesques are of a different order in
that their behavior, though equally destructive, is not depicted
as so unthinkingly natural.[5] Reinforcing the harshness and originality of their creations by an almost brutal economy of presentation, Edgeworth, Keane, and O'Faolain often remind us of
the scalding humor of their ancestor Jonathan Swift.

Narrative style most clearly connects Keane's Aroon with
Edgeworth's Thady. In *Good Behaviour* as in *Castle Rackrent*,
the reader must constantly search behind the biased, unreliable
narrator's words for—if not truth—something stable, and in
both novels, clues thrust weedlike through the textual cracks of
parataxis, contradictions, and apparent irrelevancies. These
similarities are all the more striking in view of Keane's observation that her work owes no allegiance to Edgeworth's *Castle
Rackrent*, which she had not read before writing *Good Behaviour*.[6] In part, of course, the similarities are due to the two
first-person narrations; the storytellers Thady and Aroon are su-
perbly confined by their creators to appropriate, limited perspectives. The unreliable narrator is no longer a novelty in the
twentieth century, but Keane's is, as far as I am aware, the first
work in which an Anglo-Irish protagonist/narrator adopts so
clearly the tactics of the repressed other, the Gaelic-Irish. Edgeworth's Rackrents—all but Condy, who was nurtured in the
Gaelic-Irish environs of Thady's own family—are figures of a
large rather than petty and furtive malevolence. Charlotte's
origins are doubtful, and Bowen's Naylors are serenely removed
from the consequences of their actions. But in her pettiness, in
her flattery of more powerful figures than she, and in her lies,
Aroon is matched only by Condy and Thady, is in fact an example

initially of the desperate strategies of the weak and ultimately, when she achieves power, of the arrogance of the strong. In this text, then, the fictional Anglo-Irish personality is blended totally with its Gaelic counterpart, not in Aroon's mind but in Keane's depiction of Aroon as Anglo-Irish.

The links to *Castle Rackrent* may testify to a shared inheritance rather than intertextuality, but the ties to *The Real Charlotte* seem deliberate. These ties are at once more obvious and less important, as are those to *The Last September*. In her physical and personal unattractiveness Keane's Aroon could be Charlotte Mullen's biological and social twin. But as Keane points out, Aroon is upper-class, Charlotte, middle, and that makes a great difference.[7] Indeed it is after all Aroon's exposure to the deceptive practices of upper-class "good behaviour" that allows her to shape, first in her memory, later in her text, the fiction of her successful life. Charlotte's bildungsromane would have been more overt, less tricky, less fictional. Despite the difference in style, which amounts to the difference in class in this instance, neither Charlotte nor Aroon is rich enough to compensate in the marriage market for her negative qualities. This fact decrees a similar fate in a society that continued to use women as objects of exchange.

Of the same class as Aroon, Elizabeth Bowen's Lois, on the other hand, is beautiful and therefore valuable. Nostalgia pervades Keane's text as fully as it does Bowen's, though in Keane's case the nostalgia is both pathetic and ridiculous. Keane's September could again be 1920—the year in which Danielstown and many lovely Big Houses burned. Keane's own home was burned, and she delights in telling the story. Brandishing an ancient weapon, her father accosted the arsonists. The "boys," Keane tolerantly reports, reprimanded him, advising that unless he behaved they "would *have* to shoot him."[8] In bequeathing to Aroon those character defects that previous Anglo-Irish writers reserved for the Gaelic-Irish, Keane extends the sympathetic identification her anecdote implies. Further, in setting her novel in the turbulent years of the early 1920s and in ignoring these events, Keane, like Mary Lavin, suggests the unimportance of political upheaval in the lives of her characters. Neither world nor national war affects women's lives as much as traditional social and financial constraints.

I have said that *Good Behaviour* is a masterpiece. On the most obvious level we are aware of mastery when a narrator as pompous, self-centered, and inhumane as Aroon, a liar and a matricide, wins her readers from revulsion to support. The text opens with Aroon's feeding her mother rabbit—the food that always "sickened her"—disguised as chicken quenelles, and with the mother's resistance, subsequent nausea, and death. Overtly attempting to explain her relationship with her mother (but in fact to justify her actions), Aroon begins the story of her childhood and youth. Physically unattractive and neglected by her mother, who favors her brother Hubert, Aroon is made happy by the advent of a governess, Mrs. Brock, who introduces the children to tasty food and stories of her previous charge, Richard Massingham. The happy days are cut short by Mrs. Brock's suicide, her response to being dismissed as a result of Mrs. St. Charles's discovering her husband's affair with the governess. Many years later Hubert brings Richard to visit, and Aroon imagines a love affair between herself and Richard, based primarily on Richard's coming to her bed one evening and simply placing his head on her "enormous bosoms." This affair becomes the illusionary basis of Aroon's text, an illusion preserved throughout Richard and Hubert's homosexual relationship, Hubert's death, and Richard's engagement and departure to Africa. When her father, her only ally in the family home, Temple Alice, becomes ill, Aroon is thrown back into the misery of early childhood as her mother confides in the maid Rose and cuts back on food, Aroon's sole pleasure. The first-person narration which moves us from the death scene to the early scenes of neglect is, of course, a good technique to win reader sympathy.

Of more importance, however, is the bildungsromane form itself. Through it we see the psychological abuse to which the child was subject, and as the child develops, the form also reveals the distorting effects of this abuse on her personality. Indeed the genre itself complicates Aroon's already much mentally revised text. The novel is replete with self-reflexive references to its own status as bildungsromane, references which repeatedly call our attention to genre. The opening death scene, for example, the only scene in the present tense, concludes with Aroon's explicit statement of purpose: "At fifty-seven my brain is fairly bright, brighter than ever I sometimes think, and I have a cast-iron memory. If I look back beyond any shadow into the uncertainties and glories of our youth, perhaps I shall understand more about what became of us." Moving from present tense into her statement of purpose and then into past tense, Aroon is made to emphasize the bildungsromane. In another instance, describing the visit of Richard and her brother Hubert, Aroon again calls our attention to genre and, perhaps more important, to her own previous experience with this form. The three former pupils of the governess, Mrs. Brock, Aroon tells us, constantly attempted to revive her image during the climactic summer of Richard's visit, as they recounted repeatedly "the separate childhoods, which had left us the people we were." Much later, fretting that liberty will be denied her until she is an old lady beyond even "the remembrance of time past," Aroon drops Proust's famous bildungsroman phrase as if by accident. And, perhaps most intrusively, Aroon puns that she does not need details spelled out because "I know how to build the truth."[9] Presenting Aroon as an obtuse, unreliable narrator, Keane complicates her picture by implying that this narrator is also a competent storyteller, one we might expect to be aware of the sympathy-gaining possibilities and the requirements of her chosen genre.

Further, in claiming the bildungsroman for her own, Aroon lays claim to and subverts the traditional male genre. *Bildungsroman*, as explained earlier, refers to the genre here, while *bildungsromane* refers to specific texts of women's development and maturity. In *Seasons of Youth*, generally regarded as the classic work on this genre, Jerome Buckley enumerates the characteristics of what he calls the typical work, characteristics that are listed in chapter 5. But psychological studies as well as studies of female novels of development suggest that these characteristics rightly belong to the male model of development rather than the human model. The female model, the studies argue, will valorize relatedness rather than the separation endemic to the male model. The editors of *The Voyage In* note that women's development often occurs late, frequently after conventional expectations of marriage and motherhood have been fulfilled and found wanting. Further, as noted in the earlier chapter, the exploration of environment and lovers was of course denied young women of the nineteenth and early twentieth centuries. Yet another important distinction is that female development may be chronological, as in *Jane Eyre*, for example, or in Kate O'Brien's *Land of Spices*, or may be "compressed into brief epiphanic moments," "flashes of recognition," as in *Mrs. Dalloway*. Again the development may be drawn in a subtext of dreams or memories juxtaposed against a conventional plot. Noting significant continuity as well as difference with the genre as defined by Buckley and others, the editors of *The Voyage In* summarize the results of their exploration of fictions of female development: "Belief in a coherent self (although not necessarily an autonomous one); faith in the possibility of development (although change may be frustrated, may occur at different stages and rates, and may be concealed in the narrative); insistence on a time span in which development occurs (although the time span may exist only in memory); and emphasis on social context (even as an adversary)."[10]

In this context we can read Keane's *Good Behaviour* as an ironic bildungsromane, not only ironic in the way Joyce's *Portrait* is, in that it will not allow us to simply invert Aroon's viewpoint, but also doubly ironic in its expropriation of the androcentric genre. Seizing narrative control, Aroon announces traditional bildungsromane, the genre that can only culminate for women in romance since the other opportunities of the "typical" work are denied women. Pretending to adhere to the formula, Aroon subverts and exploits its tenets, achieving her victorious conclusion through a hilarious process of conflation and substitution. The delicious fun of the creation often disguises the pervasive subversion. The process of creating the text parallels Aroon's culinary achievements, her disguising of "the rabbit foundation" of the killing quenelles with spice, a "hint of bay leaf and black pepper."[11] But the ultimate irony, which should draw attention to the fictive base of bildungsromane, is the enacting of the conventional plot (the romance) in Aroon's imagination, while the real development takes place in the constantly repressed responses to the almost Darwinian, brutal society.

Aroon's expropriation and exploitation of genre results in a change of perspective for the female protagonist, a change equivalent in consequence—to use her own phrase—to a globe's revolving.

Modern bildungsromane records the earliest stage of human development, preoedipal unity with the mother. The terms currently used to describe these early stages are common to both psychoanalysis and literature. Dorothy Dinnerstein, for example, notes that the very young child does not distinguish herself either from the people or the world around her—all are part of the one continuum. But as the child matures, she learns to see her "I"-ness in relation to another person, to an "It" which is not clearly an "I," usually the primary caretaker, the "other," mother. Having initially seen the mother as "It," children never fully allow their mothers to assume the distinctive individual status they themselves attain. Girls, however, Dinnerstein concludes, transfer some of this "It"-ness to themselves. This is the negative side of the relatedness Chodorow posits as usual for female children. Positive models and nurturance would seem of primary importance to the female child during these early stages if she is to relate positively to other human beings. Stephen Dedalus's first recorded sensations, although brief, enact the primal unity; Stephen seems to be unindividuated from the world around him.[12] Aroon's first memory, on the other hand, is that of alienation from the mother—an isolation extending indeterminately back so far as to seem natural.

The first time Aroon recalls this isolation, she seems to be invoking not a particular memory but her early, already formed sense of the world and of her own place, or lack of place, in it. The word *crusted* releases the memory:

Why do I hate the word "crusted"? Because I feel with my lips the boiled milk, crusted since the night before, round the rim of the mug out of which I must finish my breakfast milk. . . . I am again in the darkness of the nursery, the curtains drawn against the winter morning outside. Nannie is dragging on her corsets under her great nightgown. Baby Hubert is walking up and down his cot in a dirty nightdress. The nursery maid is pouring paraffin on a sulky nursery fire. I fix my eyes on the strip of morning light where wooden rings join curtain to curtain pole and think about my bantams. . . . Even then I knew how to ignore things.[13]

Only three years older than the dirty baby, Aroon is hardly more than a baby herself, yet she has already retreated into an imaginary world, isolated from both humanity and environment.

The first specific memory reinforces the reader's sense of the child's isolation, reveals the mother as the likely source of the separation, and suggests that the process of conflation and the substitution of culinary for sexual pleasure has already been effected. On an evening when the governess and all the servants are away, Aroon, compelled only by the deadly illness of her younger brother Hubert, braves the sanctuary of the dining room. There, "in spite of the desperate importance of my mission, I stood in the doorway for a whole minute, stunned and silenced by the munificent quality of their [her parents'] intimacy." Even as a child Aroon is distracted by odors as Stephen is by words; the adult Aroon will become an artist of both food and words, and the child Aroon notes, "the tide of musky, womanly scent from the wet Portugal laurels drifted in, strong against the delicate smells of strawberries and candle smoke and a breath of past roast chicken."[14] She looks to her father first:

The austere outdoor look I knew had melted from him into the air, like the glass in the cupboard. Sitting there, he seemed extraordinarily dulled, dulled and happy. Both their glasses were full and his eyes were downwards on her arms, their flesh firm as partridge breasts. He was speaking to her, asking some question I did not hear. When they saw me in the doorway, when I said, "I think Hubert's dead," he raised his eyes from her arms (it seemed a longtime, while Hubert and I were shut out) to her shoulders, to her eyes, and then he visibly let her go. If my dressing-gown had been in flames round me it would have taken them just as long to part. Although they weren't near each other I could not have walked, unless they called me, any nearer to that circle they made.[15]

This early scene establishes several themes. In the first place the unimportant, parenthetical child must pry the father's gaze from the beautiful object of his affections, from her rival. The negative presentation of the mother will be reinforced throughout the narrative, the mother constantly making circles with others designed to exclude the child, circles which enforce the child's sense of otherness, "It"-ness. On entering the room, the child is silenced, and when she is finally able to blurt out the frightening news, her mother reacts in annoyance—"My dear child—what *can* this mean?"—and ignores the narrative. Not only is Aroon not allowed to see herself as part of the continuum of mother-daughter, she is also made to feel that she alone stands outside the circle the mother makes with other members of the household. Secondly, the child's sensuous pleasure in aromas, particularly of foods, is established, a prelude to the deprived woman's lifelong obsession with and desire for culinary delight.

The intuitive awareness of the mother's sexuality, displaced by the child, is apparently still repressed by the adult narrator, mistress of both language and good behavior. The father's look is transferred to the mother's arms, but the simile "firm as partridge's breasts" betrays the intuition. Food and sexuality are almost inextricable. Food is the first love of the hungry child; sexuality, the desired quality of the unloved adult narrator. The displacement reveals both fear and fascination. The child senses her father's preference for the mother, and intuiting the mysterious nature of this preference and her personal inadequacy, she attributes its source to food. This is an interesting variant on the oedipal formula—as mother and daughter engage in rivalry, the daughter desires not the father's phallic power with which to possess the mother but rather the mother's sexuality, imaged as the power to dispense food, with which to possess the father.

Culinary and narrative powers are also intertwined. In first introducing the dead cook, Mrs. Lennon, Aroon weaves culinary, literary, and economic metaphors: "Mrs. Lennon's secrets died along with her, for she despised receipts and the ignorant and mean-minded who cooked by them; she never wrote anything down and, if possible, shut the door against any inquiring kitchen maid while she composed her greatest dishes. No inheritance was left from her years in office. She could not speak the language of her skill (nor did she wish to)."[16] Like the early nineteenth-century "primitive" or natural poets, then, Mrs. Lennon did not speak the language of her craft but composed her great dishes

without any regard for the recipes, the models which define both
the appropriate ingredients and the methods of mixing them.
Although the dishes are immediate successes, no inheritance is
left, the result of the cook's failure to record her own processes.
Mrs. Lennon serves as more than a culinary model for Aroon
and indeed for her father, Major St. Charles. Despite the sad
loss of Mrs. Lennon's gustatory triumphs, the Major and Aroon
learn a valuable lesson in the importance of inscribing their desires: although infatuated with his wife, Major St. Charles protects Aroon by willing the house to her. (Ironically the house was
Mrs. St. Charles's property, a property the "ultra-feminine"
woman placed in the hands of her competent husband.) And
Aroon too writes the apologia that excuses her crime, learning
from Mrs. Lennon the liberating power of ignoring the restrictive recipes, the methods or theories of her chosen dish, the bildungsroman.

The cook's powers, Aroon suggests, become incarnate through
the intervention of Mrs. St. Charles, an intervention that is pictured in sexual and traditional narrative terms. "Mummie expended some extreme essence of herself in bullying and inspiring
her treasured cook, Mrs. Lennon. . . . Mummie would penetrate
her cook's mind . . . demanding always more effort, a higher
standard of perfection for the Captain." Although not possessed
herself of the culinary tradition, the mother in her role as muse
penetrates the cook's mind, impregnating the cook with the seed
of the gastronomic pleasures she herself uses to attract her husband. The fruits of this handmaid's labor are essential to preserve the marriage. Upon Mrs. Lennon's death, the efforts of
the substitute cooks turn the Major from delight to disgust with
food and consequently to long visits to "some friend's sleek and
willing wife" in London. Having overlapped sexual and culinary
delight throughout this passage, Aroon can conclusively link the
mother's attraction to culinary power. "Her death made a dreadful change, a real chasm in one of his greatest pleasures, a weak-
ening of one of Mummie's unspoken influences."[17]

The fact that the father is both a gourmet and a womanizer
allows Aroon to substitute food as the source of all her rivals'
attractions. As a child and later as a young woman, Aroon is cut
off by her mother from this source, condemned to the nursery

diet of "porridge every morning, variable porridge slung together by the kitchen maid" and, in ominous foreshadowing, frequent "rabbit stews." Consequently Aroon becomes obsessed
with acquiring the powerful satisfaction of food and imagines her
father as propelled by the same desire. Seeing the Crowhurst
twins as unattractive, she ignores the Major's long private con-
sultations with one twin, attributing his frequent visits to his
delight in their good food. Similarly she equates Rose's importance with her culinary ability. Like Mrs. Lennon, Rose is apparently a "natural" cook. On an evening when the last of a series
of "undedicated cooks" leaves, Rose prepares a simple supper—
"poor Mrs. Lennon's poached eggs and rashers"—which elicits
one of the Major's devastating "embracing looks, distant, grate-
ful, promising." The visits to England become shorter, the Major
returning with presents of recipes for Rose, which he writes out
"as if marking a race-card for a chosen woman." The change in
his habits is a measure of his new interest: rather than fishing
or cleaning his gun, he is most frequently to be found now, Aroon
notes, "ordering dinner" in the kitchen. And for the first time,
Aroon sees "Wild Rose suddenly as a person" and notes the
pauses in their discussions of food, "dragging out the time of
giving and taking orders for luncheon, their voices had another
world beyond them." Refusing to examine the nature of her father's time with Rose, the familiarity to which she is an unseen
witness, Aroon cages Rose verbally, confining her influence to a
"presence" in the "beautiful smell of hot bread."[18]

Although Aroon negates the superior attractions of her rivals
by attributing them to food, she needs a supporting base on
which to build her own successful bildungsromane. The governess, Mrs. Brock, another gourmet, provides this, allowing Aroon
to glimpse alternate, if limited, possibilities. With the governess's arrival, the world and food of the dining room becomes the
children's at least for lunchtime, and Mrs. Brock introduces
warmth, treats, and fun to the schoolroom. Teaching the children
to ride through bribing the ponies with the Major's gift of choco-
late (the power of food again), Mrs. Brock earns the Major's
gratitude and not incidentally sows the seeds of friendship between Aroon and her father. Equally important for the children
are Mrs. Brock's "stories of her past pupils." Indeed the story

of Richard's childhood occupies almost half the childhood portion of Aroon's bildungsromane. The fat Aroon identifies rapidly with the fat governess, and we see Aroon begin to adopt Mrs. Brock's rather silly verbal niceties, her pleasure in designer labels, her belief in her singing ability, and ultimately her narrative methods. The positive quality of the life Mrs. Brock gives Aroon is epitomized in a recollection of one "ravingly glad day by the sea" when Mrs. Brock, seallike in her armored, black bathing dress, teaches Aroon to swim. Having swum four strokes more than Hubert, Aroon is consumed with happiness at her sense of complicity with the governess, a sense of for the first time being favored and preferred to the mother's pet, Hubert.[19] In psychological terms, the identification that takes place between Mrs. Brock and Aroon is a miniature, diluted version of that primal identification which Aroon has been denied, an opportunity to see herself in and as Mrs. Brock.

The optimistic "epiphanic flashes" that this substitute mother bequeaths Aroon, which compete in Aroon's perception of herself with the circles of isolation she inherits from her mother, are not uncontaminated. Since, as Abel, Hirsch, and Langland note, women's training was designed not to make them independent but to teach them to find someone to care for them, the lessons of sensuality are of utmost importance. These lessons are inculcated from an early age, though the code of good behavior disguises both their nature and their end. Constantly reminded by her mother of her disability in this field, Aroon is always painfully aware of the terrible fates of the Mrs. Brocks and the Miss Crowhursts. But the unspoken biology lesson of the mice, the essential feature in every 1912 schoolroom, the way "of breaking it to them nicely," seems to evade Aroon initially. Bursting with curiosity, Aroon questions the governess, to no avail, on the pregnancy of the gatekeeper's wife. Significantly the younger Hubert does not share her ignorance.[20]

The mice, or the repression of sex they come to represent, taint all the positive memories. Aware of Mrs. Brock's disappointment when the Major deserts the governess and children for a drive with Mrs. St. Charles, Aroon visits the schoolroom and, she expects, her governess. But the classroom is empty, and the mice are in an uproar as the male attempts to mate with the female. Not understanding, Aroon is terrified that the smaller mouse will be hurt. Mrs. Brock enters, however, takes care of the mice, and calms Aroon, nursing her like a baby, comforting her with milk and biscuits. Finding the governess unexpectedly happy, Aroon focuses on Mrs. Brock's lovely flowery hat, a gift of Richard's mother, now thrown on the table, looking "as if it had lain in wet grass." Although Mrs. Brock has treated Aroon so specially, the child is aware of a distance: "Again, as on an evening by the sea, I knew that a space widened between us." The day by the sea is perhaps Aroon's primary positive moment; on that day also, feeling the need to give to the beloved, Aroon confided her father's delight in the repair job Mrs. Brock had performed on his coat. Aroon remembers that as she told Mrs. Brock of his gratitude, "I knew she was tense with pleasure; and, while I glowed in its bestowal, the story was hardly out of my mouth before I knew too that her reception of it was on a different level from mine—a foreign, secret level, leaving me outside, a messenger, not a participant."[21] The moments of identification are thus tainted by an intuitive sense of the surrogate mother's stronger identification with another. Intuitively, as the linking of mice and incidents reveals, the child associates the latter identification with sexual attraction.

Sexuality, then, while essential to a woman's survival, is associated in Aroon's mind with her own exclusion and, in the climactic scene which ends the childhood section, with danger. Sensing Mrs. Brock's loneliness on the father's final rejection, Aroon comes to console her. The governess, however, betrays the code she has herself inculcated in Aroon. Angry, hurt, and almost frantic, given her latest dismissal and the absence of prospects for a genteel woman, Mrs. Brock forces Aroon to look at Minnie's "disgusting" babies. In a brutal manner, the surrogate mother now acquaints Aroon with the facts of intercourse, concluding, "It's a thing men do, it's all they want to do, and you won't like it." Although Aroon attempts to repress this memory (she reminds us frequently that she never told Richard of the mice), it haunts her text.[22] More important is Mrs. Brock's subsequent suicide by drowning. Chronologically, Aroon's identification with Mrs. Brock is followed by betrayal, by a betrayal linked to sexual attraction between the people most responsive to Aroon—her father and Mrs. Brock—and ultimately by death. Repressed throughout the text, on the one hand because they suggest frightening conclusions about her society and on the other because Aroon proposes to write a traditional bildungs-romane, an imaginative fiction which cannot comprehend these events, this frightening cluster of unexamined memories constantly directs Aroon's actual responses and shapes much of her reaction to the world.

Childhood over, the bildungsromane moves to education. In describing Aroon's schooling in only two half-sentences that refer not to the content of the education but to its encroachment on her life, Keane parodies the traditional bildungsroman interpretation of formal education as inadequate. For education, or the lack thereof, will mean less than nothing in a woman's achieving maturity, a condition associated with marriage in Aroon's society. The photographs Aroon inspects in *Tatler* demonstrate the acceptable paradigm: "A full-page picture changed all the fugitive glamour of the chase and the ballroom to a quiet contemplation of marriage and motherhood as understood by the proper sort of English family."[23] These historical realities remind us that in suggesting the unimportance of formal education, Buckley betrays a bias that only the accessibility of male education allows: Stephen Dedalus, however inimical he finds his education, is yet enabled by this training to live independently as he seeks some other life. No vocational training is available to Aroon and to all the women like her, despite the lessons of the desperate Mrs. Brocks and Miss Crowhursts. For a society that professes to cherish women and to see marriage as their destiny, such women are, like Lavin's widows, embarrassing anomalies.

The central joke in *Good Behaviour* is Aroon's apparent ignorance of the lively sexual climate and her parallel creation of romance from her exploitation. The establishment of ignorance is the necessary precondition for the creation. When the Major becomes bedridden, Rose is the only person whose ministrations he welcomes. Aroon reports Rose's massaging his "bad foot," the foot and leg he lost during the war, an activity Aroon frequently interrupts. Attributing Rose's popularity with the Major to the whisky she brings him, Aroon asks the doctor to forbid

the practice. "So that it's not just me . . . just me against them,"
she says. "Just you spoiling his bit of pleasure?" the doctor retorts, and Aroon reflects, revealing both repression and narrative
manipulation, "He understood more than I had meant." When
the shocked Rose announces the Major's death after Aroon has
interrupted a "massage," Aroon accuses Rose of killing him. "He
wanted it," Rose answers obliquely. Aroon does not ask for an
explanation but simply notes, "I told you whisky would kill him."
Aroon remembers that Rose replies: " 'Yes,' gratefully as if my
accusation were some kind of reprieve." Another suppression
takes place, but the language suggests knowledge. The Major is
the "doll" that Rose, not Aroon, plays with; Rose herself is the
"second widow" at his funeral.[24]

Faithful to form, Aroon introduces the requisite two lovers.
Mr. Kiely, the Major's solicitor, is presented as the carnal lover.
Significantly it is he who first allows Aroon to experience the
heady power of money. Stuck with a nurse unsympathetic to the
ill father's wishes because there is no money with which to pay
and dismiss her, Aroon agrees to sell Kiely the horse Richard
has, as an afterthought, left her. With the money from the sale,
she promptly pays and dismisses the nurse. Reflecting on her new-
found ability, Aroon almost betrays both the code of good behavior and the bildungsromane form with her awareness of the
actual means of her empowerment. Deflecting attention from the
means, however, she quickly turns the emphasis to her status as
a woman who is experienced, in the terms of the bildungsromane.
"You are a woman if you have had a lover in your bed as I have
had," she says, recalling her "affair" with Richard and turning
thus from the unacceptable realities of her world to the conventional plot of bildungsromane.[25] Kiely later rescues Aroon at the
disastrous ball, but he is dismissed as base despite his heroic
willingness to bring the drunken, huge girl home. Significantly
too it is Kiely who reveals the good news of the father's will. The
depiction of Kiely as the debasing lover is ironically apt, for the
connection with him threatens to reveal the monetary basis of
success in a bildungsromane and thus topple Aroon's carefully
built traditional tale.

The "affair" with Richard, on the other hand, is truly non-
carnal, the imaginative spice that conceals the foundation. Ig-

noring all the evidence of Richard's and Hubert's homosexuality, Aroon builds the memory of her illusionary affair just as she nurtured her positive memories of Mrs. Brock. The "affair" begins on another glad day at the beach of childhood, a day during which Aroon and Hubert fill Richard in on all the details of the previous trip with Mrs. Brock. Now as then, Aroon feels privileged above Hubert: as her brother calls "Come on, old Sea Cow, unpack the tea," Richard turns to Aroon. Richard's gesture is originally recalled thus: "When he pulled me up from the sand and towards himself, I shall always be sure that his lips touched the sandy, salty crook of my arm." At next airing, after a letter arrives from Richard in Africa, this becomes: "I felt as nearly as could be back in the moment when I had run along the wet sand, when he had touched the inside of my salty arm. Linked with this was the other afternoon when I had first learned to swim." Brooding on the letter, Aroon wishes that Richard had thought of her in connection with a herd of gazelles rather than a bull elephant, because then she would know that he had "remembered our running on the sands and that he had kissed my salty arm." "Had he?" she asks.[26]

The bedroom scene grows in a similar fashion. Richard comes to Aroon's room to relive, by placing his head on her "enormous bosoms," his nursery experiences with Mrs. Brock, and to talk of Hubert. Aroon's text initially betrays her sense of exploitation as she remembers how "cherished and defrauded" she felt. Rebuilding, however, she asserts, "I can never look on myself as a deprived, inexperienced girl. I've had a man in my bed. I suppose I could say I've had a lover. I like to call it that. I do call it that." This completed edifice, the basis of the traditional bildungsromane, appears, as we have seen, in the reflection substituted for the dangerous knowledge of the enabling money. Pitying the Crowhurst girls, the rivals who had easily lured the Major from Aroon, Aroon thinks they will always be "girls," whereas she is a "woman." "You are a woman if you have had a lover in your bed as I have had." Having coped with the two lovers required in the definition of bildungsroman, Aroon can assert her maturity in the only terms the genre allows a woman.[27]

But despite Aroon's creative ability, the mother is presented

as capable, until the end of the novel, of shattering the daughter's fiction. The Brock epiphanies—the memory, for example,
of the seallike Mrs. Brock and Aroon—can be dispelled as sad
illusions by the mother's scathing references to whales. The positive scenes with the father, Aroon's presentation of herself as
"mignonne" fairy princess dressed for the ball, receive similar
treatment. "Before my moment had time to live," Aroon reports
of one encounter, "it fell and shattered round me. Mummie was
sitting with him, as though she had guessed I would be doing
just this."[28] Seeming to join in the admiration the Major demands, the mother suggests that Aroon looks "stupendous," reviving, as she knows, all Aroon's fears of her immense size. The
real question is thus the source of this destructive power.

The climax of Aroon's text, in a triumph of good behavior and
narrative manipulation, reveals and conceals this source. Aroon
describes the moment when, sobbing and drunken, she is deaf
to the words of her father's will. "Do you understand?" Kiely,
the solicitor, asks, "He's left everything to you." Aroon recalls,
"I wondered if I could go on breathing naturally, through the
delight that lifted me. Twice over now this euphoria of love had
elevated my whole body; I was its host. Then the vision changed;
it was as though the face of my old world turned away from me—
a globe revolving—I was looking into a changed world, where
I was a changed person, where my love was recognized and re-
quited. . . . I was claiming what was mine—his love, his absolute love. I wanted them to understand that he had loved me
most." The convention of good behavior and the convention of
bildungsromane decree that the exultation be based on love. But
what Aroon knows of course is that now she, not her mother,
controls the means, the real base of power. This is the revolution
that reenacts in larger terms what was achieved through the sale
of Richard's horse, that turns Aroon from the frightened child,
the "It" outsider, into a competent adult. And Aroon understands
the relationship Tony Tanner discusses: this vital basis brings
control of discourse and control of narrative, as her request that
the solicitor reread that portion, "the bit about me," implies.[29]
Mrs. St. Charles protests, but receptive to the new locus of
power, the lawyer obliges. "Empowered by Papa's love," Aroon

tells her bildungsromane readers, she will be kind to her mother and Rose.

Empowered by the father's will, rather, Aroon controls discourse, and asserting love as the basis of her position, she simultaneously seizes control of the culinary tradition. Mrs. St. Charles has provided only cooking sherry for the solicitor, but Aroon turns to Rose: "This seems very nasty sherry. Would you bring the Tio Pepe?" Moving from the real and psychological chill of her isolated room, Aroon basks in the circle of heat from the glowing fire and turns her thoughts to dinner. The novice reveals her culinary sophistication, her skill apparently "natural," like that of Mrs. Lennon. Directing Rose to prepare a brace of woodcock, she advises, "Take a glass of sherry for your sauce. It's better than nothing. Thin potato chips and an orange salad, don't you think, Rose?" Fully aware of both the source and nature of power, the mother shrinks into her chair, looking, in another reversal of parts, "like a child warding off a blow."[30]

In allowing her heroine to assert that her success is the result of love, Keane allows her to succeed within the tenets of traditional bildungsromane, the genre chosen to win sympathy for the matricide. But in the pretense of adhering to these tenets, Keane allows Aroon to reveal their limits and dangers. Love as the basis of female success is an exploitive fiction, as the affair with Richard reveals—the woman imagines, the man exploits. Economic independence is the actual liberating, empowering force that allows Aroon to control her life through controlling the narrative and allows her to create an actual bildungsromane rather than to follow the confining recipes of traditional bildungsroman. Having all along conflated culinary and sexual delights, this control now allows her to equate actual possession of culinary ability with possession of sensuality and consequently to claim the love of the father. The final irony is the murder of the mother through the powers first depicted as the source of her own superiority. And the tool appropriately is rabbit. Reversing the Freudian and literary paradigms, Molly Keane suggests that erotic fulfillment is merely the spice of women's fiction—economic independence and the murder of the fictional collaborators mark the real foundation of women's texts.

8. Julia O'Faolain
The Imaginative Crucible

> The bog was pagan and the nuns saw in it an image of fallen
> nature. It signified mortality, they said, and the sadness of
> the flesh, for it had once been the hunting ground of pre-Chris-
> tian warriors, a forest which had fallen, become fossilized and
> was now dug for fuel.
> —Julia O'Faolain, *No Country for Young Men*

PROBABLY ALL parents influence their children more than the children care to admit. Some of their values are imbibed like milk;
others sour mind and heart and are rejected. Occasionally we
are mature enough to examine our opinions apart altogether
from the emotional moss they have gathered through parental
association. Writers, more than other people, mine the source
of their own reactions, or maybe they just seem to do so because
they write of this activity. Certainly Julia O'Faolain has frequently considered the influences of her writer parents, Sean and
Eileen O'Faolain, on her own work. Her father, she believes, is
an incurable romantic: indeed both her parents reacted roman-
tically and enthusiastically to the birth of the fledgling Irish state.
They Gaelicized their names, spoke the Gaelic language at home,
and embraced the original principles of de Valera's republicans.
Although he would become as disillusioned with the Republic as
with the older empire, Sean attempted to expose his own children
to "the romantic Ireland of his youth . . . which did and didn't
exist." Eileen too led her daughter to and, as happens, away
from romantic Ireland. A writer of children's stories, Eileen kept
the child Julia home from school until she was eight, audience
for Eileen's own work. When Julia finally did go to school, the
"pookas, leprachauns, magic coaches, fairy forts" of her mother's
stories were more real than the "angels and demons" the nuns
invoked. Ridiculed after rashly exposing her credulity, O'Faolain

notes that she "determined never to be caught out again and started casting a cold eye on the devils and angels too." Neither was the growing girl unaware of her father's conflicts with church and state; indeed a desire to be on his side, whatever that was, probably nurtured her resistance to and criticism of authoritarian control. Summing up her reactions to her parents' commitments, O'Faolain notes: "He and Eileen, a pair of reluctantly disillusioned romantics, made romanticism impossible for me."[1]

The reader of Julia O'Faolain's work readily consents to the truth of this statement. Valuing and employing the detachment of the eighteenth-century writers she admires, O'Faolain is a long way stylistically from her father or indeed from her Gaelic-Irish predecessors Kate O'Brien and Mary Lavin. When I first read her work, I was struck by the acid intelligence that strips away layers of tradition, affection, and affectation, exposing an often grotesque core. O'Faolain's kinship with Swift and Edgeworth remarked in an earlier chapter is evident here. It is impossible to remain passive when faced with O'Faolain's vivid and exuberant grotesques: John Mellors, for example, finds "Man in the Cellar," an early short story, "brilliantly disturbing"; Robert Hogan finds the same text "horrific." The no-holds-barred approach to sensitive political topics, to male territory in fact, also seems closer to the Anglo-Irish writers Somerville and Ross than to O'Faolain's Gaelic female predecessors. Finally, O'Faolain's cosmopolitan lifestyle—Irish herself and married to an Italian-American, she lives in London and Los Angeles—along with her nonromantic tendencies allow her to view her various societies with detachment and a cold eye for pretense, the same cold eye Molly Keane turns on the past. Indeed a hilarious bedroom scene in an early O'Faolain story "A Pot of Soothing Herbs" anticipates Keane's equally preposterous, ridiculous, and pathetic scene in *Good Behaviour*.[2]

But if Sean and Eileen were partially responsible for the substitution of an analytical rather than a romantic perspective, the early romantic deposits were not without effect. Just as the bog of the epigraph swallows, preserves, and transforms the forest, so the mind swallows, preserves, and transforms the deposits of childhood. Indeed the nuns are rightly wary, for the legends of the pagan past dwell as certainly in the imaginative crucible of the collective memory of the nation as does the forest in the bog. All the old Fenian legends, all the old historical fictions, and all the more recent romantic tales (perhaps close to those Eileen and Sean told their children) of "raids, curfews, and dancing in mountain farmhouses with irregular soldiers who were sometimes shot a few hours after the goodnight kiss" collect in, transform, and infect the national consciousness.[3]

This collection and preservation is, short of catastrophic occurrences, as inevitable as the process of nature. But if we accept the myths and legends passively, then they, like the bog, will contain and transform us, making of us mythic fuel with which to warm a future generation. Reacting against such passivity, O'Faolain the nonromantic declares an interest in demystifying, not mystifying. "Myths like lego constructions, can be taken apart: a double bonus for the writer, the magnifying effect of invoking myth in the first place, plus the energy involved in revoking its agreed values. Destruction releases energy." This, then, is often the O'Faolain project, similar to that Alicia Ostriker associates with the revisionist poets, of treating "existing texts as fence posts surrounding the terrain of mythic truth but by no means identical to it," discussed in chapter 1. O'Faolain does not limit her deconstruction to ancient or Irish tales but dismembers fictions of history and of contemporary culture alongside those of legend. Indeed one could argue that contemporary myths are more pernicious in an age or country that ignores history; consequently O'Faolain subjects both the macho Italian and the romantic Hollywood images to the same penetrating scrutiny she turns on traditional myths. Aiming to expose the cage "of assumptions," the mythic, national, religious, and familial bonds which too often imprison a people, O'Faolain releases the confined energy, the alternate materials repressed by these central cultural assumptions.[4]

The early story mentioned already, "A Pot of Soothing Herbs" (1968), enacts the problems facing the writer who would find her own voice despite restrictive traditional patterns. The protagonist of the story, Sheila, is depicted as attempting to understand both her own and her country's approach to sexuality, to experience. The story is prompted by the mother's anger at Sheila's spending the night with a fast crowd. She little knows that Shei-

la's detested virgin status was unthreatened when she shared a
bed with the homosexual Aiden and the lovers, the Anglo-Irish
Rory and the English Claudia. To protect Sheila, Aiden had
placed a "barricade" of pillows down the bed; Sheila had lain
between pillows and wall, bitterly aware that Aiden's hand,
reaching under the pillows to grasp hers, was extended only in
a "fraternal" clasp. Neither was her knowledge of the mechanics
of love increased: her head prudently covered by Aiden, Sheila
intuited the activity of Rory and Claudia only by "the heavings
of the mattress." Sheila tries to understand why her mother,
who with her peers thrills to tales of remembered romance and
adventure "as if sex, in Ireland, were the monopoly of the over-
fifties," should upbraid her so. And revealing the scars the national contradiction has cut through her own psyche, she ponders
why she has been unable to make love for the experience only
as would, she thinks, the rational eighteenth-century fictional
figures she admires.[5]

Sheila accurately defines part of her problem as a retreat behind the covers of language. Wanting to explore and to analyze
her situation, she immediately, almost instinctively it seems, protects her privacy with a humorous, self-deprecating reference to
"the Irish." Abruptly, jerkily, the narrative halts, as the narrator
attempts to probe and justify her rhetoric: "It is typical of us to
say "the Irish" instead of "I": a way of running for tribal cam-
ouflage. I am trying to be honest here, but I can't discard our
usual rituals. In a way, that would be more dishonest. It would
mean trying to talk like someone else: like some of my friends,
sheep in monkeys' clothing, who chatter cynically all day in pubs,
imitating the tuneful recusancy of a Brendan Behan." Caught
between the Scylla of regurgitating the familiar words, the
phrases of another time that define and disguise her, and the
Charybdis of a new style also alien to her, Sheila stumbles, one
moment falling into the romantic traps of her parents' generation, the next into the cynical ones of her peers'. Her identity
shaped by styles that seem alien, Sheila's position is similar to
though more extreme than that of the diver in the Adrienne Rich
poem referred to in chapter 1: the mermaid "whose dark hair /
streams black, the merman in his armored body."[6]

It is as if language shapes Sheila, not she it. Considering her refusal to make love with the elegant Robert, she notes, "I only know that I am attracted where I sense tensions and dissatis-factions—I prefer the fat, panting Hamlet to Hotspur." She thus resorts to the abstractions of literature to explain her refusal. Later, feeling sympathy toward the upset party-giver, Edna, Sheila looks back to the solitary figure: "But he was an unap-petising sight: mouth caked with the black lees of Guinness, sparse, pale stubble erupting on his chin, and a popped button on his chest revealing the confirmation medal underneath."[7] In this instance Sheila resorts to specific language as if she observes only the negative outward aspect, which apparently marks her as an objective, even cynical, observer. But the rhetoric is de-ceptive: Sheila is a romantic. The outward appearance and the confirmation medal are potent, not because Sheila is modern, in search only of experience, but because these aspects of Edna effectively neutralize her potentially romantic reactions.

In linking the myth of Cuchulain, the stories of Sheila's par-ents, and the story of Edna, the text suggests an equivalence in all three situations. As Sheila leaves the party with Aiden and Rory, Edna, the grandson of a 1916 hero, attempts to detain her, brandishing his grandfather's gun and threatening Aiden and Rory. Removing the gun, Rory pushes it barrel-down into a pot of geraniums, admonishing, "Steady, now, fellow, steady! Re-member that old Irish hero, Cuchulain, whose weapon used to get out of control and had to be put in a pot of soothing herbs? I think that's what *we* need here." Ribald weapon jokes pervade the saga of Cuchulain. One story tells how Aife, a woman war-rior, defeats Cuchulain and smashes his "weapon." All she leaves him, it concludes, is "a part of his sword no bigger than a fist." Another story tells of the king's calming of Cuchulain's war-fever by standing the maidens of Ulster naked between the mad war-rior and the city. On seeing the maidens, the saga continues, Cuchulain quivers in shame and is quelled finally when the war-riors of King Conor plunge him into three vats of cold water.[8] The warrior Cuchulain, like the warrior Edna who wears the confirmation medal of a soldier of Christ, becomes a figure of comic impotence rather than one of romantic potency.

The Cuchulain/Edna gloss colors the evocative, stirring sto-ries of the parents. When Edna's gun is first mentioned, Sheila wonders whether guns are "dangerous after three generations."[9] The answer is obviously no, as Edna, armed with the weapon of the 1916 warrior, becomes a figure of bathos rather than power, his weapon, like Cuchulain's, immobilized. The tales of the troubles can also be seen as brandished leftover weapons that retain their power only when unquestioned, when not put to the test. O'Faolain's linking of the 1916 heroes and Cuchulain is not simply humorous. A statue of the mythic hero adorns the general post office in Dublin, center of the 1916 resistance—Cuchulain, the warrior, was the inspiration of this resistance.

The tales the parents tell—like those they are based on—belong to the fantasy world of myth. Although Sheila suggests this, she fails to realize it, perhaps because, dreamily confusing life and art, her mental life like that of the young Elizabeth Bowen has been shaped so much by tale. Characters from life are seen as characters from fiction; fictional or historical characters are replaced by those from life. Thus Sheila sees the tortured, insecure Aiden as Hamlet but replaces Yeats's Maud Gonne and Proust's Odette de Crécy with Claudia Rain. Her mother's upbraiding sounds like a "foreign language" because, misreading her parents' tales for reality, Sheila has mistaken their values. Their talk, like that of all the Irish she identifies initially, "is not about activity. It is about talk."[10] Retreating behind the barrier of language, Sheila is concealed but is also unable to pierce the barrier, to uncover the activity hidden by language. Like the barricade that Aiden erected, the language of Irish myth effectively conceals experience, ironically projecting a romantic image rather than the "fraternal" clasp with which Aiden penetrated the pillows.

In *No Country for Young Men* (1980), O'Faolain uncovers multiple layers of myth—ancient, historical, and contemporary—and, enacting in the development of her novel the preservation and transformation of these deposits, tests the myths. Further, *No Country for Young Men* suggests that a nation's cultural myths are differently received by men and women. The title revises the Yeatsian myth of an Ireland exuberant with life and rejecting its "aged monuments." The young, not the old, are threatened in O'Faolain's Ireland, a country that, *pace* Yeats, valorizes history, or a particular version of history, rather than humanity. Indeed by aligning himself in "Sailing to Byzantium" with Oisin, Yeats collaborates with a figure that is negative in both O'Faolain's novel and her personal pantheon. The poet of the Fianna, Oisin, like Yeats, sought a nonhuman land, a land of eternal—static—youth, and released in his poems the myths that would shackle future generations.

Concentrating on the two recent sequences of Troubles, those of the 1920s and 1970s, O'Faolain traces a pattern that reaches back through Irish history into Irish myths and is ultimately destructive. Cuchulain of "A Pot of Soothing Herbs" was merely sterile, a domesticated hero in a particular tribe, but Fionn, whose myth shadows *No Country for Young Men*, and his warrior Fianna were a group of fighting men, not part of any tribe but lending their services where needed. Grainne O'Malley, the protagonist in O'Faolain's novel, alerts the reader to the myth when she tells the American filmmaker James Duffy that she is named after the central figure in the Diarmuid and Grainne legend. According to legend, Fionn Mac Cumhall, the general of the Fianna warriors, decided to assuage his loneliness by marrying Grainne, the beautiful daughter of King Cormac. But Grainne, reluctant to marry the aged Fionn because she loved Diarmuid, one of Fionn's young warriors, put a *geasa* (similar to an Arthurian obligation of necessity and of honor) on Diarmuid, and the lovers fled together. Furious, Fionn pursued them with hosts of the Fianna. Years of war ensued; men and land were destroyed before Fionn succeeded through magic in killing Diarmuid. But the Fianna was still demoralized, for its leader remained away wooing the reluctant Grainne. Finally, for the sake of her children, Grainne returned with Fionn to the warriors. Oisin, Fionn's son and Yeats's model, bitter at the destruction, blamed not Fionn for the indulgence, despite honor and duty, of his whim, but Grainne.[11] The myth itself, despising the obvious logic of the events it recounts, thus concludes with an irrational masculinist interpretation.

The restoration of order to the Fianna, then, depends on Grainne—whose name, as Grainne O'Malley notes, means love—forgoing her own desires and accepting the principle of conquest. As a woman, Grainne (of myth and of O'Faolain's novel)

is related to Ireland—"Mother Ireland," "the old woman," or
"Dark Rosaleen" in much Irish literature. Exemplifying in miniature the intoxicating and addictive power of national myth,
O'Faolain has a young warrior sing "Dark Rosaleen" at the
Clancy house during the civil war. When "in the last verses, the
softer sentiment disappeared and menace pounded on alone," a
listener remembers, "the boy had caught the mockers in his cadences. Rapt, they nodded to his beat and even the Da [who
loathes the violence] applauded." Jennifer Johnston too, as we
shall see, considers this mindless, emotional espousing of war
disguised as love to be a form of intoxication. The image of Ireland as injured woman whose wounds call her sons or lovers to
war is not unlike the sexual paradigm of territorial conquest that
Annette Kolodny "unearths" in American "herstory," and O'Faolain's and Johnston's work suggests a universality in this pattern.
The Irish mythmakers, whether lauding mythical or historical
Irish leaders, pictured Ireland as a woman constantly in need of
male protection and represented woman on her own, Ireland or
Grainne without a lord or without the one "righteous" lord, as
a source of disorder.[12]

When O'Faolain's novel opens in the 1920s, Ireland and the
Irish women have little choice but to submit to the demands of
the competing forces of warriors. But within the country, as
within women themselves, uncertainty, perhaps the residue of
another order, stirs. This potential disruption is configured initially in the person of Judith Clancy, Grainne's great-aunt and
the connecting link between each period. We first meet her as
a young woman contemplating the untamed aspects of nature
from the rigorously ordered garden of her convent school:

This region [the bog] was as active as a compost heap and here the
millennial process of matter recycling itself was as disturbing as decay
in a carcass. Phosphorescent glowings, said to come from the chemical
residue of bones, exhaled from its depths. "Bog" was the Gaelic word
for "soft" and this one had places into which a sheep or a man could be
sucked without trace.

The bog was pagan and the nuns saw in it an image of fallen nature.
It signified mortality, they said, and the sadness of the flesh, for it had

once been the hunting ground of pre-Christian warriors, a forest which had fallen, become fossilized and was now dug for fuel.[13]

A natural palimpsest, the bog can be read both as the repository of a nation's culture and as an archetypal feminine place. In the latter context the bog becomes a particularizing of that peripheral area assigned to women "outside and around" male culture and of the "wild" area, the crescent of female culture unknown to men. In its ability to devour men, the bog is also symbolic of the ancient male fear of the female, a fear perhaps of the older matriarchal tradition of the great goddess discussed in chapter 4. Here too Irish myth is relevant: the depiction in Irish legends of the overthrow of female oppressors by male heroes—Queen Maeve, for example, by Cuchulain—can also be read, as are many of the myths of the Near East, as a reenactment of the overthrow of the goddess.[14]

No Country for Young Men presents Owen Roe O'Malley as heir to this militant political tradition. Son of the "hero" Owen O'Malley who fought the British government in the early 1920s and then his own countrymen when they accepted the treaty negotiated with England, Owen Roe is a devious politician. The first Owen arrogantly refused to accept his government's and his people's wishes and, like his mythic ancestor Fionn, insisted on fighting a war that would devastate his country. Carrying on the tradition of the poet Oisin, Michael O'Malley, Owen's grandson and Grainne's husband, writes the revisionist history of the first Owen. Owen Roe also contributes to the glorification of his father, expecting to inherit the mantle of Owen's political office and willing, like his ancestor, to plunge the country into civil war again if this would achieve his goal. Intent, like Oisin, on squashing the potentially disrupting female account, Owen Roe attempts to have Grainne silence Judith—the reservoir of the secrets of 1920.[15]

But Judith and Grainne O'Malley are linked by Grainne's sympathy for her aunt and also referentially to bog images. Grainne, for example, thinks that "dealing with Owen Roe was like walking across a bog. You never knew when the ground might give way under your feet." She worries that Owen Roe takes her son riding on the bog, her concern extending both to the mythological bog of Irish history and the physical bog of Calary.[16] To be pulled into the bog is to accept the myths passively, to be shaped by them; to explore the bog, while still dangerous, is to question the history, the myths, to take control of one's own life. Throughout the text Judith's memory is described and portrayed as having the boglike power of absorbing, concealing for years, and regurgitating. Although James wishes to exploit Judith's memory and Owen Roe wishes to suppress it, it is appropriately Grainne who will explore that female place, crucible of individual and racial memory.

Within the bog of the Irish communal memory O'Faolain traces the patterns of the Diarmuid and Grainne myth in the male and female imaginations. The mythic triangle is represented in the 1920 grouping of Owen O'Malley, founder of the political dynasty; Kathleen Clancy, the woman he marries; and Sparky Driscoll, the American fund-raiser. Kathleen wishes to go away with Sparky, but her young sister Judith, who admires Owen, kills the outsider to prevent his interference with Owen's plans. The young Kathleen has loved Owen, but years in prison have made him, as Kathleen tells Judith, "cold as ice. A machine run on will power," a man who cares for causes rather than people. From the boglike depths of Judith's mind, whence most of the 1922 story comes, we are allowed to see that Kathleen is correct, that Owen is another Fionn. Determined to ignore the treaty that the legitimate representatives of the Irish party have signed, Owen, to advance his own political future, fights on despite the people's desire for peace. Explaining his stance to Sparky, who opposes fighting against the people's wishes, Owen says, "The people are clay. You can do what you like in their name but, as Aristotle said of men and women, the formative idea comes from the male and the clay is female: passive, mere potentiality. The clay here is the people who has no self and no aspiration towards determining anything at all until we infuse it into them. We are their virile soul. We are they."[17] This convenient rationalization allows Owen to act as Fionn, to ignore the resistance of women, people, and country in pursuit of individual desire.

O'Faolain suggests that just as the bog accretes materials through the centuries so too does the history of Ireland. Laid down over mythic layers, Irish history is affected by them. In 1922 we see the young Judith Clancy remembering the history lesson: "the frail morals of a woman were first responsible for bringing the English to Ireland in 1169—so women bore inherited guilt." Irish women thus carry a double load—the fall of "mankind" and the fall of Ireland. Given the placement of this wry reflection in a narrative overtly demonstrating the manipulation and reinterpretation of recent Irish history, the reader naturally reconsiders the events that led to Ireland's "fall," to "her" being "possessed" by an alien warrior. In the 1150s the woman in question, Dervorgilla, was married to the Lord of Brefni whose political rival was Diarmuid MacMurragh, Lord of Leinster. Dervorgilla left Brefni for MacMurragh, and though she did return, Brefni never forgave Diarmuid for the loss of face. In the course of the 1160s' internecine feuding, Brefni took the opportunity to invade Diarmuid's land. Diarmuid was forced to flee to England, where he sought Henry II's help and proffered his daughter, Eve, as gift to Strongbow, leader of the revenge expedition. Thus began the English occupation.[18]

Like Oisin of old, historians, Judith notes, blame Dervorgilla for the devastation wrought by her jealous lovers on country and people. Imaginative patterns, especially those that justify particular courses, change very slowly. The Aristotelian principles that Owen quotes simply justify manipulating human beings in general and women in particular for his own benefit. Control is obviously necessary, the interpretations imply: witness what unfettered women, Grainne and Dervorgilla, wrought. The ascetic Irish Catholic church, Grainne O'Malley realizes, adds its layer to the justification. Considering why neither frigid men like her husband Michael nor virile ones like her former lover Owen Roe can discuss sex, Grainne blames the church. "Monastic tradition described woman as a bag of shit and it followed that sexual release into such a receptacle was a topic about as fit for sober discussion as a bowel movement."[19] The legends of Ireland's ascetic monks—St. Kevin of Glendalough, for example—do indeed suggest the righteousness of the saint's disposing of, killing, woman, the fallen temptress.

The blame assigned, myth- and history-makers write Grainne and Dervorgilla out of their texts. O'Faolain, however, delves into the bog of Judith's memory to uncover the fate of her female characters. A quick learner, the young Judith absorbs all the lessons. She knows woman's duty, a duty reinforced in her school days by the warrior/priest home from World War I who counsels the girls to go forth as inspirations, lamps held up to light men's ways. Virtue, he tells the girls, can only be preserved by ignorance. "Desiring knowledge—Eve's sin—and naming things" are prime threats to their virtue, they (unlike Elizabeth Bowen's Lois) obediently believe.[20]

Inspired by this ideal, Judith admires what she sees as Owen's ascetic purity, what Kathleen sees as death-giving ice. When Kathleen confesses to Judith that she loves the American, Sparky Driscoll, Judith even thinks in Owen's idiom: "Sparky was a spoiler and a giver of bad advice. In Kathleen he had found soil only too receptive." Judith sets the two men up as good and evil, and Sparky "proves" her hypothesis when he kisses her, for her body behaves so wildly she wonders if she is mad. Seeing her own response as wild, Judith sees it as disordered, as the problem of women in fact, the problem of Grainne, of Dervorgilla, and of her sister, Kathleen. Ironically, then, her reaction to Sparky's kiss does not confirm her own and other women's sexuality but the ascetics' lessons, and the experience of her own body is discarded in favor of the authority of the fathers. Whether the early church fathers really believed female sexuality was evil matters little now. They promoted this useful idea and, as Phyllis Chesler shows in *Women and Madness*, psychiatrists and psychologists have continued to treat female sensuality as unfeminine and deviant, recognizing in it a threat to established institutions.[21] Having adopted the male paradigm of the good woman's asexuality, Judith sees her own reaction as a response to evil. So when Sparky would interfere with Owen's plans for war, Judith is in her own mind justified in killing the evil opponent of good.

Her psyche self-repressed, Judith is forced by Owen into a convent, where electric shock is administered to quiet the dangerous memory. But the recollections surge back, and Judith tells Owen she fears for her sanity, for not even her confessor believes her story. Fearful lest anyone should, Owen, unaware of the irony, calms Judith: the priest, he suggests, "probably thinks it's sex. . . . Half the women in here are probably suffering from suppressed sex."[22] But although Judith's adoption of the male paradigm with its subsequent repression of forbidden knowledge has driven her to the verge of madness, O'Faolain suggests a triumph. Judith does recover her story, for the bog is a potent preserver, as the "phosphorescent glowings," Judith's story in O'Faolain's work, attest.

If madness threatens Judith for accepting definitions other than those of her own psyche and her own intelligence, then deletion, another kind of madness, is Kathleen's fate, as it was Grainne's. In Judith's memory, in the bog of Irish history, no trace of Kathleen arises after her marriage but those registered by her male relatives. Years after 1922 Owen attempts to prevent Judith's leaving her convent: "What's wrong with being here? . . . You should see poor Kathleen struggling with the kids. She looks ten years older than you do." Judith asks if Kathleen is "still pretty" and if she is happy. Owen retorts, "Kathleen . . . is the mother of six children with another on the way." As for her happiness, "she has her children. She knows she is useful."[23] Owen Roe confirms this picture to Grainne many years later. Repressive marriage, then, even more than convent life, effectively negates the independent woman, neutralizes her sense of self, her sensuality, and indeed, from a male perspective, effectively solves the problem of women's disorder. Kathleen's sole purpose, a private one, is to give birth to the clay that O'Malley has infused.

In the final triad of Grainne, Michael, and James, O'Faolain takes her characters to the point of awareness but does not define, finish, or circumscribe their story. Married to Michael when she was little more than a romantic schoolgirl, Grainne has been sacrificed, albeit happily and ignorantly, to protecting the O'Malley name from the scandal her alcoholic, free-living husband might attract. Ensconced by his powerful family in a "safe" job, Michael continues his drinking and offers Grainne only a half life. Weary of this, Grainne turns to Owen Roe, not so much for erotic gratification but for "more through sex." In the tradition of the lusty warriors of myth, however, Owen Roe takes his sexual affairs lightly: "Your trouble," he tells Grainne after the affair, "was scruples. Making mountains out of molehills. . . . The wrong woman for a politician. Do you know that the Sicilians say 'politics is sweeter than sex'? Yes. Well, no reason not to combine them—until one starts to threaten the other. That happens when the woman—it's always the woman—makes a big production out of going to bed. Bed's simple really." Grainne reflects, "He talked with assurance, driving, mashing up things—love, politics—the way a garbage-disposer mashes them to unrecognizable, recyclable, grey fritters."[24] The bog transforms but does not destroy. Owen Roe destroys. His linguistic destruction is paralleled by his and Owen O'Malley's refusal to recognize sensuousness and their consequent violation and attempted annihilation of women's sexuality—Owen O'Malley by incarcerating Judith in a convent and by treating Kathleen as a "mode of production," and Owen Roe by his exploitation of women's bodies.

With the foreigner, James Duffy, however, Grainne establishes a fulfilling sexual relationship, one which Owen Roe sees as a threat to his political empire. By making this relationship primarily sexual (therefore ultimately limited), O'Faolain stresses the importance of responding to sensual needs so long denied women in Ireland. The warrior figure has not improved through the centuries: Cuchulain, the mythic hero of the 1916 Irish Republican Army, killed his only son rather than risk his own boasting honor; Fionn tricked Grainne into living with him by promising to protect her children; Grainne O'Malley promises to stop seeing James Duffy in return for Owen Roe's promise not to take her son, Cormac, to dangerous republican gatherings. When Owen Roe refuses, Grainne, like her namesake and like Kathleen, decides to escape with James. Once again, as in the case of Judith and Sparky, the irrational interferes on the side of the law. Patsy Flynn, whose madness is evident in his acute sexual suppression, kills James, much as Judith did Sparky, to preserve the O'Malley name and hence dynasty that is threatened equally by the outsider's sensuousness and by his political stance. But indeed sensuousness is political in Ireland. It is not a quality to be associated with mythical, historical, or fictional heroes, neither with Fionn nor Cuchulain, nor with, for example, Cuchulain's symbolic successor, Patrick Pearse, or Fionn's fictional successors, Owen and Owen Roe O'Malley.[25]

Yet Grainne is not absorbed as her physical and mythical ancestors were. As she shares a drink with Michael, who is deeply enmeshed in her life, Grainne feels that he is trying to "web her in." "Fate, he was implying, fatigue, habit, heritage, were stakes planted around her, holding her there, limiting her choices. Poor Michael, she thought, how wrong he was. She could go anytime she liked." What Grainne intuits here is the existential freedom Stephen Dedalus achieved when he thrust aside nets of country, religion, and family. But these stakes, though unfairly binding, are powerful, and the sexual relationship with James, like that of a later O'Faolain heroine with her foreign lover in *The Obedient Wife*, is ultimately a poor thing compared to the deep, twisted relationship Grainne has with her husband. O'Faolain sees no need to supply defining endings: the text leaves Grainne searching for James, whose body has been absorbed in another bog, the river Liffey. She may act on her existential realization, or like Carla in the later work, she may return to Michael. If the latter occurs, the text of Judith's memory awaits her. What seems important, however, is that the writer releases her character, refuses to constrict her as did the myth- and history-makers. The text, as one observer notes, falls from Grainne, not she from the text.[26]

Seeing myth as limiting, O'Faolain naturally offers no alternative tale, no simple equation of current female liberation with mythical and historical incarceration. Indeed she expresses deep fear of "myth-mongers, whether religious or political." Believing that they alone have the answers to the great questions makes them, she thinks, "dangerous, and in the end unlovable."[27] Grainne and Michael's bonds, woven over fifteen years, are elastic enough to take the strain of Grainne's defection. More independent than her ancestors, Grainne O'Malley can seize more freedom than they could. But as mythical and historical patterns cut their own shape in a nation's imagination, so long-standing relationships cut their patterns in individual imaginations. For Julia O'Faolain sees human beings as essentially social creatures.

The bond between Grainne and Michael unites their individual psyches. Returning to her home early in the novel, having left Michael for several months, Grainne feels "bereft" at finding an empty house. "Why wasn't Michael home?" she wonders. "She had a physical illusion that she would be whole again only when she held him in her arms. Did that merely mean that he was to her as routine was to laboratory mice." Michael too, when he suspects Grainne will leave him, agonizes at the idea of a break in their pattern. Another O'Faolain character, Una of "The Man in the Cellar," tries to explain the "fetid bubble of dependence and rancour" that traps her with the wife-beating Carlo: "Between a man and a woman who are deeply involved sexually— atrocious injuries can be forgiven."[28] (The text does not, of course, suggest that Una should remain trapped; having escaped, she attempts to explain why she remained there so long.) The intimate marital relationship, it appears, carves its pattern as indelibly on individuals as does the mythic pattern on a nation.

Despite the mutual bruising endemic to long-standing relationships, the union itself is usually seen as positive in O'Faolain's work. In *The Obedient Wife*, O'Faolain depicts an Italian family temporarily residing in Los Angeles. Carla has taken a lover while her husband works and plays in Italy, and she must decide whether to remain with this considerate lover or to return to Italy to her chauvinistic husband. Reluctantly deciding in favor of her husband, when—and because—he hurries from Italy to persuade her, Carla accuses her lover, Leo, of having no real need of her: "You're invulnerable, strong, fenced in. You believing Christians have an enormous ego, massive pride. I imagine it comes from the notion that your first duty is to save your own soul—that's breathtaking egoism, after all, and yet you learn it as a duty, a maxim and foundation-stone to your moral system."[29]

Although the strands are very twisted and although the sacrifice of the individual is rejected, the O'Faolain novel ultimately valorizes communal over individual values. This, I think, separates O'Faolain from those Anglo-Irish ancestors to whom I linked her earlier—Maria Edgeworth, Somerville and Ross, and Molly Keane. This valorization contrasts too, as we shall see, with the heroines in the later Jennifer Johnston novels, heroines who believe that the communal relationship is subordinate to that soul-saving activity of writing or painting. O'Faolain's Carla refuses to stay with Leo because his "giving" does not bring them close: "Fighting and wounding," Carla asserts, do engender a human empathy. "A flowing together takes place. It's not just

rational. It's more intimate, almost tangible. I can't explain it
in words. Lots of life evades words, Leo, but you live by them."[30]
Life, O'Faolain reminds us constantly, cannot be separated into
the isolated compartments of logic or art.

Like a crucible, then, the bog melds a nation's myths and history into national imaginative patterns. All elements are preserved within this reservoir, though they are transformed by
contact with each other and by time. Thus the top layers of the
palimpsest show traces of the earlier writing: the great Danu is
not only preserved, but she has acted throughout the centuries
so that the comic Maeve, the warrior queen whom Cuchulain
fights; the repressed Grainnes and Dervorgillas; and the Judiths,
Kathleens, and latter-day Grainnes all bear her mark. Recall
Sheila's early plaint: "The depressing thing about our talk is that
it is not about activity. It is about talk." Exactly. So the literature, the stories of the historians, the myths—all the shaping
material is ultimately not the reality of the past situations but
the talk, the words, the literature about the material. And O'Faolain's texts, along with those of other contemporary women writers, add a new reviving, ameliorating, restorative layer to the
palimpsest, a layer which not only alters the future but which
also restructures the literary past. This is the optimism of O'Faolain's essentially comic image. In the feast that ends comedy,
that harmonizes without the domination of any single melody,
the contradictory visions of Cuchulain and Emer, Fionn and
Grainne, Grainne and Michael coexist and temper each other. As
I have noted elsewhere, the unexplained geasas may be nothing
more than the harmony of opposites. But what more could we
ask? The magic does not simply belong to a golden age. As O'Faolain detects the "phosphorescent glowings," the traces of her
characters in the bog of Judith's mind, so we too can uncover
our history in the bog of national literature and myth. In a typical
O'Faolain irony, Owen Roe, the suppressor and distorter of history, observes: "In memory as in matter, Nothing . . . is lost. It
comes back in another form."[31]

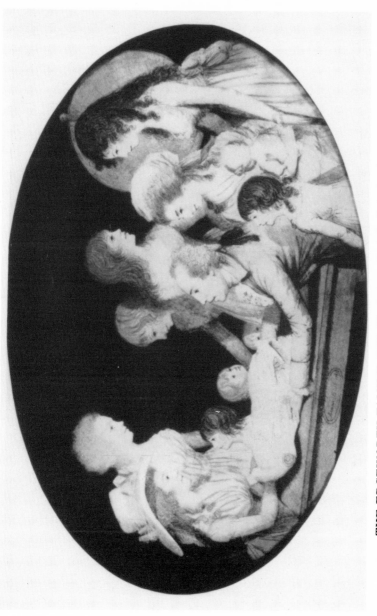

THE EDGEWORTH FAMILY, 1787. Maria is at far left. Painting by Adam Buck.

EDITH SOMERVILLE and VIOLET MARTIN (E.OE. Somerville and Martin Ross). Photo by Hildegarde Somerville. Courtesy of Curtis Brown & John Farquharson.

ELIZABETH BOWEN. Angus McBean Photograph,
Harvard Theatre Collection.

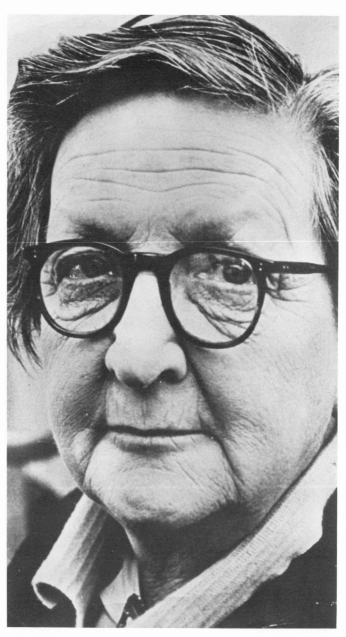

KATE O'BRIEN. Courtesy of *The Irish Times*.

MARY LAVIN. Photo by Peter Thursfield.

JULIA O'FAOLAIN. Photo by Bill Aller.

MOLLY KEANE. Photo by Ted McCarthy, Cork, Ireland.

JENNIFER JOHNSTON. © Sarah Rodway, London.

9. Jennifer Johnston
From Gortnaree to Knappogue

Perhaps . . . in a hundred years' time someone . . .
somewhere someone may read one of your books and say then
. . . say once there was this Jewish, Polish, British man called
Jacob Weinberg and today he has become a part of me. Today
I am different . . . extended.
      —Constance to Jacob in *The Christmas Tree*

IN 1977 Seamus Deane deplored what he saw as the tendency in modern Irish fiction to feed on the literary myths of the Irish revival, the most pernicious of which may be Yeats's legacy of the "greasy philistinism of the Catholic bourgeoisie and (of) the intellectual fragrance of the aristocratic Protestant tradition." In creating the myth of "no petty people," Yeats, Deane notes, ignored some very petty and vindictive people. The Protestant tradition was bourgeois, but with the fall of Parnell and the rise of Yeats's mythology, the picture that survives is that of "the Big House of the Ascendancy surrounded by the mean spirit of the gombeen Irish." Deane sees this picture reflected in Elizabeth Bowen's *The Last September* and in the novels of the seventies, Aiden Higgins's *Langrishe Go Down* and Jennifer Johnston's *How Many Miles to Babylon?* for example. The Irish novel has not, he argues, explored the "wider questions about fiction, its nature and status, its methods and its philosophy."[1] Ignoring literary innovations, contemporary Irish novelists, Deane asserts, have resorted either to the drained image of the Big House or to the glamorized one of the alienated artist, symbolized by the figure of Parnell. (After courageously and successfully leading the Irish parliamentary party in calls for land reform, Parnell was rejected by the Irish people because of his relationship with a married woman.) Deane calls for new directions, new concentration on the reality of the middle classes, and new Irish symbols. The identification and rejection of Yeats's seductive images are certainly essential in liberating the imagination. But I take issue with Deane on Jennifer Johnston's *How Many Miles to Babylon?* Contrary to his critique, I would argue that rather than repeating the patterns of her ancestors, Jennifer Johnston begins in this work to explore, reconsider, and reinterpret that tradition. Indeed the body of Johnston's work enacts pioneering textual journeys, from the Big House of traditional Anglo-Ireland in her first novel to the nameless Donegal cottage of a recent novel, journeys which—in focusing on contemporary women—range far beyond Deane's suggested exploration.

The daughter of Abbey actress Shelah Richards and playwright Denis Johnston, both prominent figures in the literary revival begun by Yeats, Jennifer Johnston is heir to the traditions and myths of Anglo-Ireland, but as she notes herself, though "nominally Protestant" she is "chiefly Irish." Set in Anglo-Irish Big Houses, however, her early work allowed critics, while admiring the poetic style that could suggest so much in so few words, to see her subject as limited, recalling in its way Jane Austen's two inches of ivory. The comparison is unfair, because from the first Johnston has not hesitated to traverse the treacherous, mined ground of Irish division, domestic and national, and to register with a continually refined instrument the depths of disturbance. Married, the mother of four, Johnston began her writing career in London, unaware, she notes, of controlling themes but aware of individual characters. Looking back, however, she identifies her first two novels, *The Gates* and *The Captains and the Kings*, as attempts to confront Protestant roots in the south of Ireland. When forced to make a hard choice in her personal life, Johnston examined and reassessed her work. *The Old Jest*, written after this decision, is the story of choice, the story of the assertion of control by the exercise of conscience and responsibility, an exercise that, Johnston notes, came late in her own life.[2]

The questioning and examining had already, I suggest, begun in her fiction. Having made her decision, however, Johnston imagines no plateau of comfortable achievement and knowledge; rather she insists on the constant need to reevaluate both the self and the situation and to move appropriately. Her fictions reflect this movement. I propose, therefore, to consider Johnston's first seven novels as a map of artistic and thematic progression. That progression is itself a fairly common paradigm in the awakening of contemporary women, an awakening both in and out of fiction that begins with acceptance and moves to recognition and frequently to rejection of inherited practices and habits. After a brief consideration of the earlier texts, texts which reflect some acceptance of traditional patterns, I turn to the questioning texts and finally to the most experimental and recent works, *The Old Jest*, *The Christmas Tree*, and *The Railway Station Man*.[3]

Perhaps in oblique acknowledgment of the ghosts of history and literature that pursue the writer, ghosts relentlessly pursue the protagonists of much of Johnston's work. All artists, frequently writers, these protagonists may be limited authorial representatives. Johnston suggests that she does indeed write about herself and cites her early, constant exposure to the variety and agility of artistic minds. Minnie, the young Anglo-Irish girl in *The Gates* who comes home to her uncle's Big House, Gortnaree, is haunted by her own ghost, which goads her from a mirror. Mr. Prendergast, the old Anglo-Irish man in *The Captains and the Kings*, is haunted by the ghost of his mother. Wordsworth's words help structure Minnie's narrative; Tennyson's, Mr. Prendergast's. The lack of development in the peripheral characters in the early novels—the overall polarization, for example, into civilized Anglo-Irish and brutal Gaelic-Irish camps and the betrayals of the Anglo-Irish friendships—is probably the source of Deane's critique and of Sean McMahon's complaint that Johnston shows a "residual inclination to take sides." The early texts also betray an acceptance of some literary types. The assertive mothers in *The Captains and the Kings* and in the later *How Many Miles to Babylon?* remind one of the destructive female figures Alicia Ostriker identifies in literary tradition.[4] Despite the apparent conformity, however, analysis reveals tensions already stirring beneath the surface.

In the first place, the Big House in the early work is more than the dilapidated relic of a past civilization, a nostalgic emblem for what might have been. Neither is it the caricaturing of a civilization, as is the case, perhaps, in that mother of Big House novels, *Castle Rackrent*. Gortnaree in *The Gates* is the site of a division which extends beyond political into class loyalties. The political waywardness of Minnie's father, his adoption of the Gaelic cause, though infuriating, is tolerated. His marriage to a tinker, "a girl he could [not] bring into the house," is unpardonable, however, and this betrayal of class results in his banishment from the family home. Again the Big House of the Prendergasts in *The Captains and the Kings* is a place of bitterness, probably resulting from what Harriet Taylor and John Stuart Mill long ago saw as the "demoralizing" effect on the characters of husband and wife of the wife's dependency, a dependency enshrined in the law of the land. Deprived of legitimate outlets, Mrs. Prendergast exercises her control viciously in the limited family arena (as does Mrs. Moore in *How Many Miles to Babylon?*), "a direct function," to quote Ostriker, "of her powerlessness to do anything else." Mrs. Prendergast prefers her romantic son, Alexander, to the more mundane Charles. Charles in his turn re-creates for his wife the misery his mother created for her husband, but there is an important difference—a wife cannot escape, being economically dependent. Johnston overtly reveals this dependence: when Charles finally acquaints his wife with news of their daughter's "double first" at Cambridge and the subsequent opening of opportunity, she observes, "She won't have to rely on getting married, then."[5]

The legacy these early characters carry is that of English literature, for they have not attempted to assimilate with Gaelic Ireland, and the historical and domestic patterns they enact are also compulsive repetitions. With seeming inevitability, war follows war in both novels as marriage follows marriage. No good reason is presented in either situation. The Anglo-Irish marriages are depicted as dreary or vicious; the Gaelic marriages, as brutish. Despite their awareness of the bitterness in the marriages they have witnessed, both Mr. Prendergast and his young Gaelic-Irish friend Diarmid see the marital situation as inevitable. War too is accepted, perhaps more than accepted. Minnie's Uncle Frank MacMahon "enjoyed" the First World War, and, exempted from the second, he pines at his exclusion from "life" while condemning his brother's activities in the Irish war against England. Mr. Prendergast and his brother Alexander engaged in World War I almost as they engaged in social activities, as the natural commitment of Anglo-Irish gentlemen.[6] And replaying for Diarmid the wars of old with toy soldiers, reciting Tennyson's absurdly romantic "Charge of the Light Brigade," willing his medals to the boy, Mr. Prendergast passes on the "romance" of the military tradition. In selecting as the title of the novel a phrase from Kipling's "Recessional"—the hymn to empire's end—Johnston seems to cast a dignified, ceremonious light on the old man's world of war and memory. Ironically it is the martial and not the marital situation that is, in retrospect, romantic.

Johnston's next novel, *How Many Miles to Babylon?*, takes a closer look at the specifics of war. Set in 1914, initially in a Big House at its height of glory, this attempt to bridge the gulf between Anglo- and Gaelic-Ireland might again seem a regression, a nostalgic glimpse into the unity that might have been. The beautifully appointed house, the ceremony of living, the swans on the lovely lake—all evoke Yeats's picture of the Gregory estate at Coole. The image is reinforced as Alexander Moore, the only child of this Big House, recites Yeats's nostalgic "Rose" poetry. However, while continuing to focus in this work on "male" subjects and to portray sensitive men and vicious, limited women, Johnston does not reify Yeats's vision of paternal accord between Big House and peasants. Further, the narrator of *How Many Miles to Babylon?* undermines the very story he tells us, his own. "I can juggle with a series of possibly inaccurate memories, my own interpretation, for what it is worth, of events." By implication, Alexander questions all stories and all memories and warns the reader to measure carefully the written word. Hatred, not Yeatsian harmony, dwells at the center of Alexander's ceremonious world. Cold dislike binds Alexander's mother to Frederick Moore, and again, as happens so often in Anglo-Irish novels, the isolated child must seek companionship outside the approved circle. Indeed, although Alexander notes his parents' friends, he never mentions their offspring, his potential friends. Instead the stable boy Jerry Crowe becomes his companion. Jerry fosters this relationship as much as Alexander does, and both the senior Moores disapprove of the friendship.[7]

While Frank MacMahon and Charles Prendergast accept British political decisions, the Anglo-Irish man in *Babylon*, Frederick Moore, sees no reason for Irishmen to become "food for

cannons" in England's war. Objecting to his wife's insistence that
service is Alexander's duty, he says, "I have never aspired to
being an Englishman. Nor have I such aspirations for my son."
This reenvisioned Anglo-Irishman regards his heritage with an
individual sense of responsibility that does not entail the auto-
matic acceptance of English perspectives. He counsels his son:
"In this country the land is our most important asset." Bidding
Alexander goodbye, Frederick Moore suggests a new day Yeats
would have deplored: "I would like to know that you will always
do what is best for the land. Not for you or her or the strange
dreams that may come into your head. Here, the land must come
first. . . . It is this country's heart. It was taken from the people.
We . . . I must be clear . . . We took it from the people. I would
like to feel that it will, when the moment comes, be handed back
in good order."[8] The image of seizure, of murder in fact (without
its heart, the country is dead), is the faulty foundation Yeats
ignores and on which his mythical ceremonious house rests
uneasily. In reinterpreting both national and literary heritage,
Johnston's text implies that the received impression of historical
events is nothing more than the product of historians and poets,
both juggling "possibly inaccurate memories."

Ironically in a work that exposes the tragic consequences of
repeating received historical patterns, but predictably in a world
where tradition and history are so important, the human being
deprived of personal and national history is lost. Although he
agrees with his father on the justice of abstaining from a war he
neither understands nor cares about, Alexander decides to enlist.
Made in despair, this decision is the result of his mother's revelation that Frederick Moore is not his father. Stripped of his
genealogy, country, tradition, history in fact, Alexander feels
"dispossessed" and by default embraces the traditions of his
mother.

As noted in an earlier chapter, the orphan is a common symbol
for the Anglo-Irish, the race who often saw themselves as "faithful to the pitch of folly" yet abandoned by the natural parent,
England.[9] The orphan's dilemma is exemplified in *How Many
Miles to Babylon?*: abandoning his Irish ties to embrace his English origins, Alexander is not nourished but destroyed. On one
level, engagement in a war for a cause one does not believe in

is degrading and destructive; on another level, embracing without question the received pattern of history is also degrading and destructive. Trapped in a system blind to human loyalties, Alexander is ordered to command the firing squad that would execute his friend Jerry Crowe. Only through death—his own and Jerry's—can Alexander preserve his own decency, his human dignity, represented by his friendship with the stable boy. When the cost is finally computed, when Alexander sees that the national machine feeds on individual human values, he refuses to cooperate. In a state of stasis, Alexander is unable any longer to chose his course, unable, too, to take the path assigned. History is circumscribed, as is Jerry's, by the relentless inhuman logic of national historic patterns, and the novel ends where it began—in the prison cell. This novel may, as Mark Mortimer asserts, be a triumphant "declaration of faith in Ireland," an attempt to bridge Lennox Robinson's awful "gulf." It is also a reexamination and a recognition of the deadliness in the mythic patterns Seamus Deane deplores, a successful wrestling of national ghosts.[10]

Moving to contemporary Derry in the next novel and focusing in part on a young woman, Johnston extends her questioning. The constriction and restriction of her early characters within the crumbling houses of marriage or the prison cells of national history symbolize the constricted routes they have followed. *Shadows on Our Skin* suggests a similar compulsion in Gaelic Ireland. Focusing on a Catholic family, on a hero who translates Gaelic poetry, on tenements rather than Big Houses, and on the ancient Celtic ruin of Grianan Oiligh, the Grianan of Ailech, Johnston suggests the universality of compulsive repetitions. Regurgitating the rebel songs of Ireland, the Logans, father and eldest son, justify their activities with the history and songs of the past, the Irish equivalent to Tennyson's paean to fruitless slaughter. The link between national and domestic violence is, in the early works, barely implied, the suggestion perhaps of the muted voice of a double discourse; but in *Shadows on Our Skin* the link is emphasized. Mrs. Logan, who works long and hard to feed her young son, responds to her husband's delight in the death of two British soldiers by denouncing his talk of "glory and heroes." "Freedom," he begins, but she cuts him off. "What's freedom?" Logan evades her question by evoking Pearse, the hero of 1916. But Mrs. Logan will not be silenced: "Have they any more freedom in the south than we have up here?" she asks. "Is there a job for every man? And a home for everyone? Have all the children got shoes on their feet? Are there women down there scrubbing floors to keep the home together because stupid, useless old men are sitting around gassing about freedom? Singing their songs about heroes?"[11]

Logan's reference to the poet Pearse is especially disturbing in light of references by other, sympathetic Johnston characters to Pearse or to his sentiments. Jerry Crowe, no mere windbag or romantic but a soldier who fights for England only to get the experience necessary to fight against it, also quotes Pearse. Angus Barry, a positive character in *The Old Jest*, echoes these views.[12] History, or rather the stories of the past, the received impression of history, become—as in Julia O'Faolain's texts— weapons, for the trace of history itself is faint, contained in the possibly inaccurate memories. Thus a dilemma: Johnston herself and many people of conscience probe and explore the muddied pages, attempting to uncover a true text or at least, like O'Faolain, to reveal the distortions in the texts. But to champion a particular text, to insist on its primacy, is to engage in the errors of the Logans, of the British major in *How Many Miles to Babylon?* of Owen Roe O'Malley in O'Faolain's *No Country for Young Men*.

Shadows on Our Skin also introduces Kathleen, Johnston's first fully drawn ethical woman. Engaged to a British soldier, this orphan comes from the Republic, and in coming to the wartorn north, she attempts, like Alexander, Mr. Prendergast, and Minnie, to reach across national divisions. Kathleen is finally defeated, not by the inevitable forces of history but by human jealousy and failure, by young Joe Logan's anger and his brother's jealousy. Marriage is now seen not as economic necessity but as mindless ritual. When Joe comforts her with talk of her forthcoming marriage, Kathleen sighs: "That's not purpose, though. It's a sort of routine, really. The birth, marriage, death routine."[13] Remembering the imprisoning routine of history, the reader is concerned. Although betrayed by those whom she had loved, Kathleen kisses and forgives Joe. Her optimistic gift of

A Golden Treasury of Verse to the translator of Gaelic poetry suggests a blending of traditions not possible for Kathleen herself, but willed by her to Joe. The volume of poetry, in contrast with Mr. Prendergast's gift to his betrayer, encourages the poetic rather than the military imagination. Kathleen's gift, then, coupled with her forgiveness and Joe's sorrow, suggests that history which seems so repetitive is not inevitable but simply the product of independent, unimaginative human beings.

The next Johnston novel, that written after her own difficult choice, returns to 1920 to the south of Ireland. This novel does not focus on the male response to the political confrontation, but on a young woman's interaction with history, as if the whole period must now be reseen, the scenario itself reshaped by the author's new, wider perspective. The protagonist in *The Old Jest*, another Anglo-Irish orphan, finally takes responsibility for her own life, not ignoring but not bound by her history. Born to the daughter of the Big House (who is long since dead) and to an inappropriate father whom she has never met, Nancy Gulliver has always sought to find this father, to marry her lifelong friend, the staid Harry, and to continue to live in the Big House the Dwyer family has inhabited for centuries. In a way, then, Nancy's attempted journey into the received history of the past parallels that of the author in the early fiction. Nancy begins to write a diary on her eighteenth birthday, the day she says, "I first began to look at the world." Johnston, too, notes that writing forces her to live consciously, to think, to explore.[14]

Like the author, then, Nancy in writing her journal reexamines and rethinks her life. "There always seems to have been a war," she writes, as if looking back not only over her personal memories—the Black and Tans, the Easter Revolution, World War I, and her grandfather's stories of the Crimea—but also over Ireland's history, or indeed Johnston's texts.[15] The young Nancy, despite her resolve to begin being a person, sees this development as a re-creation of the domestic gender patterns of her family. Further, in her unthinking acceptance of her Uncle Gabriel's stand at Ypres and her grandfather's actions in the Crimea, Nancy also accepts unquestioningly the political patterns. Like Alexander, Nancy seeks her identity in her genealogy and nationality. Into Nancy's world, however, Johnston introduces a sympathetic representative of opposition views, Angus Barry, himself a son of Anglo-Ireland who served England well in the World War. But Angus now speaks and acts against British forces because he believes Britain denies Irish people their liberty. Conversations with this alternate father figure and with the surrogate mother, Aunt Mary, and reflections in her journal will finally lead Nancy to become an independent thinking person.

Although the slogans of war are always suspect in Johnston's work whether they are Mrs. Moore's "Dulce et Decorum est" or Mr. Logan's "A Nation Once Again," Angus Barry in *The Old Jest* and Mr. Keating in *The Christmas Tree* speak reasonably of the need to oppose those who suppress freedom. The suppression of a people's liberties is overtly connected here, as in Julia O'Faolain's work, with the suppression of individual liberty. Like their author for whom they might be spokesmen, these figures, though they engage in political violence, respect personal freedom of conscience in their associates. Angus questions Nancy's assertion that "it's the killing" she cannot tolerate in the Irish struggle against England. Nancy's own grandfather, the Crimean hero, he notes, was also a killer: "He wasn't even killing to defend his own fatherland, indeed the very opposite. He was taking other people's land away from them. Creating an empire." The Misses Brabazon also insist on equating the activity of the Irish guerrillas against England with that of England against Germany in World War I. Indeed Angus connects the violence of legal repression with the violence of war: "There are conscienceless men," he tells Nancy, "utterly unscrupulous, who will go to any lengths to make sure that the world remains the way they want it to remain. . . . They crush and destroy . . . aspirations." Similarly Mr. Keating in *The Christmas Tree* tells Constance that, though he is not an Englishman, his enlistment in 1939 "was a very personal decision . . . To defend, in my own small way, democracy. . . . There are many who would totally condemn it, but it was the one thing that gave us [Ireland], the freedom to remain neutral, gave me the freedom to choose."[16] The struggle must be judged on its own terms, then, not simply condemned because it entails death.

Nancy's intuitive resistance to change aligns her with the

"conscienceless men" whose real ends, Angus suggests, are masked by the veneer of established civilization. In the circumstances of war, Nancy's trust in the stranger she meets at the beach is surprising—a measure of her anxiety to find the missing father, to find her place in the political/literary or literary/political tradition. Angus, who has renounced the loyalties implicit in his own parentage, advises Nancy to "get on with the job of maturing, exploring, and expanding" her own "faculties." Background and parentage are of limited importance in this quest. But finding the father, Nancy suggests, will mean knowing who she is, will make the world "less . . . full of dark corners." Feeling as undirected as Bowen's Lois, the orphan Nancy imagines the father's recognition as the catalyst which would in some symbolic way call forth and authenticate her identity in a patriarchal world. And, as Lois was fearful of exploring her own femaleness so Nancy, too, is afraid of penetrating the surface of her world. "I've always hated caves," she tells Angus, remembering her childhood: "They all used to go rushing into any caves that might be around. Hurray, they'd shout, lovely, lovely caves! I couldn't bear it. I used to stay outside. I could hear them calling and laughing inside. I knew I was missing something, but I couldn't go in. They used to tease me when they came out. You sometimes find terrible things in caves."[17]

Central symbol of the feminine principle, the cave, Erich Neumann reports in his extensive study *The Great Mother*, functions both positively and negatively in the collective unconscious, both "shelters the unborn in the vessel of the body" and "takes back the dead into the vessel of death."[18] As symbol, the cave thus images the power of life and death that early humans associated with women and with the goddess they worshiped in different guises. The overthrow of the goddess and the repression of women by the disciples of the male gods is also implicit in the cave reference. Fearful of the gender mysteries suggested by the cave, Nancy would embrace the safe world of her class, the repetitive security of father, husband, home, and politics, the values that the Dwyer women with the exception of her mother have embraced for centuries.

But the civilized Yeatsian drawing room of the Dwyers is both source and product of national and domestic violence in *The Old*

Jest. Producing his gun to jolt Nancy into an awareness of the potential violence underlying the veneer, Angus warns: "Life isn't full of sweetness and light and gentlemen standing up when ladies come into the room. On the contrary, it's full of violence, injustice and pain. That's what you're afraid of seeing when you open those locked doors, peer into caves. The terrible truth." The cave, female repression, is the truth obscured by the artifice of the drawing room. That gender injustice is connected to, indeed may be indigenous to, the "violence, injustice and pain" of the national struggle. Virginia Woolf, too, identified the "inferior" woman/mirror in the drawing room as the essential male enlarger without which "the glories of all our wars would be unknown." Living exemplum of Angus's words, Nancy's aunt recognizes—too late for herself—that, clinging to the traditions passed on to her, she has never lived. Like Angus, she comes to believe that Nancy has cause to celebrate the sale of the Dwyer home, a sale which frees her to select her own role in a world that has begun increasingly to open its doors to women, the doors of the university and of economic and social independence.[19] Far from mourning the passing of this world, Jennifer Johnston, in the novel she wrote after the passing of her own particular world, celebrates the beginning of women's liberation that was released by the demise of the structured world of pre–World War I, the stratified world of Anglo-Ireland included.

For Nancy's is the first Johnston bildungsromane, the first Johnston text in which a female character is fully awakened to and consequently freed from the constraints of national and gender traditions. Shari Benstock, seeing Johnston's world of the "hunting games, chivalric and heraldic codes, puberty rites, and the law of primogeniture" as masculine, suggests that Nancy's story "is taken over by the events of *his* [Angus's] life and death" and becomes in fact a male bildungsroman. Since Angus dies, however, it may more appropriately be argued that his life and death is the text that partially leads Nancy to adulthood. The author sacrifices Angus's life—as Woolf did Septimus Smith's, as Bowen did Gerald Lesworth's—in the interest of her heroine's education. The activities in which Nancy engages—acting as messenger, covering-up to the police, attempting to help Angus escape—activities that Benstock sees as the paradigmatically male activities of war, are not ultimately the source of Nancy's awakening but its consequences. The awakening itself is engendered in the conversations with Angus and with Mary, conversations in which Nancy explores the limits to the world she has inherited and that she would—initially—preserve untouched.[20]

This awakening is also the result of the conscious process of analysis demanded by the writing of the journal. For although Nancy complains of her inadequacy on this account and although each new section begins with only a brief journal entry in first person, the remainder of the text is not set off physically from the journal and is rendered almost exclusively from Nancy's perspective. This structural innovation, similar to the form of Johnston's early work, *The Gates*, suggests that the entire text is a convenient representation of Nancy's journal, of Nancy's exploration of the boundaries of her life. In this exploration Nancy moves from obsession with the "bruised ghosts" in the dark corners to acceptance of her father's death and to "not minding" about her own "anomalous position." "It is hard," she observes, "to be young and not quite grasp what it is you are trying to understand, but exciting." Finally deciding to help Angus and to accept Harry and Maeve's engagement and the sale of the Big House, Nancy both exercises and enjoys her right "to choose," to determine her personal and national destiny. She is neither oblivious to nor, like Alexander, trapped by history.[21]

Nancy's development, then, follows the chronological steps and time sequences that theorists of bildungsromane have identified in works such as *Jane Eyre*. Subsequent Johnston heroines, however, follow the pattern of later development, the pattern Johnston associates with her own life and that identified by Elizabeth Abel as the dominant female mode.[22] Two recent novels, *The Christmas Tree* and *The Railway Station Man*, move away from the reexamination of the historical past but still reach back into this past, rather as O'Faolain reaches into the bog, with intertextual echoings and formal variations. Still struggling with ghosts, these texts suggest that history must always be reevaluated, but they also begin exploration of the different possibilities, the alternate life-styles, open to women.

Forty-five years old when we meet her, the mother of a nine-month-old baby, Constance Keating of *The Christmas Tree* is dying of leukemia and writing her own story. Formally, then, Constance seems to be in the same position as Alexander Moore, circling back from the confinement her story has led to but ending where she begins—in her father's house. Like Alexander again or like Molly Keane's Aroon, Constance attempts "to make a little sense out of" her past.[23] Born in the Republic of Ireland in the 1930s, Constance is, of course, scarred by history but removed in time and space from violent upheavals. Moving frequently between the narrative written in first person, usually in the present tense, and memories in the third person, Constance's text swings back and forth through loose associations, forcing the reader to adjust without introduction to new settings and new characters, much as Constance herself must adjust to the frequent changes wrought by her dreams and drug-induced hallucinations. Like Alexander's, then, Constance's text structurally models her situation. But there is an important concluding difference to which we shall return.

In Constance, Johnston's figure of the artist develops significantly, both as narrative device and as reflection of an alternative writing role. This figure, as suggested earlier, has a problematic history in Irish art. Yeats, for example, believed that Irish fiction was public and centered on the ancient Gaelic tradition of the storyteller, exemplified, as Thomas Kilroy notes, in the fiction of the editor's transcribing Thady's "unvarnished tale" in *Castle Rackrent*. But this public form of art, Denis Donoghue points out, is antithetical to the private art of novelists. This may be the reason that many Irish writers embrace the Parnell image; the solitary figure, which F.S.L. Lyons sees as messianic, allows them to incorporate the dichotomy by delivering the essentially private word publicly, resigned to the knowledge of ultimate rejection. In some instances, Lyons notes of Yeats and Joyce, this image "allowed them to use him [Parnell] as an ideal against which the meanness and inadequacy of the society that rejected him and *them* could be measured." This transference, of course, leads to what Deane has called the "glamorization of the artist," which "frees him from the responsibility of actually *seeing* the middle classes."[24]

Considering the artist figure in the Johnston novels preceding *The Old Jest*, Shari Benstock asserts that the impulse to tell stories in Johnston's work is not social. Indeed she sees the "metaphor of trench warfare" in many of the texts as representing the furthest reaches of artistic alienation, suggesting a pessimistic conclusion "about the survival of human beings in general and of the literary artist in particular." Johnston's fiction has been, of course, that of private stories up to this point. Minnie of *The Gates* wrote a journal, as did Nancy in *The Old Jest*. Mr. Prendergast's story is told in traditional third person, but it is framed by the activities of the police who set out for his house in the introduction and arrive there at the conclusion. Joe's story in *Shadows on Our Skin* is also told in third person, and Alexander Moore in *How Many Miles to Babylon?* writes his story only, we understand, to "kill" time, for he concludes, "They will never understand. So I say nothing." The pretext then is private, though the framing and changing points of view seem to emphasize the artificial, structured nature of the texts. But Constance, the would-be writer whom publishers rejected, insists that she writes her story for publication, writes it despite the pain that cripples her fingers. She asks her friend Bill to deliver it to publishers, and finally she has Bridie, the young Gaelic-Irish orphan who comes to help her, write the last pages and deliver the manuscript safely to Bill. Constance then is, unlike the Parnell image, a social writer, one who, like Johnston herself, believes in a community somewhere that can respond to her words, as she has assured Jacob Weinberg that someone may respond to his.[25]

To return to the important difference in the structuring of Constance's and Alexander's texts: in entrusting Bridie to complete the story she has begun and to oversee its safe delivery, Constance has ensured that the manuscript cannot follow only the limited structure of her life, as did Alexander's. The structure, however, does mirror the plot of the completed novel, *The Christmas Tree*, the composite work of the Anglo-Irish Constance and the Gaelic-Irish Bridie—a duet, then, rather than an individual, private effort. This is important, since Johnston's texts constantly reflect, refract, restate, and reinterpret the literature, songs, folktales, and folkwisdom of her ancestors, of her culture. "Masterpieces," Virginia Woolf wrote, "are not single and solitary births; they are the outcome of many years of think-

ing in common, of thinking by the body of the people, so that
the experience of the mass is behind the single voice."[26] All of
Johnston's work pays tribute to the many years of common thinking; *The Christmas Tree* in particular pays tribute to the ability
of women to both think and mother in common.

The structure of *The Christmas Tree* reflects both the pattern
of the novel and the alternative, composite pattern of mothering
which Constance embraces. The orphan Bridie leaves Ireland
with Jacob to mother the child of the dead Constance. Indeed
Constance's pursuits of both a writing and a mothering career
show significant resemblances: as a young woman, in much the
position of Nancy at the end of *The Old Jest*, Constance initially
refuses secure marriage with a man she respects. She then has
to fight the inertia of tradition to win the right to live her own
life as an apprentice writer in England, a fight which receives
the emotional but not the financial support of her father. At age
forty-four, Constance exercises what she believes is again her
right: promising nothing, she engages in a brief relationship with
Jacob Weinberg, refuses to remain with him, and does not inform
him of her pregnancy. When she discovers her leukemia, however, Constance does notify Jacob, assuring him at the same time
that the baby will be emotionally and financially secure should
he not wish to claim her.[27]

As she was responsible for her own life and work as a writer,
so Constance, a positive, assertive woman, also embraces independent, responsible motherhood. Actually, of course, Constance has already linked parenting and authoring. In the
quotation used as epigraph to this chapter, she comforts Jacob
on his lack of descendants: "Perhaps in a hundred years' time
someone . . . somewhere someone may read one of your books
and say then . . . say once there was this Jewish, Polish, British
man called Jacob Weinberg and today he has become a part of
me. Today I am different . . . extended."[28] Bridie's completion
of Constance's text and the new family group of Jewish, Polish,
English, and Irish heritage, extend the work outward in time
and space, moving it far from the limited boundaries that confined Alexander's story. Further, Constance's suggestion on the
value of Jacob's books can be read as Johnston's tribute to the
books that changed her, to all the mothers and fathers she has

read back through, and as the self-reflexive gesture of the social
artist who finds her values in art.

Framed by the first-person memory of the death of Helen's
husband on one side and the first-person memory of the deaths
of her lover and son on the other, the intervening text in *The
Railway Station Man* enacts the same old patterns of war and
marriage, only the emphasis differs. Like the heroines of early
twentieth-century fiction, Helen Cuffe lived through marriage
and motherhood without achieving any significant personal development. When her husband is shot by the Irish Republican
Army in Derry, a victim of mistaken identity, Helen experiences
"an amazing feeling of relief, liberation." Moving from both the
city and the house she had shared with her husband and son to
a small, nameless cottage in the village of Knappogue in Donegal,
Helen, reversing Constance's pattern of career first and motherhood second, begins to paint. When her son Jack becomes involved in the apparently endless circle of war, Helen does not
attempt to force or dissuade him. She is reminded by her sensitive English lover, Roger Hawthorne, that he too had engaged
in this activity. Indeed he remains physically and mentally
scarred from his experiences at Arnhem.[29] Although Roger
qualifies his comfort by admitting that he, unlike Jack, had no
choice, the reader remains shocked by the implied acceptance.

The compulsion to war is again connected with the compulsion
to marriage—almost as if the two were primitive forces emerging from the depths of the racial unconscious, forces which rational people must constantly question. However accidental and
ironic, the violence of war approaches Helen only through the
men in her life—her husband, son, and lover—a fact she seems
to understand as she paints the male figure out of her work.
Entitling her four paintings "Man on the beach, 1, 2, 3, and 4,"
Helen has painted a figure on the beach in the first, in the sea
in the second, swimming in the third. In number four, only the
discarded clothes remain on the beach—the sea and sky are
empty. Associating the painted swimmer with the figure of her
husband, we can link the irrational, insensate force of nature that
sweeps the swimmer out of the canvas with the accidental and
also irrational force that killed the husband, that will kill Roger.
On viewing the finished paintings, Roger tells Helen that she is

a remarkable woman, "to have held all that inside you for so long, without driving yourself into some state of insanity."[30] The hell of war drove Roger into mental hospitals, but unexpectedly liberated from the hell of her dreary marriage, Helen treats herself through her paintings, the depiction of her accidental release and of the cast-off clothes—or habits—that she abandoned on moving to Donegal.

But Roger is not so easily painted out. Love comes when Helen least wishes it, when she faces, she believes, her last chance to express her individual vision. But Roger, despite his awareness of Helen's response to her first marriage, automatically aligns love with traditional marriage. Indeed the terms he uses to propose marriage suggest that the institution, so much more attractive to the later Johnston men than to the women, still carries traditional negative connotations of possession and control:

"I don't want to take anything away from you. I only want to *give* you whatever you want. Everything."

"I only want one thing, you know."

"I know what you're going to say . . . freedom. . . . I'll give you freedom."

"I don't want you to give me anything. I want my own space. I don't want anyone to give me anything. All that kindness, all that giving that you talk about, offer me, it could be like a prison" [my italics].[31]

The notion that freedom is something a man can give a woman in marriage is the logical result of centuries of acculturation based on primitive kinship structures. The real goal of these structures, as Claude Levi-Strauss has shown, was the extension of male bonding systems. Ironically, Levi-Strauss sees the kinship patterns as a generally successful attempt to curtail the compulsive violence of war, yet he fails to recognize the centuries of female repression begotten in them.[32] Johnston's text on the other hand, recognizing the patterns, suggests that women, if they are to live at all, must live in the interstices of violence, which sometimes translate into the interstices between marriages.

The structure in Johnston's work—in particular, the echoes, the frames, and the double-voiced narratives—like that in Mary

Lavin's work, deserves comment because it so clearly serves a thematic function. Echoes, as the earlier discussion implies, shadow all Johnston's work—echoes of poetry, rhymes, novels, music. Even the titles reveal debts—*The Captains and the Kings, How Many Miles to Babylon?, Shadows on Our Skin, The Old Jest.* Kipling, Turgenev, and the nursery rhyme are familiar; "Shadows" is from a song by an Irish band, Horslips. At one level, Johnston uses the echoes to evoke characteristic mental states and preoccupations: Helen, for example, in *The Railway Station Man* shouts the opening lines of Shelley's ode "To a Skylark" at the bird that sings so "unperturbed" as her world begins to shatter. Besides the obvious situational irony, the echo also reveals a mind responsive to Shelley's music. Not one to collect or catalog, however, Helen is unable to remember more than the first few lines and confuses the poem with Keats's "Ode to a Nightingale."[33]

On another level, the recurrence of old songs, stories, and poems highlights the recurrence of behavior, the often unconscious repetition in the one instance suggesting a similar unconsciousness in the repetition of actions. And finally, these overt echoes in calling attention to themselves also call attention to the debt the writer—and of course all readers—owe to the past. Johnston is not, as was Alexander Moore, rendered mute, powerless, by the anxiety of influence. Rather, reading back through her mothers and her fathers enables her and not only permits "another world to radiate into the self-contained world of the novel" but also colors that past world with the world of the novel. The "harmonious madness" that Roger dislikes in Shelley becomes shadowed by the discordant madness of Arnhem, and Helen's apostrophe to the "blithe spirit" is colored in turn by this altered Shelley.[34] The layers in the bog recur. In the Irish context, the echoes reveal our heritage—we Irish are both Anglo and Gaelic. We are shaped, colored, and composed by English and Irish linguistic and cultural parents. Diving into the wreck of our past, we find the doubleness Adrienne Rich discovered. To paraphrase, we are us: we are them. We cannot begin anew. We cannot even fictionalize or verbalize such a condition.

The other overt elements, frames and double-voiced narratives, are closely related to the echoes. Changing from first to

third person liberates, as suggested already, the narrator to comment on her own reactions; more important, it introduces another perspective, another voice. Negating any authorial
definitiveness, this qualifying second voice by its presence implies the potential existence of others. The heteroglossia, or
many voices, that Bakhtin sees as inherent in the modern novel
thus erupt structurally and thematically in Johnston's texts.
The double-voiced narrator and the echoes suggest the constant
need to place one text, one view, one voice, beside another.[35]
But failure always threatens: there are too many texts, views,
voices. The frame that seems to cut the text away, out from the
bog of potentially conflicting voices, also draws attention to its
own action, to its arbitrariness, and hence undermines its apparent authority. The prison cell that confines Alexander Moore
also confines a partial, thus distorted, perspective of the older
Moores, Jerry Crowe, and the British major.

   The Christmas Tree seems to offer the most positive vision
of Anglo- and Gaelic-Irish cooperation. The young orphan Bridie
fulfills her promise to the dead Constance, records the last few
hours of the dying woman's life, and saves her text from the
potentially destructive hands of her family. The orphan figure,
usually a young Anglo-Irish woman who represents the Anglo-
Irish situation, is now a young Gaelic-Irish woman. This fact may
suggest the author's perception of the similarities in the experiences of Anglo- and Gaelic-Irish women. It may also suggest
the orphaned situation of women in contemporary Ireland. Bridie's voice at the end of Constance's text is tentative. Constance
has asked that she record "everything" but has warned against
"flights of fancy." As readers, we believe that Bridie honestly attempts to meet her commitment: "These last few pages are written by me Bridie May, beginning on Christmas Eve 1978. I
haven't made anything up, nor have I left anything out . . . at
least I don't think I have." This then is the best human beings
can do: present a plurality of tentative perceptions. Bridie's
words recall for us Alexander's presentiment and warn us about
the doubly unreliable basis of all texts, grounded on "possibly
inaccurate memories" and clothed in inaccurate language. As she
watches Doctor Bill, the man whose proposal Constance rejected
some twenty years previously, hesitate outside the dying wom-

an's door, Bridie notes: "I wondered if there had ever been anything between them. Anything romantic." Catching herself, however, she amends, "But she wouldn't like me to be writing that."[36] The double-voice, then, allows Johnston to present not only an optimistic tableau of Gaelic- and Anglo-Irish cooperation, it also allows her to depict in a quiet and compelling fashion the difficulties in rendering another's story. As in Somerville and Ross's *The Real Charlotte*, perception does not act as an accurate divining rod but as a mist or veil that obscures or distorts the other.

Even the optimistic reverberations are undercut. The text achieves its harmony, its union of Anglo- and Gaelic-Irish perspectives, only through Constance's death. This fact parallels the tragic pattern of too-late acceptances throughout Irish history, parallels, too, many of Johnston's other texts. The Anglo-Irish man Alexander Moore and the Gaelic-Irish man Jerry Crow must die to preserve their friendship. Angus Barry's death is the lens through which Nancy Gulliver perceives the priorities of the colonizer. "You poor bloody old sod," Guard Deveney murmurs, extending his sympathy too late to the dead Charles Prendergast.[37] An expression of the natural idiom of Ireland, the words also reflect sadly and ironically on the country itself and on the whole history of waste and mistrust. Poor bloody old sod, indeed.

10. Irish Women Writers
The Experience of the Mass

> For masterpieces are not single and solitary births; they are
> the outcome of many years of thinking in common, of think-
> ing by the body of the people, so that the experience of the
> mass is behind the single voice.
> —Virginia Woolf, *A Room of One's Own*

FINALLY, THEN, from the vantage point of the most recent text,
Jennifer Johnston's *The Railway Station Man*, we look back to
ask what constitutes a tradition. Several times during this study
I referred to the tradition of *aislingi* poetry, poems written by
Gaelic-Irish poets during the years of suppression. The subject
of these poems was the pitiful state of Ireland, wronged by England, and the commitment of Gaelic-Irish people to again achieve
independence. The distribution of these poems was possible only
because the poets disguised their subject by envisioning Ireland
as a young maiden coerced by a strong warrior. In this instance,
then, similarity in subject matter and technique constitutes tradition. We cannot expect to find such unanimity of subjects and
techniques in our exploration of Irish women writers; the time
span is too great, and the political and cultural backgrounds vary
too much. We must, however, discover some similarities to claim
a tradition.

The most frequently recurring theme in the women's writing
we have examined seems to be the link between domestic and
political violence. The Rackrent men in Maria Edgeworth's *Castle Rackrent* are equally appalling as husbands and as landlords.
E.OE. Somerville and Martin Ross present an unappealing and
amoral character in *The Real Charlotte*, but depict her nevertheless as a victim of an unjust society. The Eden of Anglo-Ireland, as Elizabeth Bowen presents it in *The Last September*,
depends upon Anglo-Irish women and the Gaelic-Irish population

accepting without question the word of domestic or colonizing fathers. The security of the Gaelic-Irish society in Kate O'Brien's *Without My Cloak* also rests upon the sacrifice of women, as does the independent state posited in *The Land of Spices*. The Gaelic-Irish warriors of 1922 and 1979 are both equally willing to exploit women in Julia O'Faolain's *No Country for Young Men*. And domestic repression reflects national repression in almost all Jennifer Johnston's work, most overtly in *Shadows on Our Skin*.

The traditional representation of the assertive woman as destructive, discussed in chapter 1, appears in some of the texts, but the move is definitely toward an independent rather than passive heroine. Only self-assertion, for example, saves Maria Edgeworth's Jessica. Somerville and Ross see Pamela Dysart's passivity as personally annihilating, and Elizabeth Bowen warns against a similar acquiescence in *The Last September*. Were Anna Murphy not to speak for herself in *Land of Spices*, she would have no future. Mary Lavin's positive characters know and act on what is right for themselves. Aroon is both aggressive and negative in *Good Behaviour*, but the only possibilities presented by her society are repression or manipulation. Female passivity or acquiescence effectively erases women in *No Country for Young Men*. Charles Prendergast's mother in *The Captains and the Kings* and Mrs. Moore in *How Many Miles to Babylon?* are examples of the tradition of destructive assertive women, but women in later Johnston texts prove their maturity and integrity by reaching and acting upon personal decisions.

Re-visioning in Irish women writers functions thematically and technically. Elizabeth Bowen's use of *Paradise Lost*, for example, and Julia O'Faolain's use of the Cuchulain and Diarmuid and Grainne myths reveal the repression of women entailed in both the Milton version of the Judeo-Christian myth and the Celtic myths. But the myths are not totally discarded: their presence enriches and complicates the texts. Maria Edgeworth's re-vision of Shakespeare and Julia O'Faolain's of Irish history reveal the negation of women's autonomy central to the dramatic and historical perspectives. Again, the presence of the dramatic or historical dimension adds a poetic and allusive quality to each woman's work.

Re-vision of genre also suggests thematic as well as technical goals. Maria Edgeworth's reversal of the traditional romance pattern, for example, implies both a critique of literary form and a belief that women's lives are not contained/completed by marriage. The re-working of bildungsroman form is the most pervasive genre play: Elizabeth Bowen's Lois, Kate O'Brien's Anna, Molly Keane's Aroon, and Jennifer Johnston's Nancy do not attain maturity through fulfilling sexual relationships. Indeed Lois, Aroon, and Nancy must banish traditional romantic expectations before they can free and develop themselves. Perhaps even more dramatic is the late development Jennifer Johnston depicts for her most recent heroines, Constance and Helen, a development that replays that of Mary Lavin's widows. If we see Constance, Helen, and the Lavin widows as experiencing the anguish of adolescents, we understand something of the position of many contemporary middle-aged women. For, as the statistics on divorce, late mothering, single parenting, and women's assumption of new careers show, these patterns are also those of many contemporary women.

Mutual thematic interests do not, of course, necessitate actual sympathy between Anglo- and Gaelic-Irish women. In fact *The Real Charlotte*, as I suggest in chapter 3, reveals the authors' aversion to both the slum-poor and the middle class of Gaelic-Ireland. But the mutual thematic interests do attest to the common ground Irish women occupied, excluded alike in Anglo-Irish and Gaelic-Irish cultures. Neither do these mutual interests lead necessarily to the most rewarding areas of the texts. Chapters on the individual writers have attempted to point to the richness, originality, and humor of their work; this chapter merely summarizes the components of the tradition.

Differences in preferred or optimistic conclusions exist, however, from one writer to the next. These may reflect basic differences in outlook, in the writers' perceptions of the role of the individual in the community. Maturity for Johnston's heroines seems to entail the independence of living alone—Nancy gives up her dream of marrying Harry; Constance and Helen refuse to live with their lovers. Similarly, Maria Edgeworth, in the one text she wrote to entertain rather than instruct in acceptable behavior, releases her female characters from marriage. Although Charlotte desires to marry Roddy in *The Real Charlotte*, marriage is presented throughout the text not as source of companionship and love but as solitary confinement. Elizabeth Bowen's Lois, having attained some level of maturity, wishes to cultivate her own talents, not to marry. Aroon St. Charles expresses her desire to be married, but her text suggests that this traditional wish masks her real desire for economic independence.

Turning from Anglo-Irish writers of Protestant descent to Gaelic-Irish writers of Catholic heritage, we find that Kate O'Brien pictures women as largely restricted in marriage. The beautiful, nurturing Molly in *Without My Cloak* is rewarded by the love and attention of her family, but Molly dies—fictionally she has nowhere to go. Anna, however, child of a later period, realizes that she must "spin" her future from her own intelligence and efforts, not from marriage. Mary Lavin, on the other hand, seems to value communion over independence. Failure in Lavin is failure to love, and love is always worth the price: the envious, grudging Bedelia in "Frail Vessel" taunts her pregnant sister Liddy that she'll never see her husband/lover again: "I think you've seen the last of him—do you hear me—the last of him."[1] But the text celebrates:

But she couldn't make out whether Liddy had heard or not. Certainly, her reply, when it came in a whisper, was absolutely inexplicable.
    "Even so!" Liddy whispered. "Even so."[2]

In Julia O'Faolain's work, positive conclusions also entail a recognition of the richness in deeply flawed human relationships: Grainne's ties to the alcoholic Michael cannot be easily broken; Carla returns to her chauvinistic husband, her ties to him more valuable than those to her lover. Una in "Man in the Cellar," aware of the strength of the emotional bond, must put her own life in danger, were she to remain with husband, as insurance that she will leave her abusive partner.[3]

A comparison of two scenes in which O'Faolain's and Johnston's heroines respectively refuse to live with their lovers reveals differences in authorial perspectives. At the end of *The Obedient Wife*, Carla prepares to leave her lover Leo and return to her husband. She explains to Leo that he never really needed her; had he done so, he would have "been less forbearing" and would have pressured her for a commitment. Yes, she knows he was "being sensitive," but she continues: "I've been waiting, staying very quiet like an animal on the watch, for you to get . close to me, to show yourself a bit—and you never did. You probably can't. You can't help it. You're invulnerable, strong, fenced in. You believing Christians have an enormous ego, massive pride. I imagine it comes from the notion that your first duty is to save your own soul—that's breathtaking egoism, after all, and yet you learn it as a duty, a maxim and foundation-stone to your moral system." Carla asserts that "a flowing together takes place . . . in fighting and mutual wounding." She says, "It's not just rational. It's more intimate, almost tangible." In Johnston's *The Railway Station Man*, on the other hand, Helen values the independence Carla rejects. Aware of the misery of Helen's first marriage, Roger attempts to justify his marriage proposal: "I only thought that perhaps we could push a bit of loneliness away. Yours as well as mine." But Helen replies, "Marriage isn't a cure for loneliness anyway. Sometimes it makes it more painful. I suppose some sort of close relationship with God is the only real answer to that."[4] Helen rejects the human relationship Carla seeks; Helen admires the spiritual independence Carla rejects.

Helen and Carla might be exempla of the Protestant and Catholic perspectives David Bakan identifies in *The Duality of Human Existence*. Bakan's theories were discussed briefly in chapter 1; now we will apply them to Johnston's and O'Faolain's texts. The reader should refer to the fine distinctions Bakan draws; I generalize in the interest of space, ignoring both Bakan's distinctions and the vast differences that always exist within any formal group. Helen acts in accordance with Bakan's agentic, Carla rejects it. The agentic, we remember, entails "the existence of an organism as an individual, and communion . . . the participation of the individual in some larger organism of which the individual is a part." Within Protestantism, Bakan notes, following Weber: "Each person is on his own with respect to grace. The major business of life is a private affair between each person and God. This is associated with a considerable alienation of each individual from other persons, including the members of his family. His relationships with other people are not *gemutlich*, and in place of sociability he substitutes formal social organization."[5] Though neither Helen nor Carla is overtly religious, both act in accordance with the tenets of their traditional religions as identified by Bakan; Helen espouses the idea of the individual alone with her God, and Carla embraces the idea of human communion. Ironically, while she acts in the mode Bakan identifies as Catholic, Carla accuses the Catholic priest of acting in the mode identified as Protestant.

In discussing her childhood, Johnston herself suggests that the physical aspects of the two churches correspond in some ways with Bakan's identifications. The atmosphere of the Church of Ireland she remembers as being "antiseptic" and empty, the clatter of her feet on the metal grilles making her feel "terribly alone and confronted with God, whereas the Catholic church was warm and embracing and I loved that."[6]

Nancy Chodorow, as noted in chapter 1, uses Bakan's concepts of individuality and communion to characterize the difference in the early training of boys and girls. Edgeworth, Somerville and Ross, Bowen, Keane, and Johnston would have been exposed to Protestant perspectives of individuality from the religious affiliations of their families. The perspective would persist, of course, whether or not individual members were churchgoers. In addition, I suggest that the childhood training of girl children in the relatively wealthy group of Anglo-Irish Protestants was closer to that Chodorow characterizes as male than was the training of girl children in the Gaelic-Irish Catholic homes. Early closeness to the mother and to female relatives forms, Chodorow believes, the communion pattern, the blending of ego boundaries between female children and their mothers. But girl children of the ascendancy were, like their brothers, generally cared for by a nurse and later by a governess in a nursery at some distance from the adult regions. Although differences would have existed (Hubert in *Good Behaviour*, for example, has more early freedom than has his sister Aroon), the big differences—the boy going away to school while the girl remained at home—would generally have occurred after the time of personality formation. And, of course, neither the female nor the male children had the opportunity to identify with their mothers in the manner Chodorow describes, though we might perhaps see the female child as identifying more with the female nurse or governess than the boy did.

The texts of the Anglo-Irish women examined do tend to support, in their preferred resolutions, Bakan's and Chodorow's theories of differences, as do the texts of the Gaelic-Irish Kate O'Brien. If we, aware of the generalizing danger in so doing, view the resolution as evidence of the writer's perspective, then O'Brien's texts, which, like the Anglo-Irish writers', assert the individual's duty, would suggest that the home rather than religious orientation is of primary influence on personality. Though reared as a Catholic, hence a recipient of the ideals of communion, O'Brien was not raised by her mother, who died while she was a child.[7] Lavin and O'Faolain, on the other hand, growing up in Catholic traditions with mothers as primary care-givers, celebrate the virtues of communion identified as Catholic by Bakan, as female by Chodorow.

When asked about traditions, Jennifer Johnston notes that she does not see her writing nor that of Julia O'Faolain, whom she admires, as part of an Irish female tradition, yet she does 'see Irish writing as distinct from English. She suggests that the root knowledge within Irish people of both a double grammatical and a double cultural mode enriches and energizes their work, allowing their Irish readers to respond, as outsiders cannot, to the always-present undertones and qualifications of the second culture. But women's work in the past was, Johnston says, too scarce and too constrained to serve as a model.[8]

Perhaps contemporary Irish women writers do not consciously look to their predecessors, but they have nevertheless imbibed the fruits of their mothers' labor. The influence I see is most often a matter of unconscious heritage, similar to the awareness Johnston sees in Irish writers and readers of the double culture, or the dialectic of the muted voices. Because women's experiences in childhood and in marriage are remarkably similar across racial, religious, and class lines, and because women, like colonized peoples, have had to repress their desires, women's fiction has been subject to the same kinds of repressions as women themselves, repressions which forced early writers to encode their concerns in a muted voice. Just as Irish readers of both sexes incorporate and respond to messages of the double culture, so women respond to this repression by creating a level of feminine discourse that encodes comments, jokes, and criticisms—implicit or explicit—about their own condition. Indeed, this discourse may have been so widely practiced that it seemed instinctive.

On another level, of course, Jennifer Johnston is absolutely correct in insisting that she and Julia O'Faolain are engaged in pioneering novel work, are "beginning a tradition."[9] The woman's plot, however subversive or ironic, was in early texts always the muted second voice of discourse; whereas, in contemporary women's work, the woman's plot is enacted at dominant as well as subordinate and subtextual levels. Not that these writers begin to write propaganda. The reader of both Johnston's latest work and O'Faolain's is pervaded by a deep sense of regret at the demise of an institution that despite its injustices is often seen as a source of human warmth and communion in the face of a hostile world. Given Johnston's emphasis on her dual heritage of English and Irish literature, we should not expect her to reject an institution that has served well a great portion, albeit a gender-imbalanced portion, of human beings. What we might see in the writings of contemporary Irish women is an appropriate and natural reversal, a discourse in which the traditional plot—the war and marriage—has itself become the muted or marginal voice, has figuratively become Freud's woman in a corner. As the dialogue focuses more securely and more emphatically on women, on their choices, roles, and relationships not as these relate to men only but as they relate to the world, the literature of Anglo- and Gaelic-Irish women presents a unified tradition of subjects and techniques, a unity that might become an optimistic model not only for Irish literature but also for Irish people.

Notes

1. Seeking a Tradition

1. William Butler Yeats, *Cathleen Ni Houlihan* (1902; reprinted in *The Collected Plays of W.B. Yeats* [New York: Macmillan, 1953]), 53.

2. Nuala O'Faolain, "Irish Women and Writing in Modern Ireland," in *Irish Women: Image and Achievement*, ed. Eilean Ni Chuilleanain (Dublin: Arlen House, 1985), 129.

3. See, for example, Eilean Ni Chuilleanain, "Women as Writers: Danta Gra to Maria Edgeworth," in *Irish Women*, ed. Ni Chuilleanain, 111-26. This brief study differs from my own in analyzing female figures in love poems, in a famous lament, and in several of Edgeworth's novels.

4. Virginia Woolf, *A Room of One's Own* (1929; New York, Harcourt, Brace and World, 1957), 77.

5. Frank O'Connor, "The Girl at the Gaol Gate," in *The Lonely Voice: A Study of the Short Story* (Cleveland: World Publishing Co., 1963), 202, 204.

6. M.H. Abrams, gen. ed., *The Norton Anthology of English Literature*, 4th ed. (New York: Norton, 1979) included Mary Shelley; the fifth edition includes more women writers; and Sandra M. Gilbert and Susan Gubar, eds., *The Norton Anthology of Literature by Women* (New York: Norton, 1985) attempts to compensate for the long absence of women's work in the Norton anthologies. Susan Hardy Aiken, "Women and the Question of Canonicity," *College English* 48 (1986): 290.

7. Robert Hogan, "Old Boys, Young Bucks, and New Women: The Contemporary Irish Short Story," in *The Irish Short Story*, ed. James F. Kilroy (Boston: Twayne, 1984), 202; Ellen Moers, *Literary Women* (Garden City, N.Y.: Doubleday, 1976); Elaine Showalter, *A Literature of Their Own: British Women Novelists from Brontë to Lessing* (Princeton, N.J.: Princeton Univ. Press, 1977); Nina Baym, *Woman's Fiction: A Guide to Novels by and about Women in America, 1820-1970* (Ithaca, N.Y.: Cornell Univ. Press, 1978); and Sandra M. Gilbert and Susan Gubar, *The Madwoman in the Attic: The Woman Writer and*

the Nineteenth-Century Literary Imagination (New Haven, Conn.: Yale Univ. Press, 1979).

8. Sigmund Freud, "Female Sexuality," in *The Standard Edition of the Complete Psychological Works of Sigmund Freud*, ed. and trans. James Strachey in collaboration with Anna Freud, vol. 21 (1931; reprint, London: Hogarth Press, 1975), 225-43; Claude Levi-Strauss, *The Elementary Structures of Kinship*, rev. ed., trans. James Harle Bell, John Richard von Sturmer, and Rodney Needham, ed. (1949; reprint, Boston: Beacon Press, 1969).

9. Gayle Rubin, "The Traffic in Women: Notes on the 'Political Economy' of Sex," in *Toward an Anthropology of Women*, ed. Rayna R. Reiter (New York: Monthly Review Press, 1975), 157-210; Sherry B. Ortner, "Is Female to Male as Nature Is to Culture?" in *Women, Culture, and Society*, ed. Michelle Zimbalist Rosaldo and Louise Lamphere (Stanford, Calif. Stanford Univ. Press, 1974), 67-87.

10. Margaret Mead, *Male and Female* (New York: William Morrow, 1949).

11. See, for example, Nancy Chodorow's "Family Structure and Feminine Personality," in *Women, Culture, and Society*, ed. Rosaldo and Lamphere, 43-66, and *The Reproduction of Mothering* (Berkeley: Univ. of California Press, 1978); Dorothy Dinnerstein, *The Mermaid and the Minotaur: Sexual Arrangements and Human Malaise* (New York: Harper and Row, 1977); and Carol Gilligan, "In a Different Voice: Women's Conceptions of Self and of Morality," *Harvard Educational Review* 47 (1977): 481-517. Chodorow, "Family Structure," 44, 45.

12. Chodorow, "Family Structure," 53.

13. Ibid., 43-58; David Bakan, *The Duality of Human Existence* (Chicago, Ill.: Univ. of Chicago Press, 1966), 15.

14. Chodorow, "Family Structure," 43-58; Carol Gilligan, "Woman's Place in Man's Life Cycle," *Harvard Educational Review* 49 (1979): 431-46; Chodorow, "Family Structure," 58.

15. Michelle Zimbalist Rosaldo, "Woman, Culture, and Society: A Theoretical Overview," in *Women, Culture, and Society*, ed. Rosaldo and Lamphere, 19.

16. Gilbert and Gubar, *Madwoman*, 3-44; Harold Bloom, *The Anxiety of Influence: A Theory of Poetry* (New York: Oxford Univ. Press, 1973); Gilbert and Gubar, *Madwoman*, 45-92; Edward Said, *The World, the Text, and the Critic* (Cambridge, Mass. Harvard Univ. Press, 1983), 46; Edward Said, *Beginnings: Intention and Method* (New York: Basic Books, 1975), 172; Roland Barthes, *The Pleasure of the Text*, trans. Richard Miller (New York: Hill and Wang, 1975), 10; and M.M. Bakhtin,

The Dialogic Imagination, ed. Michael Holquist, trans. Caryl Emerson and Michael Holquist (Austin: Univ. of Texas Press, 1981).

17. Woolf, *Room*, 8; Elaine Showalter, "Women and the Literary Curriculum," *College English* 32 (May 1971): 855.

18. *Critical Inquiry* 10 (Sept. 1983); Christine Froula, "When Eve Reads Milton: Undoing the Canonical Economy," *Critical Inquiry* 10 (Dec. 1983): 321-47.

19. Aiken, "Question of Canonicity," 298; Showalter, "Literary Curriculum," 859; Nancy Miller, "Arachnologies: The Woman, the Text, and the Critic," in *The Poetics of Gender*, ed. Nancy Miller (New York: Columbia Univ. Press, 1986), 274; Siobhan Kilfeather, "Beyond the Pale: Sexual Identity and National Identity in Early Irish Fiction," *Critical Matrix* 2 (1986), no. 4: 1-31.

20. Edmund Curtis, *A History of Ireland* (1936; reprint, London: Methuen, 1970), especially chaps. 17 and 18.

21. Denis Donoghue, "One-Way Communication," in *Image and Illusion in Anglo-Irish Literature and Its Contexts: A Festscrift for Roger McHugh*, ed. Maurice Harmon (Dublin: Wolfhound Press, 1979), 131.

22. Ibid., 136; James Joyce, *A Portrait of the Artist as a Young Man* (1916; reprint, Middlesex: Penguin, 1983), 188.

23. See Katharine Simms, "Women in Norman Ireland," in *Women in Irish Society: The Historical Dimension*, ed. Margaret MacCurtain and Donncha O Corrain. (Westport, Conn: Greenwood Press, 1979), 14-25, esp. 18.

24. J.J. Lee, "Women and the Church since the Famine," in *Women in Irish Society*, ed. MacCurtain and O Corrain, 37; Gearoid O Tuathaigh, "The Role of Women in Ireland under the New English Order," in ibid., 26.

25. Lee, "Women and the Church," 43; Curtis, *History of Ireland*, 373-74.

26. Curtis, *History of Ireland*, 373-74; Lee, "Women and the Church," 38.

27. Seamus Heaney, "Act of Union," in *Selected Poems 1965-1975* (London: Faber and Faber, 1980), 125-26.

28. *The Mentor Book of Irish Poetry* (New York: New American Library, 1965), 269-71, 401-2; Joyce, *Portrait of the Artist*, 203; Robert Hogan, ed., *Dictionary of Irish Literature* (Westport, Conn: Greenwood Press, 1979), 45-46; Patrick Pearse, "The Rebel," *Mentor Book of Irish Poetry*, 319-20.

29. The proclamation has been widely reprinted. See Ruth Dudley Edwards, *Patrick Pearse: The Triumph of Failure* (1977; reprint, London: Faber and Faber, 1979), 279-81.

30. Mary Wollstonecraft, *A Vindication of the Rights of Woman*, ed. with an introduction by Miriam Brody Kramnick (Middlesex: Penguin Books, 1975), 197; John Stuart Mill, "The Subjection of Women," in *Essays on Sex Equality*, ed. Alice S. Rossi (Chicago, Ill.: Univ. of Chicago Press, 1970), 154-58; Wollstonecraft, *Vindication*, 100-108; Mill, "Subjection of Women," 150-53.

31. Elizabeth Janeway, *Powers of the Weak* (New York: Knopf, 1980), 5, 172; Louise Lamphere, "Strategies, Cooperation, and Conflict among Women in Domestic Groups," in *Women, Culture, and Society*, ed. Rosaldo and Lamphere, 97-112; Elaine Showalter, "Feminist Criticism in the Wilderness," *Critical Inquiry* 8 (1981): 179-205; Janeway, *Powers of the Weak*, 210-11, 300.

32. Karl Bottigheimer, *Ireland and the Irish* (New York: Columbia Univ. Press, 1982), 144.

33. Adrienne Rich, "When We Dead Awaken: Writing as Re-Vision," in *Adrienne Rich's Poetry*, ed. Barbara Chalesworth Gelpi and Albert Gelpi (New York: Norton, 1975), 92-93; Maria Edgeworth, *Castle Rackrent* (1800; reprint, London: Oxford Univ. Press, 1964), 100-114, 97; E.OE. Somerville and Martin Ross, *The Real Charlotte* (1894; reprint, London: Quartet Books, 1982), 44-49; Elizabeth Bowen, *The Last September* (1929; reprint, New York: Avon Books, 1979), 52-54, 240-46, 28.

34. Eileen Ni Chuilleanain, *The Second Voyage* (Winston-Salem, N.C.: Wake Forest Univ. Press, 1977), 120. For examples of poetry, see Eavan Boland, *The War Horse* (London: Gollancz, 1975), and Medbh McGuckian, *On Ballycastle Beach* (London: Oxford Univ. Press, 1988).

35. E.OE. Somerville and Martin Ross, *Some Experiences of an Irish R.M.* (London: Longmans, Green, 1889; previously serialized in the *Badminton Magazine*).

36. Terence de Vere White, *The Anglo-Irish* (London: Gollancz, 1972), 36-51, 262; Yeats quoted, 45.

37. Marilyn Butler, *Maria Edgeworth: A Literary Biography* (Oxford: Clarendon Press, 1972), 171; see Maria Edgeworth, *The Absentee* (1812; reprint, London: Dent, 1893).

38. Lady Morgan, *The Wild Irish Girl* (London: Phillips, 1806); Butler, *Maria Edgeworth*, 452; Emily Lawless, *Hurrish* (Edinburgh: Blackwood, 1886).

39. George Moore, *Drama in Muslin* (1886; reprint, London: Colin Smythe, 1981).

40. Janet Madden-Simpson, ed., *Woman's Part: An Anthology of Short Fiction by and about Irish Women, 1890-1960* (Dublin: Arlen House, 1984).

41. A body of criticism has grown apace of the novels on the Big House. See, for example, Brian Donnelly, "The Big House in the Recent

Novel," *Studies* 64 (Summer 1975): 133-42. Kate O'Brien, *Without My Cloak* (Garden City, N.Y.: Doubleday, Doran, 1931), *The Anteroom* (Garden City, N.Y.: Doubleday, Doran, 1934), and *The Land of Spices* (Garden City, N.Y.: Doubleday, Doran, 1941).

42. Lord Dunsany, Preface to *Tales from Bective Bridge*, by Mary Lavin (1942; reprint, Dublin: Poolbeg Press, 1978), 8-12. In "Mary Lavin's World: Lovers and Strangers," Thomas J. Murray suggests that Lavin, unlike Joyce, Beckett, or Flann O'Brien, does not "lyricize self through poetry into some grand design which creates out of minutest parts cosmological and metaphysical schemes of reality" (*Eire-Ireland* 7, no. 2 [Summer 1972]: 123). In a personal interview in June 1985, however, Lavin suggested, and I agree with her, that this is just what she does do.

43. Molly Keane, *Good Behaviour* (1981; reprint, New York: Dutton, 1983).

44. Brenda Maddox, "The Romantic and the Realist," *Sunday Times Magazine*, 1 April 1984, 8-9; and Julia O'Faolain, "Sean at Eighty," in *Fathers: Reflections by Daughters* (London: Virago, 1983), 120-31. Gene A. Barnett, "Dennis Johnston," in *Modern British Dramatists, 1900-1945*, vol. 10 of *Dictionary of Literary Biography* (Detroit: Gale Research Co., 1982), pt. 1, 254; and Jennifer Johnston, "Jennifer Johnston," in *A Portrait of the Author as a Young Girl* (London: Methuen, 1986), 49-62.

45. Julia O'Faolain, *No Country for Young Men* (Middlesex: Penguin Books, 1980). Jennifer Johnston, *The Captains and the Kings* (1972; reprint, Glasgow: Fontana, 1982); *The Gates* (1973; reprint, London: Coronet, 1974); *How Many Miles to Babylon?* (1974; reprint, London: Coronet, 1975); *Shadows on Our Skin* (Garden City, N.Y.: Doubleday, 1978); *The Old Jest* (1979; reprint, Glasgow: Fontana, 1980); *The Christmas Tree* (1981; reprint, Glasgow: Fontana, 1982); and *The Railway Station Man* (London: Hamish Hamilton, 1984).

46. Bakan, *Duality of Human Existence*, 20-21.

47. Elaine Showalter, "Feminist Criticism in the Wilderness," 200.

48. Tony Tanner, *Adultery in the Novel: Contract and Transgression* (Baltimore, Md.: Johns Hopkins Univ. Press, 1979), 64.

49. Bakhtin, *Dialogic Imagination*, 20, 12, 55, 76, 77.

50. Edwin Ardener, "The 'Problem' Revisited," in *Perceiving Women*, ed. Shirley Ardener (London: Malaby Press, 1975), 19-27; Elaine Showalter, "Feminist Criticism in the Wilderness," 201; Tanner, *Adultery in the Novel*, 52; Bakhtin, *Dialogic Imagination*, 228.

51. Nancy Miller, "Emphasis Added: Plots and Plausibilities in Women's Fiction," *PMLA* 96 (1981): 36-48; Freud quoted, 40.

52. Ibid., 44-45, 42, 43.

53. Ibid., 46; Elizabeth Abel, Marianne Hirsch, and Elizabeth Langland, Introduction to *The Voyage In: Fictions of Female Development*, ed. Elizabeth Abel, Marianne Hirsch, and Elizabeth Langland (Hanover, N.H.: Univ. Press of New England, 1983), 11, 7.

54. Abel, Hirsch, and Langland, Introduction to *The Voyage In*, 12.

55. Ellen Moers uses the term "undercurrent" in her book *Literary Women*. Rich, "When We Dead Awaken," 90; Adrienne Rich, "Diving into the Wreck," in *Adrienne Rich's Poetry*, ed. Gelpi and Gelpi, 67.

56. Susan Gubar, "Mother, Maiden and the Marriage of Death: Women Writers and an Ancient Myth," *Women's Studies* 6 (1979): 306.

57. Charlotte Brontë, *Shirley* (1849; reprint, Middlesex: Penguin Books, 1975); Woolf, *Room*, 118; Froula, "When Eve Reads Milton," 327.

58. Alicia Ostriker, "The Thieves of Language: Women Poets and Revisionists Mythmaking," *Signs* 8 (1982): 72, 76, 78.

59. Ibid., 87; John Hollander, *The Figure of Echo: A Mode of Allusion in Milton and After* (Berkeley: Univ. of California Press, 1981).

60. Personal interviews were conducted with Jennifer Johnston in Derry, Northern Ireland, June 1985; with Molly Keane in Ardmore, county Waterford, Republic of Ireland, June 1985; with Mary Lavin in Dublin, Republic of Ireland, June 1985; and with Julia O'Faolain in Los Angeles, California, Nov. 1985.

61. Julia O'Faolain and Lauro Martines, eds., *Not in God's Image: Women in History from the Greeks to the Victorians* (London: Temple Smith, 1973); Julia O'Faolain, *The Obedient Wife* (1982; reprint, Middlesex: Penguin Books, 1983).

62. Molly Keane, *Molly Keane's Nursery Cooking* (London: Macdonald, 1985).

2. Maria Edgeworth

1. Butler, *Maria Edgeworth*, 477, n. 477, 420. Several volumes of Edgeworth's letters have been published, unfortunately no complete set as yet. As Butler notes in her introduction, there are problems in relying on the letters because the Edgeworth family selected them. There is no debate, however, about Maria's need to be reassured, to be loved. See Augustus J.C. Hare, ed., *The Life and Letters of Maria Edgeworth* (Boston: Houghton Mifflin, 1895); also, *Chosen Letters*, ed. with an introduction by F.V. Barry (London: Cape, 1931).

2. *Memoirs of Richard Lovell Edgeworth, Esq.*, begun by himself and concluded by his daughter, Maria Edgeworth (London: Hunter,

1820), 184; Butler, *Maria Edgeworth*, 37; Edgeworth, *Memoirs*, 1: 272-326.

3. Butler, *Maria Edgeworth*, 47.

4. Ibid., 52, 56.

5. See Edgeworth, *Memoirs*, vol. 11.

6. Butler, *Maria Edgeworth*, 90-91; Edgeworth, *Memoirs*, 344-45; Butler, *Maria Edgeworth*, 209.

7. See Emily Lawless, *Maria Edgeworth* (London: Macmillan, 1905); Maria Edgeworth, *Ennui* (London: Johnson, 1809); *Absentee*; *Memoirs*, vol. 2, chap. 2; Edgeworth Papers, 10166: 425, National Library of Ireland; Butler, *Maria Edgeworth*, 271-304.

8. Butler, *Maria Edgeworth*, 180-81, 178.

9. Hare, *Letters*, 21-24, 26, 47, 65, 78, 95, 171; Edgeworth Papers, 287, 417, 425.

10. Hare, *Letters*, 21, 30; Butler, *Maria Edgeworth*, 174; Hare, *Letters*, 432-33.

11. Hare, *Letters*, 112-16; Butler, *Maria Edgeworth*, 192-96, 217-18.

12. Butler, *Maria Edgeworth*, 240.

13. George Watson, Introduction to *Castle Rackrent*, by Maria Edgeworth, (reprint, London: Oxford Univ. Press, 1964), vii-xxv; Edgeworth, *Memoirs*, vol. 2, chap. 2. See J.C. Beckett, *The Making of Modern Ireland, 1603-1923* (London: Faber and Faber, 1981), 161-86; and Curtis, *History of Ireland*, 226-34, 252-55, 372.

14. Thomas Flanagan, "Castle Rackrent," in *The Irish Novelists: 1800-1850* (1958; reprint, Westport, Conn: Greenwood Press, 1976), 78; Bruce Teets, Introduction to *Castle Rackrent*, University of Miami Critical Studies no. 4 (Coral Gables, Fla.: Univ. of Miami Press, 1964), 23; James Newcomer, *Maria Edgeworth the Novelist: A Bicentennial Study* (Fort Worth: Texas Christian Univ. Press, 1967), 151; W.B. Coley, "An Early 'Irish' Novelist," in *Minor British Novelists*, ed. Charles Alva Hoyt (Carbondale: Southern Illinois Univ. Press, 1967), 25; O. Elizabeth M. Harden, "Castle Rackrent," in *Maria Edgeworth's Art of Prose Fiction* (The Hague: Mouton, 1971), 43-71; Gerry H. Brookes, "The Didacticism of Edgeworth's *Castle Rackrent*," *Studies in English Literature* 17 (Autumn 1977): 593-605.

15. John Cronin, "Castle Rackrent," in *The Nineteenth Century*, vol. 1 of *The Anglo-Irish Novel* (Belfast: Appletree Press, 1980), 36; W.J. McCormack, *Ascendancy and Tradition in Anglo-Irish Literary History from 1789 to 1939* (Oxford: Clarendon Press, 1985), 97-122; Robert Tracy, "Maria Edgeworth and Lady Morgan," *Nineteenth-Century Fiction* 40 (June 1985): 3. *Family Chronicles: Maria Edgeworth's Castle Rackrent*, ed. Coilin Owens (Dublin: Wolfhound Press, 1987) is an ex-

cellent, much-needed collection of Edgeworth criticism. The new entries in this volume, however, also fail to consider the domestic plot.

16. Gilbert and Gubar, *Madwoman*, 149-50; Butler, *Maria Edgeworth*, 489; Showalter, "Feminist Criticism in the Wilderness," 179-205.

17. Watson, Introduction to *Castle Rackrent*, xix; Janeway, *Powers of the Weak*; Joanne Altieri, "Style and Purpose in Maria Edgeworth's Fiction," *Nineteenth-Century Fiction* 23 (1968): 265-78; Miller, "Emphasis Added," 36-48.

18. Tanner, *Adultery in the Novel*, 62, 63-64; Lee Holcombe, *Wives and Property: Reform of the Married Women's Property Law in Nineteenth-Century England* (Toronto, Ont.: Univ. of Toronto Press, 1983), 20-46; Tanner, *Adultery in the Novel*, 104.

19. Edgeworth, *Castle Rackrent*, 16, 14-15.

20. Edgeworth, *Memoirs*, 16-20; Edgeworth, *Castle Rackrent*, 16.

21. Edgeworth, *Castle Rackrent*, 12; Holcombe, *Wives and Property*, 20, 13; Edgeworth, *Castle Rackrent*, 18.

22. Edgeworth, *Castle Rackrent*, 12, 15, 12, 17; Simms, "Women in Normal Ireland," 18; Edgeworth, *Castle Rackrent*, 17-18.

23. Edgeworth, *Castle Rackrent*, 18, 12.

24. Ibid., 32, 20-21.

25. Ibid., 16-17; Butler, *Maria Edgeworth*, 83-85; Edgeworth, *Memoirs*, 16-42; Edgeworth, *Castle Rackrent*, 20-23; Edgeworth, *Memoirs*, 17-18; Edgeworth, *Castle Rackrent*, 23.

26. Edgeworth, *Memoirs*, 19. See Beckett, *Making of Modern Ireland*, 161-86; and Curtis, *History of Ireland*, 226-34, 252-55, 372. Edgeworth, *Castle Rackrent*, 21.

27. Edgeworth, *Castle Rackrent*, 23-24, 36, 29, 31.

28. Ibid., 32; Holcombe, *Wives and Property*, 21-23; Edgeworth, *Castle Rackrent*, 32.

29. Edgeworth, *Castle Rackrent*, 32, 33, 31, 35, 36.

30. Ibid., 26, 108, 40; Tanner, *Adultery in the Novel*, 13.

31. See Harden, "Rackrent," 57; Cronin, "Rackrent," 35; and Flanagan, "Rackrent," 76. Edgeworth, *Castle Rackrent*, 56, 61-62; Butler, *Maria Edgeworth*, 181-84. Condy's settlement on Isabella is the only action he plans and carries through himself, yet he tells Jason, with Thady's blessing, that he acted "without a moment's thought" (Edgeworth, *Castle Rackrent*, 76).

32. Edgeworth, *Castle Rackrent*, 41, 35-61, 40.

33. Ibid., 55, 39; Edgeworth, *Memoirs*, 31; Edgeworth, *Castle Rackrent*, 79.

34. Edgeworth, *Castle Rackrent*, 48, 65, 66.

35. Holcombe, *Wives and Property*, 21, 39-40; Edgeworth, *Castle Rackrent*, 70, 90-91.

36. Edgeworth, *Castle Rackrent*, 49, 51, 43, 51, 41, 50.

37. Ibid., 50, 66.

38. Flanagan, "Rackrent," 70; Harden, "Rackrent," 62; Edgeworth, *Castle Rackrent*, 45.

39. Gilbert and Gubar, *Madwoman*, 7; Edgeworth, *Castle Rackrent*, 31.

40. Maria Edgeworth again expressed both the power and the potential value of literary role models in *Ormond* (London: Hunter, Baldwin, Cradock and Joy, 1817). Emulating *Tom Jones*, young Harry Ormond attempts a life of roguery but changes his mind after reading Richardson's *Sir Charles Grandison*.

41. Edgeworth, *Castle Rackrent*, 42, 47, 42-43, 44, 48, 66.

42. Ibid., 87, 92; Sigmund Freud, "The Relation of the Poet to Day-Dreaming," in *On Creativity and the Unconscious*, sel. with an introduction and annotations by Benjamin Nelson (New York: Harper, 1958), 44-54; Miller, "Emphasis Added," 46.

43. Butler, *Maria Edgeworth*, 306.

44. Ibid., 240.

3. Somerville and Ross

1. E.OE. Somerville and Martin Ross, *Irish Memories* (London: Longmans, Green and Co., 1918), 53, 236; Terence de Vere White, private communication, 1986; and V.S. Pritchett, "Hunting Ladies," *New Statesman*, 24 May 1968, 688. See John Cronin, "Dominant Themes in the Novels of Somerville and Ross," in *Somerville and Ross: A Symposium* (Belfast: Queen's Univ., 1968), 8-19; *Somerville and Ross*, Irish Writers Series (Lewisburg, Pa.: Bucknell Univ. Press, 1972); John Cronin, "The Real Charlotte," in *The Anglo-Irish Novel* 1: 135-53; Thomas Flanagan, "The Big House of Ross-Drishane," *Kenyon Review* 28 (1966): 54-78; Sean McMahon, "John Bull's Other Ireland: A Consideration of *The Real Charlotte* by Somerville and Ross," *Eire-Ireland* 3, no. 4 (Winter 1968): 119-35; and Alan Warner, "Somerville and Ross," in *A Guide to Anglo-Irish Literature* (New York: St. Martin's Press, 1981), 50-60. E.OE. Somerville and Martin Ross, *The Big House of Inver* (London: Heinemann, 1925).

2. Alicia Ostriker, "Thieves of Language," 68-90.

3. Although Edith always called her cousin "Martin," I refer to the women in relation to each other and to their families by their given names, Edith and Violet, simply to avoid confusion. I refer to the literary collaborators by the names they themselves selected and used,

the male-sounding E.OE. Somerville and Martin Ross. Somerville and Ross, *Irish Memories*, 28.

4. Curtis, *History of Ireland*, chap. 19; Robert E. Kennedy, Jr, *The Irish: Emigration, Marriage, and Fertility* (Los Angeles: Univ. of California Press, 1973), 193, 198; Hilary Robinson, *Somerville and Ross: A Critical Appreciation* (New York: St. Martin's Press, 1980), 5-6.

5. Somerville and Ross, *Irish Memories*, 154; Robinson, *Somerville and Ross*, 16.

6. Violet Powell, *The Irish Cousins: The Books and Background of Somerville and Ross* (London: Heinemann, 1970), 2; Robinson, *Somerville and Ross*, 18; Maurice Collis, *Somerville and Ross: A Biography* (London: Faber and Faber, 1968), 268-69.

7. Somerville and Ross, *Irish Memories*, 326; Robinson, *Somerville and Ross*, 19, 20.

8. Robinson, *Somerville and Ross*, 86; Sir Patrick Coghill, "Opening Address," in *Somerville and Ross: A Symposium*, 5-7; Hilary Mitchell, "Somerville and Ross: Amateur to Professional," in *Somerville and Ross: A Symposium*, 21.

9. Robinson, *Somerville and Ross*, 16-17; Somerville and Ross, *Irish Memories*, chaps. 1, 6, and 7.

10. Robinson, *Somerville and Ross*, 85; Somerville and Ross, *Irish Memories*, 133, 137; Bakan, *Duality of Human Existence*.

11. Somerville and Ross, *Irish Memories*, 32, 91.

12. Flanagan, "Big House," 57.

13. Ann Power, "The Big House of Somerville and Ross," *The Dubliner* 3 (Spring 1964): 45; Somerville and Ross, *Irish Memories*, 52; Bakhtin, *Dialogic Imagination*.

14. Somerville and Ross, *The Real Charlotte*, 176.

15. Gilbert and Gubar, *Madwoman*, 6.

16. Somerville and Ross, *Real Charlotte*, 176, 63.

17. Ibid., 322; Miller, "Emphasis Added," 36-48.

18. Somerville and Ross, *Real Charlotte*, 6-7.

19. Ibid., 8, 2-5.

20. Somerville and Ross, *Irish Memories*, 229-31; Somerville and Ross, *Real Charlotte*, 147-62; Ostriker, "Thieves of Language," 87; Somerville and Ross, *Irish Memories*, 229.

21. Somerville and Ross, *Real Charlotte*, 24, 100, 29, 17, 314, 66.

22. Ibid., 98, 225.

23. Ibid., 134, 135-36; Phyllis Chesler, *Women and Madness* (Garden City, N.Y.: Doubleday, 1972).

24. Somerville and Ross, *Irish Memories*, 21, 23; Janeway, *Powers of the Weak*; Somerville and Ross, *Real Charlotte*, 140.

25. Somerville and Ross, *Real Charlotte*, 47.

26. Somerville and Ross, *Irish Memories*, 237.

27. Somerville and Ross, *Real Charlotte*, 47.

28. Ibid., 48.

29. See Powell, *Irish Cousins*, 54; and Cronin, "Real Charlotte," 147. Somerville and Ross, *Real Charlotte*, 12, 16, 166, 259, 339, 225, 226.

30. Somerville and Ross, *Real Charlotte*, 67, 70.

31. Bakan, *Duality of Human Existence*, 16.

32. Somerville and Ross, *Real Charlotte*, 70, 175, 67.

33. See Conor Cruise O'Brien, *Writers and Politics* (New York: Pantheon Books, 1955), 111; McMahon, "John Bull's Other Ireland," 132; and Mitchell, "Somerville and Ross," 27. Somerville and Ross, *Real Charlotte*, 83, 184, 314, 55, 209.

34. Somerville and Ross, *Real Charlotte*, 176, 11, 60, 173-74, 260.

35. Ibid., 312.

4. Elizabeth Bowen

1. Elizabeth Bowen, "Herbert Place," in *Seven Winters and Afterthoughts* (New York: Knopf, 1962), 4; Elizabeth Bowen, *Bowen's Court* (1942; reprint, New York: Ecco Press, 1979), 423-24, 402, 416, 417.

2. Bowen, *Bowen's Court*, 403, 425; Spencer Curtis Brown, Foreword to *Pictures and Conversations*, by Elizabeth Bowen (New York: Knopf, 1975), xxxi.

3. Bowen, *Bowen's Court*, 426-34, 432, 433-34.

4. Elizabeth Bowen, "The Big House," in *Collected Impressions* (New York: Knopf, 1950), 197; Bowen, *Bowen's Court*, 20, 453; Elizabeth Bowen, Preface to *The Last September* (1929; reprint, New York: Avon Books, 1979), vii.

5. Bowen, Preface to *The Last September*, xii, viii.

6. Bowen, *Bowen's Court*, 416; Elizabeth Bowen, "Origins," in *Pictures and Conversations*, 19.

7. Bowen, *Bowen's Court*, 417. Although Elizabeth Bowen received her first reading lessons at Bowen's Court, the occasion was on a visit after the first sojourn in England and was hence associated in time with the traveling period. Elizabeth Bowen, "Out of a Book," in *Collected Impressions* (New York: Knopf, 1975), 264, 267, 268.

8. Elizabeth Bowen, "Disloyalties," in *Seven Winters and Afterthoughts*, 67; Elizabeth Bowen, "Sources of Influence," in *Seven Winters and Afterthoughts*, 79; Elizabeth Bowen, "Truth and Fiction," in *Seven Winters and Afterthoughts*, 246; Bowen, "Out of a Book," 269, 268.

9. Bowen, Preface to *The Last September*, ix; Bowen, *Last September*, 158.

10. Thomas Flanagan sees the Irish struggle as a war between the Big Houses and the cabins in "Big House," 54-78.

11. Bowen, *Last September*, 78.

12. Ibid., 79; Heaney, "Act of Union," 125-26.

13. Robert Graves, *The White Goddess: A Historical Grammar of Poetic Myth* (1948; reprint, New York: Farrar, Straus and Giroux, 1984); Merlin Stone, *When God Was a Woman* (New York: Harcourt Brace Jovanovich, 1976). See also Erich Neumann, *The Great Mother: An Analysis of the Archetype* (New York: Pantheon, 1955). Mary Condren, *The Serpent and the Goddess: Women, Religion and Power in Celtic Ireland* (San Francisco: Harper and Row, 1989). Stone, *When God Was a Woman*, chap. 3.

14. Stone, *When God Was a Woman*, 84-86; The female deity, which the name of the early Irish people suggests, had of course been suppressed long before the plantation of Ireland by England; the Anglo-Irish in this paradigm simple replace one patriarchal religion with another. Nature does seem to shelter the Gaelic-Irish rebels, who in their turn will continue the social and religious patriarchal dominance. For tales of the Tuatha de Danann, see Tom Peete Cross and Clark Harris Slover, eds., *Ancient Irish Tales* (New York: Holt, 1936), 1-126.

15. Bowen, *Last September*, 3, 4.

16. Ibid., 37, 172, 197, 211, 249.

17. Tanner, *Adultery in the Novel*; Bowen, *Last September*, 26; John Milton, *Paradise Lost* (1674; reprint, *John Milton: Complete Poems and Major Prose* [Indianapolis: Bobbs-Merrill, 1975]) 9: 803-4.

18. Bowen, *Last September*, 26, 27. *Black and Tan*: The poorly disciplined irregulars, co-opted by a British army diminished by war, were hated by the Irish and nicknamed after the colors of their uniforms.

19. Ibid., 66-67, 27, 67, 226, 236-38.

20. Bowen, *Bowen's Court*, 20; Bowen, *Last September*, 49-50, 100.

21. Bowen, *Last September*, 50, 253, 219, 128.

22. Milton, *Paradise Lost*, 8: 547-48. My reading of this section of *Paradise Lost* is indebted to Froula.

23. Ibid., 9: 265-69.

24. Ibid., 9: 294-97, 335-36; Froula, "When Eve Reads Milton," 332.

25. Milton, *Paradise Lost*, 4: 477-82, 490; Froula, "When Eve Reads Milton," 334-35.

26. Bowen, *Last September*, 57-60, 121, 208, 58, 163, 60, 36, 121, 154.

27. Ibid., 120, 122.

28. Ibid., 56, 57.

29. Ibid., 114, 115, 201.

30. Harriet Blodgett, *Patterns of Reality: Elizabeth Bowen's Novels* (The Hague: Mouton, 1975).

31. Bowen, *Last September*, 152, 155.

32. Ibid., 153.

33. Heaney, "Act of Union"; Bowen, *Last September*, 154, 156.

34. Bowen, *Last September*, 158-59.

35. Bowen, "Out of a Book," 264; Bowen, *Last September*, 158.

36. Bowen, *Last September*, 202, 212, 159; Milton, *Paradise Lost*, 8: 460-99.

37. Bowen, *Last September*, 213.

38. Ibid., 153, 236.

39. Ibid., 236-37.

40. Ibid., 250.

41. Ibid., 250-51, 252.

42. Ibid., 114-15; Milton, *Paradise Lost*, 9: 358-59.

43. Bowen, "Out of a Book," 264.

44. Bowen, Preface to *The Last September*, xii; Bowen, *Last September*, 255, 245.

45. Bowen, *Last September*, 256; Blodgett, *Patterns of Reality*, 25.

5. Kate O'Brien

1. Kate O'Brien, "Imaginative Prose by the Irish, 1820-1970," in *Myth and Reality in Irish Literature*, ed. Joseph Ronsley (Waterloo, Ont.: Wilfred Laurier Univ. Press, 1977), 305-15.

2. Kate O'Brien, *Presentation Parlour* (London: Heinemann, 1963), 13.

3. Ibid., 14.

4. O'Brien, "Imaginative Prose," 307, 314.

5. Ibid., 311; Seamus Deane, "The Literary Myths of the Revival: A Case for Their Abandonment," in *Myth and Reality in Irish Literature*, 319; O'Brien, "Imaginative Prose," 312; Lorna Reynolds, *Kate O'Brien: A Literary Portrait* (Gerrards Cross, Bucks.: Colin Smythe, 1987).

6. *Without My Cloak* (Garden City, N.Y.: Doubleday, Doran, 1931); *The Anteroom* (Garden City, N.Y.: Doubleday Doran, 1934); *The Land of Spices* (Garden City, N.Y.: Doubleday, Doran, 1941); *Mary Lavelle* (Garden City, N.Y.: Doubleday, Doran, 1936); *As Music and Splendour* (London: Heinemann, 1958); *Pray for the Wanderer* (Garden City, N.Y.: Doubleday, Doran, 1938); *The Last of Summer* (Garden City, N.Y.: Doubleday, Doran, 1943); *The Flower of May* (New York: Harper, 1953); *That Lady* (London: Heinemann, 1946), republished as *For One Sweet*

Grape (Garden City, N.Y.: Doubleday, Doran, 1946). Reynolds, *Kate O'Brien*, 70-74.

7. Margaret Lawrence, "Matriarchs," in *The School of Femininity* (Toronto: Musson Books, 1972), 244.

8. Bakhtin, "Epic and Novel" in *The Dialogic Imagination*, 14-20. The gods intervene in Homer's epic to arrange the elements of plot; the Greek playwrights who followed Homer used arbitrary devices, not always gods, to shape their plots. In *Oedipus Rex*, for example, the timely arrival of the messenger, the only person who can tell Oedipus that his father was not Polybos, turns the tale. *The Oedipus Cycle*, trans. Dudley Fitts and Robert Fitzgerald (New York: Harcourt, Brace and World, 1949), 50-53.

9. O'Brien, *Without My Cloak*, 3, 4. Regarding the importance of the horse in Anglo-Irish tradition, see Somerville and Ross, *Irish R.M.* Brendan Behan's explanation of an Anglo-Irish man as "a Protestant on a horse" is widely quoted; see de Vere White, *Anglo-Irish*, 17. O'Brien, *Without My Cloak*, 3-5, 469, 417.

10. O'Brien, *Anteroom*, 101, 107.

11. O'Brien, *Without My Cloak*, 452.

12. Ibid., 469.

13. Levi-Strauss, *Elementary Structures of Kinship*; Rubin, "Traffic in Women," 157-210; O'Brien, *Without My Cloak*, 310. Lorna Reynolds finds the marriage of Denis and Anna "one of the few flaws in this impressive novel" (*Kate O'Brien*, 50). The marriage is a flaw if we read the text as realism, not if we read it as epic. As epic undercut, the marriage, while validating the epic structure, ironically underscores the winners and losers in the configuration—Christina loses, Denis wins. Anna is no more than a cipher, the necessary device, the contrived reward for Denis's conformity.

14. Lawrence, "Matriarchs," 244.

15. Reynolds, *Kate O'Brien*, 43; O'Brien, *Without My Cloak*, 317, 159, 160, 158.

16. Reynolds, *Kate O'Brien*, 57.

17. Mill, "Subjection of Women," 238.

18. Benedict Kiely, *Modern Irish Fiction: A Critique* (Dublin: Golden Eagle Books, 1950), 87; Kate O'Brien, Introduction to *Impressions of English Literature*, ed. W.J. Turner (London: Collins, 1944), 18; Susan Vander Closter, "Kate O'Brien," in *British Novelists, 1930-1959*, vol. 15 of *Dictionary of Literary Biography* (Detroit: Bruccoli Clark Books, 1983), 392.

19. O'Brien, *Anteroom*, 6, 271, 269.

20. Ibid., 32, 98, 286, 90-92, 183, 244, 245, 239.

21. Ibid., 103-6; Thomas Bulfinch, *The Age of Fable* (1855; reprint, New York: Signet Classics, 1962), 66; O'Brien, *Anteroom*, 104.

22. O'Brien, *Anteroom*, 244-45, 270, 272, 274-77.

23. Simone de Beauvoir, *The Second Sex*, ed. and trans. H.M. Parshley (1952; reprint, New York: Vintage Books, 1974), 301; Jerome Buckley, *Seasons of Youth: The Bildungsroman from Dickens to Golding* (Cambridge, Mass.: Harvard Univ. Press, 1974), 16-17.

24. Abel, Hirsch, and Langland, Introduction *The Voyage In*, 3-19. O'Brien was as familiar with her material as Joyce was with his. The aunts in *Presentation Parlour*, for example, share many qualities of character with Mother Superior, and, as Lorna Reynolds's biography shows, many of the scenes, characters, and events in the novels are close to those in O'Brien's own life.

25. Joyce, *Portrait of the Artist*, 163; James Joyce, *Ulysses* (1922; reprint, London: Bodley Head, 1960), 312-13; Charlotte Brontë, *Jane Eyre* (1847; reprint, New York: Airmont Books, 1963), 292; O'Brien, *Land of Spices*, 187.

26. In her essay "Women in the Novels of Kate O'Brien: The Mellick Novels," in *Studies in Anglo-Irish Literature*, ed. Heinz Kosok (Bonn: Bouvier Verlag Herbert Grundmann, 1982), 330, Joan Ryan notes that Anna is paralleled to Stephen in her love of words and that O'Brien employs stream of consciousness and even echoes Joyce. O'Brien, *Land of Spices*, 304, 91, 97, 118, 146-47, 40, 221, 192, 226-29, 221; Joyce, *Portrait of the Artist*, 7, 226; O'Brien, *Land of Spices*, 52, 236-40, 66, 249, 277-78.

27. O'Brien, *Land of Spices*, 250.

28. Chodorow, "Family Structure," 43-66; O'Brien, *Land of Spices*, 102, 103, 16, 102-3, 233-34.

29. O'Brien, *Land of Spices*, 218, 230, 218, 221, 288.

30. Ibid., 293, 187, 233, 235.

31. Ibid., 257, 235-98.

32. Ibid., 253, 141.

33. Edgeworth, *Castle Rackrent*, 97; Somerville and Ross, *Irish Memories* 310-11 and elsewhere; Somerville and Ross, *Real Charlotte*; Bowen, *Last September*, 53.

34. O'Brien, *Anteroom*, 216-19.

35. Joyce, *Portrait of the Artist*, 188-89, 202-3, 253.

36. O'Brien, *Land of Spices*, 210, 188-91, 109, 210.

37. Ibid., 10, 16, 103, 108, 93, 236-40.

38. Ibid., 304; Joyce, *Portrait of the Artist*, 203, 253.

39. O'Brien, *Land of Spices*, 318, 317, 298, 187.

40. Lawrence, "Matriarchs," 244.

6. Mary Lavin

1. *Tales from Bective Bridge* was published in 1942; "Happiness" first appears in a collection in 1969, but these themes are continued into Lavin's most recent collection, *A Family Likeness* (London: Constable, 1985).

2. Elizabeth Peavoy, "Life Styles," *Inside Tribune*, 24 March 1985, 4.

3. For biography see A.A. Kelly, *Mary Lavin, Quiet Rebel: A Study of Her Short Stories* (New York: Barnes and Noble, 1980); Richard F. Peterson, *Mary Lavin* (Boston: Twayne, 1978); and Zack Bowen, *Mary Lavin* (Lewisburg, Pa.: Bucknell Univ. Press, 1975). See also the author's own account, "Mary Lavin," in *A Portrait of the Artist as a Young Girl* (London: Methuen, 1986), 79-92.

4. Personal interview with Mary Lavin, Dublin, June 1985; Bonnie Scott Kime, "Mary Lavin and the Life of the Mind," *Irish University Review* 9 (Autumn 1979): 265; Lavin interview; Janet Dunleavy, "The Making of Mary Lavin's 'A Memory,' " *Eire-Ireland* 12, no. 3 (Autumn 1977): 96.

5. Lawrence, "Matriarchs," 216.

6. Mary Lavin has frequently expressed this sentiment. See, for example, Marianne Koenig, "Mary Lavin: The Novels and the Stories," *Irish University Review* 9 (Autumn 1979): 244-61.

7. Mary Lavin, "Happiness," in *Mary Lavin: Collected Stories* (Boston: Houghton Mifflin, 1971), 411.

8. Ibid., 403.

9. Ibid., 407.

10. Ibid., 406.

11. Ibid., 409.

12. Ibid., 408, 416-17.

13. Ibid., 417.

14. Ibid.; Susan Hardy Aiken, University of Arizona, private communication with the author, 1986.

15. Aiken communication; Dunleavy, "Making of Mary Lavin's 'A Memory,' " 90; Janet Dunleavy, "The Making of Mary Lavin's 'Happiness,' " *Irish University Review* 9 (Autumn 1979): 230; O'Connor, "Girl at the Gaol Gate," 203-4.

16. Dunsany, Preface to *Tales from Bective Bridge*. Robert W. Caswell makes a similar point about Irish literary luminaries in "Irish Political Reality and Mary Lavin's *Tales from Bective Bridge*" *Eire-Ireland* 3 (Spring 1968) no. 1: 59. O'Connor, "Girl at the Gaol Gate," 203.

17. Lavin interview; Dunleavy, "Making of Mary Lavin's 'A Memory,' " 96.

18. Augustine Martin, "A Skeleton Key to the Stories of Mary Lavin," *Studies* 52 (Winter 1963): 400; O'Connor, "Girl at the Gaol Gate," 209; Mary Lavin, "The Little Prince" and "A Cup of Tea," in *The Stories of Mary Lavin* (London: Constable, 1964); Mary Lavin, "Frail Vessel," in *Mary Lavin: Collected Stories*.

19. Kelly, *Mary Lavin*, 77; Seamus Deane, "Mary Lavin," in *The Irish Short Story*, ed. Patrick Rafroidi and Terence Brown (Lille, France: Univ. of Lille, 1979), 245.

20. Mary Lavin, "In a Cafe," in *The Stories of Mary Lavin*, 359; Mary Lavin, "In the Middle of the Fields," in *Mary Lavin: Collected Stories*, 373.

21. Catherine A. Murphy, "The Ironic Vision of Mary Lavin," *Mosaic* 12 (Spring 1979): 69; V.S. Pritchett, Introduction to *Mary Lavin: Collected Stories*, ix-xiii; Mary Lavin, "Villa Violetta," in *A Memory and Other Stories* (London: Constable, 1972).

22. Rosaldo, "Women, Culture, and Society," 32-34. See also Mary Daly, *Gyn/Ecology: The Metaethics of Radical Feminism* (Boston: Beacon Press, 1978).

23. Lavin, "In a Cafe," 348, 347.

24. Ibid., 351.

25. Ibid., 353.

26. Charlotte Brontë, *Shirley* (1849; reprint, Middlesex: Penguin Books, 1975); Woolf, *Room*, 118; Lavin, "In a Cafe," 349; Mary Lavin, "The Cuckoo-Spit," in *Mary Lavin: Collected Stories*, 387; Lavin, "Middle of the Fields," 368.

27. Lavin, "In a Cafe," 358, 359, 360.

28. Lavin, "Cuckoo-Spit," 383.

29. Ibid., 374.

30. Ibid., 380; Lavin, "Middle of the Fields," 357.

31. Lavin, "Middle of the Fields," 359, 373.

32. Murphy, "Ironic Vision," 76; Lavin, "Cuckoo-Spit," 381, 399.

33. Chodorow, "Family Structure," 43-66; Mary Lavin, "Senility," in *The Shrine* (London: Constable, 1977), 116-37.

34. Lavin, "Senility," 129, 130.

35. Ibid., 127, 128, 127.

36. Ibid., 135-36, 132, 116.

37. Mary Lavin, "A Family Likeness," in *A Family Likeness* (London: Constable, 1985), 7-19; quote on 10.

38. Ibid., 11, 12, 14.

39. Ibid., 14, 15.

40. Lavin, "Happiness"; Lavin, "Cuckoo-Spit," 374; Lavin, "Middle of the Fields," 359.

7. Molly Keane

1. Polly Devlin, Introduction to *The Rising Tide*, by Molly Keane (1937; reprint, London: Virago Press, 1984), v. See also author's own account of her childhood, "Molly Keane," in *Portrait of the Artist as a Young Girl*, 61-78. Keane's remarks remind one of Terence de Vere White's more serious comments on the Anglo-Irish quoted in chapter 1 and also, of course, of Maria Edgeworth's representations in *Castle Rackrent*. Molly Keane, "Elizabeth of Bowenscourt," *Irish Times*, 20 March 1985, 19.

2. Devlin, Introduction to *The Rising Tide*, ix, vii, ix.

3. Molly Keane, *Good Behaviour* (1981; reprint, New York: Knopf, 1983); Rachel Billington, "Fictions of Class," *New York Times Book Review*, 9 August 1981, 13.

4. We might say that Aroon is the victim of the "scoptophilic lens" Luce Irigaray describes in *This Sex Which Is Not One*, trans. Catherine Porter and Carolyn Burke (1977; reprint, Ithaca, N.Y.: Cornell Univ. Press, 1985), 23-26.

5. J.G. Farrell, *Troubles* (1970; reprint, London: Fontana, 1984); Julia O'Faolain, *Man in the Cellar* (London: Faber, 1974); Julia O'Faolain, *Daughters of Passion* (Middlesex: Penguin, 1982).

6. Personal interview with Molly Keane, Ardmore, County Waterford, June 1985.

7. Keane interview.

8. Keane has Aroon allude to Keane's own favorite Bowen novel when obliged to sell Richard's gift—"It was the death of my heart" (*Good Behaviour*, 167). Keane interview.

9. Keane, *Good Behaviour*, 10, 31, 219, 142.

10. Buckley, *Seasons of Youth*, 17; Abel, Hirsch, and Langland, Introduction to *The Voyage In*, 3-19; see also Gilligan, "Different Voice," 481-517.

11. Keane, *Good Behaviour*, 3.

12. Dinnerstein, *Mermaid and the Minotaur*; Joyce, *Portrait of the Artist*, 1-2.

13. Keane, *Good Behaviour*, 13.

14. Ibid., 15.

15. Ibid., 15-16.

16. Ibid., 72.

17. Ibid., 12, 71-73.

18. Ibid., 12-13, 74, 76, 115.

19. Ibid., 55, 17, 10-63, 18, 17, 20, 44, 49-50.

20. Abel, Hirsch, and Langland, Introduction to *The Voyage In*, 8; Keane, *Good Behaviour*, 28, 57.

21. Keane, *Good Behaviour*, 59, 50-51.

22. Ibid., 62, 19, 91.

23. Ibid., 65-67, 206.

24. Ibid., 189, 213, 222, 234.

25. Ibid., 172.

26. Ibid., 100, 137, 141.

27. Ibid., 107, 108, 172, 211.

28. Ibid., 180, 194.

29. Ibid., 243-44; Tanner, *Adultery in the Novel*.

30. Keane, *Good Behaviour*, 244, 245.

8. Julia O'Faolain

1. Maddox, "Romantic and Realist," 8-9; O'Faolain, "Sean at Eighty," 130.

2. John Mellors, "Kites and Aeroplanes," *The Listener*, 26 September 1974, 416; Hogan, "Old Boys," 202; Julia O'Faolain, "A Pot of Soothing Herbs," in *Melancholy Baby* (1968; reprint, Dublin: Poolbeg Press, 1978), 53-70.

3. O'Faolain, "Soothing Herbs," 54.

4. Personal interview with Julia O'Faolain, Los Angeles, Nov. 1985; Ostriker, "Thieves of Language," 72; Julia O'Faolain, *The Obedient Wife* (1982; reprint, Middlesex: Penguin Books, 1983), 33.

5. O'Faolain, "Soothing Herbs," 68, 54, 55.

6. O'Faolain, "Soothing Herbs," 53; Rich, "Diving into the Wreck," *Poetry*, 67.

7. O'Faolain, "Soothing Herbs," 57, 66.

8. O'Faolain, "Soothing Herbs," 66. Sources of the Cuchulain sagas vary in details, but see the acclaimed Irish epic, *The Tain*, trans. Thomas Kinsella (London: Oxford Univ. Press, 1969), 32; and Cross and Slover, *Ancient Irish Tales*, 167. *The Tain*, 91-92; Cross and Slover, *Ancient Irish Tales*, 151. Even children's versions betray the sexual ambiguity; see Rosemary Sutcliff, *The Hound of Ulster* (Leicester: Knight Books, 1967), 69.

9. O'Faolain, "Soothing Herbs," 62.

10. Ibid., 53.

11. O'Faolain, *No Country for Young Men*, 170; Cross and Slover,

Ancient Irish Tales, 420. Again, see the children's version for the firmly stated lesson: Eoin Neeson, "Diarmuid and Graine," in *The Second Book of Irish Myths and Legends* (1966; reprint, Cork: Mercier Press, 1975), 109.

12. O'Faolain, *No Country*, 224; Annette Kolodny, *The Lay of the Land* (Chapel Hill: Univ. of North Carolina Press, 1975). Recent studies demonstrate the contradiction in the conception of woman as a potential instrument of public disorder, and hence best confined, and as the instrument for inculcating morality in the home. Indeed in " 'The Disorder of Women': Women, Love, and the Sense of Justice," *Ethics* 91 (October 1980): 20-34, Carole Patemen goes further, demonstrating that the family itself "is simultaneously the foundation of the state and antagonistic to it."

13. O'Faolain, *No Country*, 12.

14. Ortner, "Is Female to Male," 85; Showalter, "Feminist Criticism in the Wilderness," 200-205. "Palimpsest" is the word Gilbert and Gubar use to describe the layers of women's fiction in *Madwoman in the Attic*. Helen Lanigan Wood, "Women in the Myths and Early Depictions," in *Irish Women*, ed. Ni Chuilleanain, 17; and Curtis, *History of Ireland*, 1-3; see also early chapters in Cross and Slover, *Ancient Irish Tales*.

15. O'Faolain, *No Country*, 152.

16. Ibid., 165, 151.

17. Ibid., 323, 314.

18. Ibid., 34; Curtis, *History of Ireland*, 43-46.

19. O'Faolain, *No Country*, 155.

20. Ibid., 302.

21. Ibid., 312, 332, 260; Chesler, *Women and Madness*, especially chaps. 1 and 2.

22. O'Faolain, *No Country*, 189.

23. Ibid., 192, 193, 194.

24. Ibid., 147, 151.

25. See Edwards, *Patrick Pearse*.

26. O'Faolain, *No Country*, 327; Lynda Zwinger, University of Arizona, private communication, 1986.

27. O'Faolain interview.

28. O'Faolain, *No Country*, 89, 47; Julia O'Faolain, "The Man in the Cellar," in *Man in the Cellar* (London: Faber and Faber, 1974), 40, 30.

29. O'Faolain, *Obedient Wife*, 229.

30. Ibid.

31. Ann Owens Weekes, "Diarmuid and Grainne Again: Julia O'Faolain's *No Country for Young Men*," *Eire-Ireland* 21 (Spring 1986), no. 1: 89-102; O'Faolain, *No Country*, 164.

9. Jennifer Johnston

1. Deane, "Literary Myths," 319, 321.

2. Fleda Brown Jackson, "Jennifer Johnston," in *British Novelists since 1960*, vol. 14 of *Dictionary of Literary Biography* (Detroit: Gale Research Co., 1983), pt. 2, 445; see also "Jennifer Johnston," in *Portrait of the Artist as a Young Girl*, 49-62, the artist's own account of her childhood. Mark Mortimer, "The World of Jennifer Johnston: A Look at Three Novels," *Crane Bag* 4 (1980) no. 1: 91; personal interview with Jennifer Johnston, Derry, June 1985.

3. *The Captains and the Kings* (1972; reprint, Glasgow: Fontana, 1982); *The Gates* (1973; reprint, London: Coronet, 1974); *How Many Miles to Babylon?* (1974; reprint, London: Coronet, 1975); *Shadows on Our Skin* (New York: Doubleday, 1978); *The Old Jest* (1979; reprint, Glasgow: Fontana, 1980); *The Christmas Tree* (1981; reprint, Glasgow: Fontana, 1982); and *The Railway Station Man* (London: Hamish Hamilton, 1984).

4. Johnston interview; Sean McMahon, "Anglo-Irish Attitudes: The Novels of Jennifer Johnston," *Eire-Ireland* 10, no. 3 (1975): 140; Ostriker, "The "Thieves of Language," 68-90.

5. Donnelly, "Big House," 137; Johnston, *Gates*, 148, 80, 42; Harriet Taylor and John Stuart Mill, "Enfranchisement of Women," in *Essays on Sex Equality*, ed. Rossi, 113; Ostriker, "Thieves of Language," 78; Johnston, *Captains and the Kings*, 112, 130.

6. Johnston, *Captains and the Kings*, 49; Johnston, *Gates*, 10; Johnston, *Captains and the Kings*, 112.

7. Lennox Robinson first deplored the terrible permanence of the wide gulf between Anglo- and Gaelic-Irish in his *The Big House* (London: Macmillan, 1928); the issue became nostalgic, a recognizably rich source which writers after Robinson mined easily. Johnston, I suggest, does more than mine the already exposed seams. For an interesting view of Johnston's subjects, see Shari Benstock, "The Masculine World of Jennifer Johnston," in *Twentieth-Century Women Novelists*, ed. Thomas F. Staley (Totowa, N.J.: Barnes and Noble, 1982), 191-217. Johnston, *Miles to Babylon*, 5, 29-30.

8. Johnston, *Miles to Babylon*, 36, 39, 33, 41-42.

9. Ibid., 46; Somerville and Ross, *Irish Memories*, 91.

10. Johnston, *Miles to Babylon*, 135-37; Mortimer, "World of Jennifer Johnston," 94.

11. Johnston, *Shadows*, 66, 159.

12. Johnston, *Miles to Babylon*, 94-95; Johnston, *Old Jest*, 100.

13. Johnston, *Shadows*, 123.

14. Johnston, *Old Jest*, 10; Johnston interview.

15. Johnston, *Old Jest*, 10.

16. Johnston, *Miles to Babylon*, 39; Johnston, *Shadows*, 159; Johnston, *Old Jest*, 100, 144, 100; Johnston, *Christmas Tree*, 114-15.

17. Johnston, *Old Jest*, 56, 57.

18. Neumann, *Great Mother*, 45; see also discussion of cave imagery in Gilbert and Gubar, *Madwoman*, especially chap. 2.

19. Johnston, *Old Jest*, 59; Woolf, *Room*, 35-36; Johnston, *Old Jest*, 92-94.

20. Benstock, "Masculine World of Jennifer Johnston," 201; Johnston, *Old Jest*, 55-60, 63-64, 66-72, 91-95, 100-104.

21. Johnston, *Old Jest*, 96, 136, 158.

22. See Karen E. Rowe's discussion of *Jane Eyre*, "Fairy-Born and Human-Bred," in *The Voyage In*, ed. Abel, Hirsch, and Langland, 69-89; Abel, Hirsch, and Langland, Introduction to *The Voyage In*.

23. Johnston, *Christmas Tree*, 8.

24. Thomas Kilroy, "Tellers of Tales," *Times Literary Supplement*, 17 March 1972, 301-2; Denis Donoghue, "The Problems of Being Irish," *Times Literary Supplement*, 17 March 1972, 291-92; F.S.L. Lyons, "The Parnell Theme in Literature," in *Place, Personality and the Irish Writer*, ed. Andrew Carpenter (New York: Barnes and Noble, 1977), 78; Deane, "Literary Myths," 326.

25. Benstock, "Masculine World of Jennifer Johnston," 217; Johnston, *Miles to Babylon*, 141; Johnston, *Christmas Tree*, 63, 109-10, 158; Johnston interview.

26. Woolf *Room*, 68-69.

27. Johnston, *Christmas Tree*, 33, 2-5.

28. Ibid., 84.

29. Johnston, *Railway Station Man*, 11, 151-52.

30. Ibid., 164.

31. Ibid., 175.

32. Levi-Strauss, *Elementary Structures of Kinship*.

33. Johnston, *Railway Station Man*, 175-78.

34. I refer of course to Harold Bloom's *Anxiety of Influence* and to the many texts that agonize over the authorial shaping by the fathers. The quotation is from Herman Meyer, Introduction to *The Poetics of Quotation in the European Novel*, trans. Theodore and Yelta Ziolkowski (Princeton, N.J.: Princeton Univ. Press, 1968), 6. Johnston, *Railway Station Man*, 175-76.

35. Responding to this anxiety in *Beginnings*, Edward Said suggests that modern writers desire relationships of "adjacency" rather than linearity with previous texts.

36. Johnston, *Christmas Tree*, 161.

37. Johnston, *Captains and the Kings*, 142.

10. Irish Women Writers

1. Mary Lavin, "Frail Vessel," in *Mary Lavin: Collected Stories*, 302.

2. Ibid.

3. O'Faolain, *No Country*; O'Faolain, *Obedient Wife*; O'Faolain, "Man in the Cellar."

4. O'Faolain, *Obedient Wife*, 228, 229; Johnston, *Railway Station Man*, 176-77.

5. Bakan, *Duality of Human Existence*, 15, 21.

6. Johnston, "Jennifer Johnston," 52.

7. O'Brien, *Presentation Parlour*, 14.

8. Johnston interview.

9. Ibid.

Selected Bibliography

Note: Unless otherwise noted, all works listed are novels.

Elizabeth Bowen

Encounters. London: Sidgwick and Jackson, 1923. [Short stories]
Ann Lee's and Other Stories. London: Sidgwick and Jackson, 1926. [Short stories]
The Hotel. London: Constable, 1927.
Joining Charles. London: Constable, 1929.
The Last September. 1929; reprint, New York: Avon, 1979.
Friends and Relations. London: Constable, 1931.
To the North. 1932; reprint, Middlesex, Penguin, 1987. (By arrangement with Knopf, Penguin, U.S.)
The Cat Jumps. London: Victor Gollancz, 1934. [Short stories]
The House in Paris. London: Victor Gollancz, 1935.
The Death of the Heart. 1936; reprint, New York: Avon, 1979.
Look at All Those Roses. London: Victor Gollancz, 1941. [Short stories]
Bowen's Court. 1942; reprint, New York: Ecco Press, 1979. [History of Bowen family and home]
The Demon Lover. London: Jonathan Cape, 1945. [Short stories]
The Heat of the Day. London: Jonathan Cape, 1949.
Collected Impressions. New York: Knopf, 1950. [Pieces on writing]
A World of Love. London: Jonathan Cape, 1955.
Stories by Elizabeth Bowen. New York: Knopf, 1959. [Short stories]
Seven Winters and Afterthoughts. New York: Knopf, 1962. [Early memories]
The Little Girls. 1964; reprint, Middlesex: Penguin, 1985.
A Day in the Dark and Other Stories. London: Jonathan Cape, 1965. [Short stories]
Eva Trout. London: Jonathan Cape, 1969.
Pictures and Conversations. New York: Knopf, 1975. [Pieces collected after Bowen's death]

Maria Edgeworth

The Parent's Assistant: or Stories for Children. 3 vols. 1796; reprint, New York: Garland, 1976.
With Richard Lovell Edgeworth. *Essays on Practical Education.* 3 vols. 1798; reprint, New York: Garland, 1974.
Castle Rackrent. 1800; reprint, London: Oxford University Press, 1964.
Moral Tales for Young People. 5 vols. London: Johnson, 1801.
Belinda. 3 vols. London: Johnson, 1880.
With Richard Lovell Edgeworth. *Essay on Irish Bulls.* 1802; reprint, London: Johnson, 1803.
Popular Tales. 3 vols. London: Johnson, 1804.
The Modern Griselda: a Tale. London: Johnson, 1805.
Leonora. London: Johnson, 1806.
Ennui. 1809; reprint, New York: Garland, 1978.
The Absentee. 1812; reprint, London: Dent, 1893.
Patronage. London: Johnson, 1814.
Ormond. 1817; reprint, New York: Garland, 1978.
Memoirs of Richard Lovell Edgeworth, Esq. Begun by himself and completed by his daughter. London: Hunter, 1820.
Helen: A Tale. London: Bentley, 1834.

Jennifer Johnston

The Captains and the Kings. 1972; reprint, Glasgow: Fontana, 1982.
The Gates. 1973; reprint, London: Coronet, 1974.
How Many Miles to Babylon? 1974; reprint, London: Coronet, 1975.
Shadows on Our Skin. Garden City, N.Y.: Doubleday, 1978.
The Old Jest. 1979; reprint, Glasgow: Fontana, 1980.
The Christmas Tree. 1981; reprint, Glasgow: Fontana, 1981.
The Railway Station Man. London: Hamish Hamilton, 1984.
Fool's Sanctuary. London: Hamish Hamilton, 1987.

Molly Keane

Taking Chances. 1929; reprint, Middlesex: Penguin, 1987.
Mad Puppetstown. London: Collins, 1931.
Devoted Ladies. 1934; reprint, London: Virago, 1984.
Full House. 1935; reprint, London: Virago, 1986.
The Rising Tide. 1937; reprint, London: Virago, 1984.
Two Days in Aragon. 1941; reprint, London: Virago, 1985.

Good Behaviour. 1981; reprint, New York: Dutton, 1983.
Time after Time. 1983; reprint, New York: Knopf, 1984.
Molly Keane's Nursery Cooking. London: Macdonald, 1985.
Loving and Giving. London: Deutsch, 1988. Published in United States as *Queen Lear*. New York: Dutton, 1989.

Mary Lavin

Tales from Bective Bridge. 1942; reprint, Dublin: Poolbeg Press, 1978. [Short stories]
The Long Ago and Other Stories. London: Michael Joseph, 1944. [Short stories]
The House in Clewe Street. London: Michael Joseph, 1945.
The Becker Wives. 1946; reprint, New York: New American Library, 1971. [Short stories]
At Sallygap. Boston: Little, Brown, 1947. [Short stories]
Mary O'Grady. London: Michael Joseph, 1950.
A Single Lady and Other Stories. London: Michael Joseph, 1951. [Short stories]
The Patriot Son and Other stories. London: Michael Joseph, 1956. [Short stories]
Selected Stories. New York: Macmillan, 1959. [Short stories]
The Great Wave and Other Stories. London: Macmillan, 1961. [Short stories]
The Stories of Mary Lavin. Vol. 1. London: Constable, 1964. [Short stories]
In the Middle of the Fields and Other Stories. London: Constable, 1967. [Short stories]
Happiness and Other Stories. London: Constable, 1969. [Short stories]
Collected Stories. Boston: Houghton Mifflin, 1971. [Short stories]
A Memory and Other Stories. London: Constable, 1972. [Short stories]
The Stories of Mary Lavin. Vol. 2. London: Constable, 1974. [Short stories]
The Shrine and Other Stories. London: Constable, 1977. [Short stories]
A Family Likeness and Other Stories. London: Constable, 1985. [Short stories]

Kate O'Brien

Without My Cloak. Garden City, N.Y.: Doubleday, Doran, 1931.
The Anteroom. Garden City, N.Y.: Doubleday, Doran, 1934.

Mary Lavelle. Garden City, N.Y.: Doubleday, Doran, 1936.

Pray for the Wanderer. Garden City, N.Y.: Doubleday, Doran, 1938.

The Land of Spices. Garden City, N.Y.: Doubleday, Doran, 1941.

The Last of Summer. Garden City, N.Y.: Doubleday, Doran, 1943.

That Lady. London: Heinemann, 1946. Republished as *For One Sweet Grape.* Garden City, N.Y.: Doubleday, Doran, 1946.

The Flower of May. New York: Harper, 1953.

As Music and Splendour. London: Heinemann, 1958.

My Ireland. London: Batsford, 1962. [Guide to country]

Presentation Parlour. London: Heinemann, 1963. [Biographical sketches]

Julia O'Faolain

We Might See Sights. London: Faber and Faber, 1968. [Short stories]

Godded and Codded. 1970. Published in United States as *Three Lovers.* New York: Coward, McCann and Geoghegan, 1971.

Man in the Cellar. London: Faber and Faber, 1974. [Short stories]

Women in the Wall. 1975; reprint, London: Virago, 1985.

No Country for Young Men. Middlesex: Penguin, 1980.

The Obedient Wife. 1982; reprint, Middlesex: Penguin, 1983.

Daughters of Passion. Middlesex: Penguin, 1982. [Short stories]

The Irish Signorina. Middlesex: Viking, 1986.

Ed., with Lauro Martines. *Not in God's Image: Women in History from the Greeks to the Victorians.* London: Temple Smith, 1973.

E.OE. Somerville and Martin Ross

Some Experiences of an Irish R.M. London: Longmans, Green, 1889. Previously printed in *Badminton Magazine.* [Short stories]

An Irish Cousin. London: Longmans, Green, 1903. Revision of 1889 publication.

Naboth's Vineyard. London: Spencer Blackett, 1891.

Through Connemara in a Governess Cart. London: Allen, 1893. Previously printed in *Lady's Pictorial.* [Travel articles]

The Real Charlotte. 1894; reprint, London: Quartet Books, 1982.

Beggars on Horseback. London: Blackwood, 1895. Previously printed in *Black and White.* [Travel articles]

The Silver Fox. London: Lawrence and Bullen, 1898. Previously printed in *The Minute.*

All on an Irish Shore. London: Longmans, Green, 1903. Previously printed in magazines. [Short stories]

Some Irish Yesterdays. London: Longmans, Green, 1906. Previously printed in magazines. [Articles]

Further Experiences of an Irish R.M. London: Longmans, Green, 1908. Previously printed in magazines. [Short stories]

Irish Memories. London: Longmans, Green, 1917. [Biographical sketches]

Mount Music. London: Longmans, Green, 1919.

The Big House of Inver. 1925; reprint, London: Quartet Books, 1978.

French Leave. London: Heinemann, 1928.

Happy Days. London: Longmans, Green, 1946. Previously printed in magazines. [Travel articles]

Index